MODERN MYSTERIES OF THE UNEXPLAINED

MODERN MYSTERIES OF THE UNEXPLAINED

The Most Perplexing Events of Recent Times

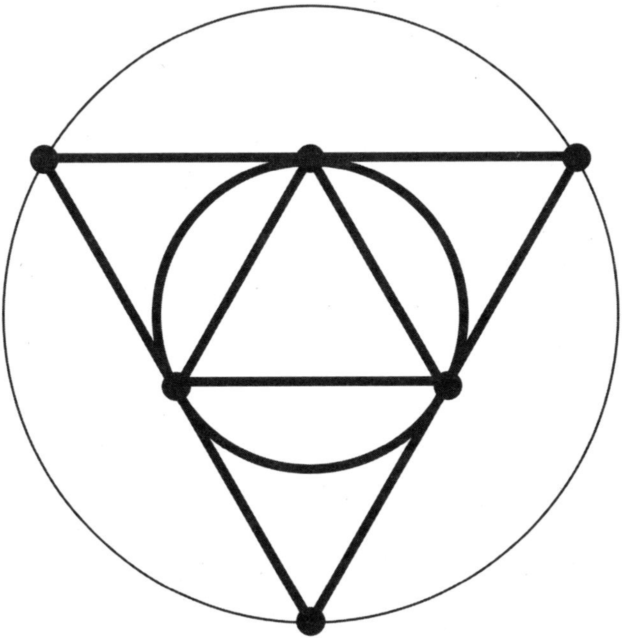

NEIL WARD

Neil Ward is the host of *The Paranormal Peepshow* on the Paranormal UK radio network and was one of the founding members of the British Visionary Artist Group. He is an active paranormal researcher and has investigated UFOs, psychic events and more in his search to learn more. He has written a number of books, including *True Tales of the Paranormal.*

This edition published in 2025 by Arcturus Publishing Limited
26/27 Bickels Yard, 151–153 Bermondsey Street,
London SE1 3HA

AD011625UK

Printed in the UK

MIX
Paper | Supporting responsible forestry
FSC® C013604

CONTENTS

INTRODUCTION

The strange stories in this book are not concerned with ancient races and archaic monuments; each one of them originated either in this century or the last, in the modern age of mass automation, mass automobile transport and, increasingly, mass communication. They occurred within the living memory of many readers: some only a few years ago, others further back. One thing unites them – they are as yet unexplained.

As humans, we are all intrigued by mysteries. They excite our imagination, curiosity, trepidation and wonder, leading us to ask could it really have happened that way, or does such a thing actually exist? We have a hardwired psychological need to find out the things we do not know – and a deep-seated fear of what we will discover when we do. And now, the answer to every mystery we could possibly imagine is no more than just a few taps away on the keyboard or screen of one of the many electronic devices that are part of everyday modern life. Or seemingly so.

Ultimately, it all comes down to belief. When we type a question into an internet search engine or click a video on a social media platform, how can we know that the information it provides is accurate and impartial? The simple answer is that we can't. Do we know who wrote it, or why? And where did they get their information from? More importantly, when they wrote their answer, opinion, or callback, what *didn't* they say? This is not such an issue so long as we treat what we read and view with a healthy dose of scepticism. But the thing about the online world is that it's a place where that is an increasingly difficult thing to do. Too often today it's a forum where opinions are presented as facts and differences of opinion dismissed as personal attacks or hate speech.

So, in an age when we are constantly in danger of drowning in a sea of information and misinformation – and when there is more information and misinformation out there than ever before – how do we find our way to a safe harbour? How can we know what is true and what is false? If the one thing we can be sure of in our 21st-century world is that we need to be wary of anyone who tells us anything with absolute certainty, does this mean that there is nothing left for us to trust?

Not quite.

What this book attempts to do, by exploring some of the most puzzling mysteries of modern times, is to ask you to believe that there is one thing in this life that you can still trust: yourself. It avoids offering absolutes and definitive answers and does not claim to possess all the facts for all the stories it tells. Instead, it discusses what may or may not have happened for each intriguing mystery and then asks you to decide for yourself what you believe took place. It sets you on a course and invites you to see where it takes you.

While this is interesting in itself and hopefully, at some points at least, fun, there's an important point at stake in all of this. Tied up in some of the mysteries presented here is the idea that someone, somewhere, may be keeping something from us. There are discussions, after all, of possible alien encounters and interdimensional time-travel. Unsolved disappearances are touched upon and grisly deaths dissected. Some, or all, of these events may involve official cover-ups and shady conspiracies. Perhaps, then, these things are only mysteries because 'they' (whoever 'they' may be) want to keep them as such.

Or possibly not.

What this book above all asks you to do is *think*. This is because thinking is the first step in freeing your mind from those who wish to control it, whether it be individuals, groups or governments. Hopefully, by the time you finish reading about the modern mysteries explored in the pages that follow, you will see the world in a different light. Or at least you will understand, if you don't already, that we should always question the 'official version' of any subject. You may end up agreeing with that official version, or you may not. Perhaps you'll still be none the wiser. But at least you will have thought about it critically and in doing so you will have a deeper understanding of the world around you. Maybe then our rapidly changing world of increasingly personalized technology and artificial intelligence – and any others that may or may not exist – won't seem like such a mysterious place after all.

CHAPTER 1

NOT OF THIS EARTH

As long as there has been a sky to look up to, humankind has wondered about the mysteries beyond it. Even in ancient times, humans made many references to it in their writings, paintings and myths. It was long thought to be home of the Gods, or God, unseen but believed to be all powerful; in many cultures everything fortunate or unfortunate, holy or evil came from the sky. It is also our gateway to other worlds and, possibly, beings that may, or may not, wish to communicate with us. Many here are convinced these beings have already spoken to us and left their wisdom upon the earth as written histories, coded messages, and religions. Our modern scientific minds now look at the skies with the benefit of wisdom and science: we predict changes in weather systems, send automated craft to explore the far reaches of our solar system, and examine minerals and the mix of gases that may even permit life on some remote planets. But there is still much to ponder and when things come from beyond Earth, they often leave their marks – not always as ancient writings but as deep scars upon the planet's surface, strange machines that we do not understand, or bizarre patterns and formations that leave us scratching our heads. Are deities still talking to us, but changing their methods of communications, or are there other supernatural explanations for the modern-day signs and encounters related here?

CROP CIRCLES

If you are British and were born in the mid-20th century or later, the chances are you have heard of crop circles. These strange patterns appear suddenly, often overnight, as if some giant force has pressed them into the ground. They are typically found in farmed fields of wheat, although other crops have also been used as a natural canvas for indentations into the plants that flatten them into an often complex and beautiful series of whorls and geometric shapes – only truly revealed when viewed from above. For obvious reasons, most crop circles in the UK tend to turn up in areas with significant swathes of agricultural land, particularly in Wiltshire and nearby Hampshire, and in the summer months. However, the United Kingdom is not alone in witnessing crop circle phenomena; crop fields in countries including Australia, Canada, Holland and the USA have also been decorated with mysterious circular crop patterns. Are they some kind of weather-driven natural phenomena, physical proof of a visit to our world by flying saucers, or even messages from the angels?

Mainstream British media started taking an interest in crop circles in the early 1980s and within a few years they had begun to attract widespread attention. By then, numerous individuals were devoting themselves to serious investigation into whether these were non-human phenomena. The veteran British crop circle researcher and author Colin Andrews, an electrical engineer by profession, takes credit for coining the term 'crop circle' after seeing a formation for the first time in July 1983. Their origins, however, are a little muddied.

In 1932, an archaeologist named E. C. Curwen recorded a sighting of four dark rings in a barley field at Stoughton Down near Chichester, West Sussex: the circles where the barley was beaten down were flat, while the centre of each ring was very slightly raised up. Earlier records of sightings are rare: they include a woman mentioning that her grandfather regularly found his crops flattened into circles and patterns in his fields around Tilshead, Salisbury in Wiltshire between 1900 and 1910. Although we don't have much information on the Tilshead crop circles in the 1920s, the then young Constance Wheeler

Crop circles became more common during the 20th century – what do they mean?

recalled that her uncle, Teddy Lawes, met a local farmer, Mr Shepherd, at the market, who reported fairy circles appearing in his fields at Ipsden near Reading. He was apparently angered at the fairies for making such circles and recalled that the same fields had similar rings around 20 years previously, again putting this to around 1900. When times changed, the term 'fairy rings' was updated as science progressed and earthlings headed to the moon. Could it be that other things also from space might be responsible for the patterns?

The early term for crop circles, 'saucer nests', arose from a growing belief that flying saucers had landed, causing the circular markings in crop fields. In 1963, respected astronomer and BBC television presenter, Patrick Moore, went to investigate so-called 'saucer nests' that appeared after a meteor crash in July, causing a crater in a potato field in Wiltshire. Near the crater were spiral patterns in the wheat that he believed were made by the force of air currents from the meteor's impact, due to their angle in relation to the crater. However, a local farmer named Mr Blanchard, who first sighted the 'saucer nests', was adamant that something had landed and taken off again. One interesting side note to this event was a letter to the *Dorset Echo* newspaper, which suggested a previous crop circle had appeared in the same field around 1952.

As public interest in crop circles grew, books, TV programmes and news items on these mysterious appearances increased, causing media sources to buzz with UFO and extraterrestrial researchers discussing their vortex or alien origin theories, which only fuelled the public's fascination.

Some of the researchers emerging around this time had technical credentials to add to their bow, such as English cereologists or 'croppies' as they are sometimes called. Colin Andrews, who was originally an electrical engineer before he became associated with crop formations, first became interested through his interest in UFOs and he was actually researching a UFO case when he happened to drive past a newly formed crop circle and took a closer look.

In his book, *Crop Circles: Signs of Contact*, he laid out theories as to what caused so-called 'genuine' crop circles. Magnetism was one chief theory that Andrews came up with after testing the Earth's magnetic field in crop circles and finding an increase of about 120 per cent above the norm. The magnetic patterns Andrews mapped out under the crop formations matched the actual design of the formations themselves. He called it a magnetic fingerprint, and he calculated that the 'dipoles' as he called them – a pair of electric charges of equal strength but opposite polarity strong enough to produce that level of magnetic field – are buried around 20 feet below the ground or alternatively somewhere around 20 feet in the air above the crop circle formation! The levels of magnetic force recorded around the crop circles remained there for several days.

Andrews, along with some of the scientific colleagues he consulted, believe that magnetism is connected to the phenomenon, though it cannot be the only force that creates the patterns. He believes some additional force combined with the magnetic fields of the Earth might be involved in flattening the stems. Another theory covered by Andrews is the Plasma Vortex Theory. He compares Plasma vortices, which are spinning columns of electrified air, to electrocution. The vortices pass through the field and electrocute the wheat stems, causing them to collapse into a circular form.

In their 1990 book, *Crop Circles*, author Jenny Randles and co-writer Paul Fuller also concluded that the formations were similarly produced by atmospheric phenomena. But while some circles might have been caused in this way, it would not explain the more intricate designs that have been recorded. Besides, Andrews later dropped this theory on the basis that animals, too, could be injured by electrical columns of spinning plasma and there was no evidence of that.

Researchers of a more religious bent, such as the late Arthur Eedle, writer and Christian, suggested that the more complex crop circles and formations are created by fallen angels of God. He wrote: 'The Bible does give us a sufficient warranty for assuming an invasion, not of extraterrestrials, but of those from a higher dimensional level, simply because *it has happened once before*, when some of the angels transgressed God's command and forsook their higher dimensional level to live on the earth, cohabit with human women, and generate a race of giants. This happened in Noah's day, created untold violence, and led to the judgment of the Flood. I believe Crop Circles are yet another manifestation of interference from the fallen angelic world.' From his perspective, they were created for the purpose of destroying the Earth and turning people away from the truth of the Christian God.

Those who don't subscribe to the Christian doctrine might interpret crop formations in a more New Age light and see it perhaps as the Earth itself sending messages through its own eco systems. The so-called Gaia New Age theory suggests that the Earth itself is a living being and is attempting to communicate through natural energies. The original idea of the living planet Earth was first proposed by scientist, Timothy Zell, in the 1970s and later expanded upon by British chemist, James Lovelock. These two academics suggested that the Earth responded to damage inflicted on it by throwing up biochemical processes to heal itself. In the same way that our bodies produce bruises and scars when injured, it was hypothesized that crop formations are the attempts of the living earth to heal itself against the pollution of industrialization. Andrews, while not quite endorsing this particular theory, at least supports the general idea of caring for the planet and considers that the Gaia approach goes some way towards making people aware of environmental concerns. Andrews also co-wrote a book with a retired aeronautical engineer, Pat Delgado, *Circular Evidence: A Detailed Investigation of the Flattened Swirled Crops Phenomenon*, which sold 50,000 copies in the 1980s. He met Andrews at a crop circle site and they started working together. However, Delgado blundered when shown a newly formed circle by a member of the press, by saying how much he admired it, only to be told later that it was faked. It was at this point that Delgado decided to withdraw from the centre stage of crop circle research. His co-author, Andrews, continued, however, braving the storm, so to speak.

Other researchers took up the cause after Delgado dropped out of the limelight. They included Roy Dutton, David Cayton and Robert Hulse. Dutton and Cayton both worked for British Aerospace and it was Dutton who introduced Cayton to some intriguing crop circle photos during a lunch break at work. Fascinated, he decided to find out more. Both Cayton and Dutton were very much UFO enthusiasts and crop circles seemed to them like a natural extension of their interests. Besides, Cayton saw the crop markings as tangible evidence of alien activity, something much more solid than anything you got with a UFO, which might just zip away into the distance after a brief sighting. Hulse met Dutton and was later introduced to Cayton, who he joined forces with.

Hulse believed he had had contact with ETs all his life, going back to childhood. All three put together reports of sightings of UFOs near crop circles supported by eyewitness accounts. A man called Win Keech claimed to have filmed the formation of crop circles in Wiltshire in 2007. Using five video cameras, Keech apparently filmed a 1,000-foot-long crop circle appearing over a period of nearly two hours.

In an effort to co-ordinate serious research, the Centre for Crop Circle Studies came into being in 1990, offering international membership and annual conferences.

By now, the public was hooked. There was a steep rise in the number of reports of circles appearing in Britain in the 1980s and 1990s, accompanied by the complaints of farmers that their fields were being damaged by the crop circles and the number of visitors who wanted to walk among the patterns. It seemed as if every weekend a new pattern would appear, usually overnight. The patterns included spirals, stripes and circles, as well as diamond shapes, squares, grooves and every kind of variation. They were often found in fields within easy reach of towns, which led some researchers to conclude that they were likely to have been made by human hands. In some cases at least, this would prove to be true.

Two hoaxers go public

An ITN *News at Ten* broadcast in September 1991 featured a duo who confessed to venturing out in the middle of the night and creating crop circles with planks of wood and string. They would flatten crops by pressing the wooden boards down with their feet and pulling up tightly on the attached strings, while walking around in circles. Doug Bower and Dave Chorley, from Southampton and Winchester respectively, explained that they were inspired by a 1966 account of a flying saucer near Tully in Queensland, Australia, in which the craft is said to have landed in a lagoon, leaving behind a round depression in the reeds.

The hoaxers, both retired, claimed to have produced more than 200 crop circles since 1976, and showed journalists plans for their designs, stored in their garden sheds. Embarrassingly, Pat Delgado, mentioned earlier, was told on camera that a recent crop circle he had pronounced genuine, perhaps even extraterrestrial, was in fact the work of Doug and Dave.

More recently, some individuals and groups have openly admitted to creating crop circles – and even explained how they did it: for example, Circlemakers is a group established by crop circle artist and film-maker, John Lundberg, and others, which proudly details its work and even offers a beginner's guide. Lundberg says that the group, or arts collective, explores the phenomenon of crop circles and the role of deception in the process of artistic creation. One art critic described it as 'crop-circle making as the basis for an enquiry into the conditions of modern mythology'. Over the years, Circlemakers has become quite a commercial venture, with many companies hiring them to produce brand logos for them in fields.

Nowadays, any mainstream article on crop circles tends to conclude they are all human-made, which means for many members of the general public that the 'mystery' of the crop circle is now solved. But what about all the other thousand or so circles not created by Doug and Dave or the self-confessed 'circlemakers'? And why, if crop circles are fake, have those in government investigated them seriously and come up with ideas about what might be causing them?

In the 1980s, it seems that the British government took an active interest in crop circle phenomena. Nick Pope, a former Ministry of Defence (MoD) employee who investigated UFO sightings for the government department, was reported as saying that the MoD became aware of crop circles in 1985 after a farmer complained about damage to his crops caused by downdraughts from military helicopter rotary blades. The MoD investigated and found their helicopters were not responsible, but by now they were aware of crop circle formations. In the late 1980s, the Centre for Crop Circle Studies (a 'civilian' organization representing crop circle investigators) provided samples of soil and stems from crop circles to the research arm of the (then) Ministry of Agriculture, Fisheries, and Food. These were analysed by a laboratory in Wolverhampton, and the results proved similar to those found by an American biophysicist, Dr William Levengood, who had also been looking into circles on behalf of the CCCS. According to later tests done under the banner of Project Argos, the CCCS found no traces of radiation beyond the normal levels found in nature. Levengood later published research indicating, 'Some crop circles have been deliberately man-made, (but) the observed thickening and lengthening of herbaceous plant nodes found in spontaneous crop circles have not been explained and remained incomprehensible anomalies.' Critics of Levengood have suggested he was not a proper scientist but a partisan 'crop-circle believer'. The modern-day equivalent of the Ministry of Agriculture, Fisheries, and Food, The Department for Environment, Food and Rural Affairs reported that they cannot locate any records of crop circle tests due to closures of various departments and employees retiring. But it did not say they didn't test samples. After David Cayton said questions were asked in the House of Commons about public money being wasted on 'silly' crop circles, the Wolverhampton scientists' work was ended. In July 1989, MP Michael Colvin asked Douglas Hurd, the then Secretary of State, about investigations into Crop Circles. Colvin said his intention was 'To ask the Secretary of State for the Home Department if he will call for a report from the chief constables of Hampshire and Wiltshire on their investigations into the cornfield circles in Hampshire and Wiltshire; what is the estimated cost of these investigations; and if he will make a statement.' Mr Hurd's answer was to the point. He said, 'I understand from the chief constables of Hampshire and Wiltshire that there have been no investigations into the cornfield circles by their officers.'

In his question to Hurd, Michael Colvin seemed to imply that he was already aware of an investigation in his constituency by police, as it was likely instigated by concerned farmers who possibly contacted Colvin who in turn may have been working with local police to try and come up with answers. Yet Hurd denied that any investigations were taking place. Nonetheless, later on, the MoD itself were given authority to look into the phenomenon under the scrutiny of TV companies.

Operation Blackbird

In the summer of 1990, there appeared to be a change of mind in government, as the MoD allowed a television project named 'Operation Blackbird' to be filmed on British Army land at Bratton Camp, Westbury near Warminster in Wiltshire, an area of high crop circle formation activity.

In this joint project between the BBC and a Japanese broadcaster, crop circle researchers, Pat Delgado and Colin Andrews, would attempt to solve the mystery for the benefit of TV viewers by keeping watch round the clock over fields in the hope of seeing a circle formed. By the second day, a crop circle had appeared, apparently formed overnight, much to Andrews' obvious delight. However, it was revealed later during the project that this poorly constructed pattern was in fact a hoax. By way of confirmation, the crop circle hoaxer had left a crop circle board game and crudely made cross in the centre of the circle to underline the fact that humans were responsible. In hindsight, researchers wondered if they were deliberately left there to pin the blame on 'New Age' or 'occult' groups. The hoaxers, whose presence was never detected, seemed to have known that, at half a mile's distance, they were just out of the effective range of the image-intensifying equipment, which was used to try and detect any activity in the nearby fields. Was this a set-up perhaps?

Some crop circle researchers have alleged that Andrews and Delgado were deliberately made to look like gullible fools, and that Operation Blackbird was aimed at undermining serious crop circle investigation, dismissing the whole subject as nothing more than a hoax. One of the soldiers taking part in Operation Blackbird, Corporal Darren Cummings, was reported to have told the press: 'We are here to prove that they (the Circles) are caused by people; the scientists are here to prove otherwise.' It has also been suggested by a researcher called George Wingfield that the BBC managed to film a genuine crop circle around this time, known as the 'Question Mark', but did not air the material and made no public mention of it at the time. There's a further allegation that, unknown to TV viewers and the general public, the British Army had a separate team 19 miles away at Silbury Hill, Avebury, that was making a secret study of the crop circles. Colin Andrews alleged that the military unit there captured on film a large shiny orb over fields to the south of the hill.

According to Colin Andrews, the television project did yield some interesting results: for example, at 4 am on 25 July, eyewitnesses reported seeing a triangular formation of lights hovering over one of the fields. (Later, it emerged that the businessman Richard Branson had flown his airship over the area, which could account for the lights.) In the early hours of the same day, Andrews and Delgado entered the field under surveillance from long-range cameras, but according to Andrews BBC cameras and other media crews were kept out of the field as four aircraft, possibly military, suddenly came in from the east and flew very low directly over their heads. Andrews spotted that they were light aircraft carrying passengers with cameras.

On his website, Andrews also insisted that one of the media companies present was about to report the incident live on the radio when it received an instant Category D notice to stop its broadcast. (In the UK, the government can issue a 'D notice' to order media not to print, publish or broadcast on subjects deemed sensitive for reasons of national security.) Presenter Dave Barret, who was back in the TV studio awaiting the live coverage, confirmed to Andrews that a 'D notice' had suddenly been issued to them. Whatever was in that field, it seems the MoD did not want the nation to know about it. A few days later, it was reported that a woman in Wiltshire, Elizabeth Price, had called in to the Blackbird team to report that she had seen a bright flash in the night sky, followed by tall columns of some kind of mist in a field, and that she felt that something or someone was nearby. This was in a new circle to the east of the existing site under observation. She heard rustling in the field and also saw a light nearby. She instinctively felt that the columns of mist were to do with circle formations.

In the daylight, Andrews investigated the new circle formed by these misty columns and the BBC also tried to work out where it had come from. Engineers Steve Dunn and Tony Pearce, using dowsing techniques taught by Pat Delgado, managed to pinpoint two areas in the circle where the dowsing rods crossed, indicating potential hot spots. They explained on camera that these two spots indicated shifts in DC or Direct Current, under the ground presumably. They then placed normal RF (radio frequency) aerials in those spots connected to an audio tape recorder, and they managed to record a series of unusual tones. What this indicated was that there was some kind of energy in the circle. Would a fake circle have this kind of hotspot?

As we will see later, this is not the only time an eyewitness had seen tall columns in fields where crop circle activity was found. Once Operation Blackbird had finished, rumours circulated that during the project cameras had managed to film the formation of a circle, but the MoD again stepped in and stopped the evidence from being aired. These rumours cannot be substantiated, but the incident could have been confused with an event captured by Nippon TV from Japan. On 18 August 1991 in Alton Barnes, England, Andrews stood alongside a crew from Nippon Television and witnessed the flight of a UFO, which began interacting with their torch lights. Andrews telephoned Air Traffic Control and they confirmed there were no regular aircraft in the area at the time. But could the UFO have had anything to do with crop circles?

Operation Blackbird, in the eyes of some, was a government media campaign designed to debunk crop circle research by openly fabricating a crop circle during the programme, thereby making the public think that there was absolutely nothing unusual going on. Could Doug and Dave have been part of Blackbird, too? Andrews recalled seeing them at many crop circles before they went public in 1991. The timing of Doug and Dave coming on the scene as Crop Circles Fever was reaching a peak was almost scripted you might think. Perhaps it was just a coincidence and, with all the publicity, Doug and Dave maybe just decided to come clean. Interestingly, they were never arrested and charged for any damage done to crops they had flattened. Operation Blackbird was the last time the British government was publicly involved in crop circle detection.

Intelligence interest

There are, however, indications that MI5, the British internal security service, may have maintained a continuing interest in crop circles. Crop circle authors, David Cayton and Robert Hulse, believe that the British and American security services are still involved to this day in researching circles. AWACs (airborne warning and control) aircraft and military helicopters have been seen by crop circle researchers passing overhead and inspecting newly created patterns. Hulse has said he filmed Apache attack helicopters investigating crop circle fields over the Vale of Pewsey in Wiltshire, proving to him at least that the government is still curious about the phenomenon.

In his own research, Cayton had on two occasions detected types of radiation in the circle patterns he was investigating. Do man-made crop circles involve radiation? It would be a fairly dangerous practice if they did, which could arguably justify the need for monitoring by responsible agencies. The radiation could, though, turn out to be normal amounts that are often detected in nature. Another factor could be that researchers often take video cameras into circles and these also emit small amounts of electromagnetic radiation, safe for humans but still detectable by sensors. In this way, it may be just misinterpretation of everyday background emissions.

Nick Pope, formerly of the MoD's 'UFO desk', has said that many military aircraft would overfly crop formations, merely because the pilots were curious. However, would such highly trained and disciplined service people be allowed to change flight plans purely out of curiosity? Besides, according to Hulse, unmarked helicopters have been seen to chase small orbs of light which have appeared over certain crop circle patterns. Hulse believes the government does still investigate circles on a 'need-to-know' basis. While most MoD staff would probably be unaware of such investigations, it's feasible that a small unit could be tasked with responsibility for investigating new circles as they appear.

In addition, Hulse has suggested that the Circlemakers organization was created to show that behind all crop circles were hoaxers purely in order to throw the public off the scent. Its website contained references in the past to M15, albeit joking about a connection to the security services and linking to MI5's recruitment page (the link no longer works).

In an interview with a UFO magazine in 2002, Colin Andrews claimed he was contacted by the CIA or Central Intelligence Agency (the US government agency that collects information on foreign countries and events) in 1989. He was told the unnamed operative was assigned to involve him in a plan to promote high-profile crop circle researchers in turn, then debunk them publicly. This individual allegedly offered Andrews a large sum of money on one condition – that at some point in the future, he would go on television and announce that through his research he had found crop circles were a complete hoax. Obviously concerned, and finding the idea completely abhorrent, Andrews decided to contact someone he knew in the MoD, who advised him to ignore the contact. The 'CIA operative' (if this is what the caller really was) kept calling Andrews, but he ignored the calls and eventually they stopped.

Recognizing the fakes... and the real thing?

Experienced crop circle researchers like Hulse and Cayton believe they know what to look for in the human-made circles. With the rope-and-board techniques demonstrated by hoaxers Doug and Dave, the board is pressed down onto the crops and the edge of the board creates an indented crease or bend mark in the crop. This 'scar' takes approximately 12 to 20 hours to show up, usually as a white line going horizontally across the stalk of the wheat plant. A board or plank of wood about 60 cm (2 ft) long would create many of these white lines or crease marks.

On the other side of this coin, is it possible to tell if a circle is made by someone or something that is not human? For Robert Hulse, genuine crop circles look like the one he identified as genuine in 2005, which was located at Alton Priors in Wiltshire in a field of rapeseed oil plants. It had a natural-looking 'flow' of pressed-down plants, bent smoothly but not crushed or flattened. He pointed out that it is possible to see a pattern in oilseed rape where the flattened flowers are not crushed but almost laid down; in contrast, the bright yellow flowers are destroyed by the board-stomping process done by humans. Genuine formations in this crop are better presented than human ones – the display looks similar to pressed flowers in a book. In addition, there would be no tell-tale bend marks in the stalks from the edge of the boards.

Another genuine formation, according to Hulse, was the Ogbourne St George circle in Wiltshire, spotted in 2003. This pattern featured lines that were formed like grooves in a record, where the crop had not been laid flat to the ground, but only slightly reduced below the height of the crop, to show a slight shadow when viewed from above. Hulse also talks about 'blown nodes', where heat from whatever is making the crop circle formation warms up moisture in the stems of the plants at a natural 'knuckle' point where the stalk is usually strongest. As this moisture heats up, it becomes steam, which like a pressure cooker, builds up inside the stem. It eventually blows a hole in the node, similar to breaking a joint; this causes the stem to bend, flex and lie down, helping to form the patterns. Neither of these elements, according to Hulse, are found in faked crop formations made with boards.

Who – or what – is forming crop circles?

The late Roy Dutton, who was a professional aeronautics engineer, believed that there are genuinely supernatural crop formations out there. He used his mechanical and engineering skills in an attempt to work out what kind of method was being employed to create the swirls in the crops. His first clue was the sequence of spiral strips that feature in many crop circles. He thought some force was moving outwards from the centre of the circle, then sweeping back and forth, rotating as it did so. He constructed a model to demonstrate his hypothesis; it had a small brush on the end of a metal rod, or arm, sweeping radially back and forth over chalk powder and marking swirls in it. The arm was supported by a tall central rod that slowly rotated clockwise. Dutton's machine gradually rotated the brush in a circle and, after a minute, it had made a miniature image of a crop circle. After studying other patterns using a computer, he came to the conclusion that he had solid proof that some kind of scanning technology was making the crop patterns.

Dutton also proposed that during the creation of crop circles, something had to come from a sufficient altitude to make a beam, or some kind of long projection from the sky coming down to the ground. This was supported by Dutton's first personal experience of a crop circle, which was located on a hill. Instead of a perfect circle, he noticed that it was elliptical, that is, slightly more oval than round in shape. In his view, whatever caused it was projecting a circular pattern downwards, but the angle of the hill meant the circle was stretched into an oval – similar to how a torch beam would look if shone on to a sloped surface. A faked crop circle would probably not be made on a hillside in the first place and neither would it be likely to be an elliptical shape.

Another fascinating part of Dutton's evidence related to an event that happened in the daytime –remembering that hoaxers tended to admit making their circles at night, away from prying eyes. Dutton interviewed a farmer named Albert Bull from Exeter in southwest England, who claimed to have seen something very strange in one of his fields in August 1990. Bull said he witnessed huge black vertical tubes appear out of the cloudy sky before making contact with the ground, just short of the woods behind his fields. He estimated the tubes to be about 60 cm (2 ft) wide and approximately 300 m (1,000 ft) or more in height. He could not see the top of the tubes, as it was an overcast day and they reached up into the clouds. Albert initially saw one tube on the left-hand side of the field, about 100 m (330 ft) away, which was black in colour. Eventually, he said, the first one dematerialized and another tube appeared only a few metres in front of him, so he was able to get a long look at it. It looked rather like a large drill bit, rotating and turning the ash on the soil of his barley field round and round, but not sucking it up like a pump might. He said this long tube was there for about three or four minutes, spinning constantly, then eventually it 'died away'. A short while later, either the same tube or another one appeared in the field next to the barley field where Bull was standing and it went through the same process. Although no crop circles appeared anywhere in the fields, Dutton believed these mysterious tubes might be connected to the phenomenon. Perhaps the entity responsible for the strange tubes was attempting without success to produce a crop circle. Albert Bull told Dutton he had worked those same fields for nearly 50 years and had never seen anything like it before.

Dutton thought that Bull might have seen the kind of beam that he had theorized would be required to produce crop circles. He thought the farmer's sighting was an unfocused beam and, had it been more focused and not as wide, it might actually have pushed the crops down. Dutton hypothesized that the beam might have been microwave or gravitational high-frequency radiation that, given the right focus, could actually pick things up. (As mentioned, Cayton claimed to have picked up the presence of radiation at crop formation sites.) Dutton also referred to a later report, thought to have happened around 2000, of two Japanese boys playing in their village and seeing what they described as a 'trumpet-type cone' appear in the field next to them. This strange cone apparently made a humming noise and left circular marking in the grass. (However, Dutton didn't give any more specific details on this report.) Like the Bull case, this appeared to have happened in daylight.

Dutton postulated that whoever or whatever was controlling those beams in the field could in theory connect them to some kind of graphics programme, then produce any kind of image in the fields they liked – like an advanced laser printer printing on to plants instead of paper. Of course, the wider question is why? Are these visually mesmerizing patterns in crop fields actually a form of communication with a message for viewers?

But do crop circles actually mean anything? David Cayton and Robert Hulse are of the opinion that some kind of higher intelligence is at work on at least some of the formations. Andrew Collins, while not trying to prove an ET hypothesis, mentions a bizarre feature surrounding many circles or patterns. He says, 'The most significant real mystery of all are the "High Strangeness" events which have constantly taken place around the crop circles and those making and researching them since the beginning.'

But are aliens really trying to send messages via crop formations?

Crop circle messages

Incredibly, there does seem to have been one obvious extraterrestrial message left in crop circles. The Arecibo interstellar radio message was a transmission sent on 16 November 1974 from a radio telescope known as the Arecibo telescope, located at an observatory in Puerto Rico, to a group of stars called Messier 13. The message itself consisted of seven parts that encoded information like formulas for human DNA, our place in our solar system, being the third planet from the Sun, the height of humans and so forth. The scientists and astronomers who sent it did not do so in expectation of a reply, but to show what their technology was capable of at that point in time. The Messier 13 star cluster is so far away from Earth in deep space that it would take a message travelling at the speed of light 25,000 years to arrive. If some alien civilization there sent a similar message back using the same technology, it would take the same time to reach Earth.

However, in 2001, a strange crop marking of rectangular patterns was discovered next to the radio telescope at the Chilbolton Observatory in Hampshire. The pattern was almost a perfect copy of the graphical

One crop circle pattern resembled an image transmitted by the Arecibo telescope in 1974.

image transmitted from the Arecibo telescope in 1974. There were some slight discrepancies in the new image, however, such as the DNA configuration and the location of the supposed sender of the reply. If those theoretical aliens at Messier 13 had decoded the message, they had also added details about themselves. For instance, instead of Earth being listed as the third planet from the Sun, in the Chilbolton Observatory crop formation reply a planet was shown to be the fourth planet from the Sun. The original message estimated the height of humans at around 1.8 metres and this crop circle reply showed the height for an alien to be around half the size.

The Centre for Crop Circle Studies, headquartered in the UK, had its own US office. Doug Rogers, the US co-ordinator, studied the new formation at Chilbolton and gave presentations about it, believing it to be a genuine message from the cosmos. In 2001, he declared, 'The cat is out of the bag', indicating his belief that 'we have company, and the company is intelligent'. If it was true and that aliens did compose the message in some way, it is feasible that the 'reply' in the crops could have come from other extraterrestrial beings that did not necessarily come from the Messier 13 cluster. They could have hacked into the Arecibo telescope's transmission if they had been operating covertly over Earth. If the crop circle was a hoax, how would the hoaxers have had access to this level of detail within a message sent from thousands of miles away?

There is, however, a more down-to-earth explanation for the reply since the original message, although transmitted to the stars, also found its way to many astronomers and scientists through a variety of media, so it would only take a crop circle maker a short time to find the original message online or in a science periodical. Anyone with an astrophysics background would have been able to concoct an exciting thought-provoking design like this.

Another person who believes crop circles are messages from other worlds is Carole Cochrane, a cheirologist (one who reads palms), crop circle researcher and former chairman of the Centre for Crop Circle Studies. She believes the names of villages where crop circles are created contain hidden interstellar messages from the Sirius star system. (Sirius A is the brightest star in our night sky and one of the closest star systems at only 8.6 light years from Earth.) More specifically, through crop circles, its inhabitants want to convey the message that humankind is not alone in the universe.

Cochrane claims to have decoded a circle located at Alton Barnes in Wiltshire by identifying a 'letter bar', the number of times the same letter appears in the place name. Using this guide, you can in theory make up new words from the letters of 'Alton Barnes', the letter bar would allow you to use two letters As, the A in Alton and the A in Barnes. From the letter bar, she reconstructs as many new words as possible, rather like making anagrams, and then attempts to use an intuitive and/or telepathic connection with the alien message that is encrypted within the new, reconstructed words. Using this process, Cochrane has 'decoded' messages connected to Alton Barnes, including: 'We are Siriun, we twirl the wheat, we are the real artists.' She based her method on a system devised by an astrologer, Linda Goodman, called 'lexigramming', fine-tuning her version of the process over 20 years. It's quite a complex process, but it is explained in more details on her web site at www.thesiriusletters.com. Whatever your opinion of crop circles, or the theories around them, one thing is certain: they are intriguing enough to pull many people into their orbit, individuals who are dedicated to finding answers to the key questions of 'Who?' and 'Why?'

Many so-called 'croppies' will no doubt continue to stand firm in their belief that crop formations are evidence of angels, aliens or other non-human phenomena, while other enthusiasts and investigators will continue to accept that at least some circles are fakes. For most of the general public, though, the crop circle enigma has already been filed away under 'human-made hoax', albeit one that's often marvellous to look at and impressive in its ingenuity and symmetry.

However, it does seem rather odd that hoaxers were suddenly keen to admit to their activities publicly, especially at the risk of legal or criminal action from annoyed farmers or the authorities. Maybe

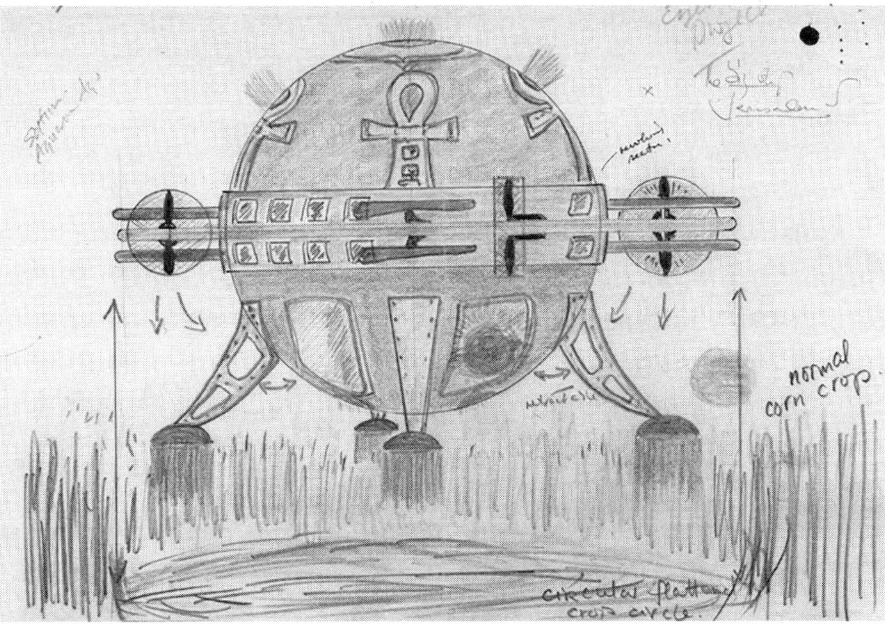

An image sent to the UK Ministry of Defence, explaining how UFOs could create crop circles.

someone higher up the ladder was more than happy to compensate farmers whose fields had been trampled or destroyed. And with individuals like farmer Albert Bull giving such detailed descriptions of long vertical tubes over his crops, we are left confused as to what might really be going on. We can only hope that all the years of hard work by dedicated amateur investigators – some of whom are no longer with us – will be taken up by younger generations and eventually lead to a breakthrough on the intriguing questions of whether these are genuine phenomena or not. Or maybe, if an intelligent extraterrestrial force has been leaving us messages, it will perhaps rethink its methods and develop a new way of attracting our attention.

THE ROSWELL MYSTERY

Did a UFO really crash near Roswell, New Mexico in July 1947? The US Army Air Forces (USAAF), the predecessor of the US Air Force, issued a press statement on July 8, 1947, indicating that it had recovered a crashed 'flying disc', the description used at that time for extraterrestrial craft. However, the following day the USAAF retracted this statement. It insisted that the object was in fact only a weather balloon. This story could easily have faded away and disappeared for ever, had it not been for an off-camera discussion decades in the future between a television show producer and one of the show's guests.

As illustrated by strange events such as the Aldeburgh Platform (see Chapter 3), unidentified flying objects (UFOs) had been sighted as far back as 1917, and there are indications that other sightings go back further, perhaps even centuries. However, the modern phenomenon of UFOs – or as many experts now call them 'unidentified anomalous phenomena' (UAPs) – came to prominence with a number of sightings during the Second World War. Then, small orange spheres, nicknamed 'Foo Fighters', were spotted flying alongside both Allied and enemy aircraft on bombing raids.

The concept of UFOs was first officially recognized just after the war in June 1947, when an American businessman and private pilot named Kenneth Arnold reported to the *East Oregonian* newspaper that he was flying his light aircraft near Mount Rainier, Washington State when he saw nine shiny flying unidentified objects that appeared to be racing across the skies at around 1,900 kph (1,180 mph). He said the objects appeared to skim and bounce through the sky like saucers skipping across a pond, and a journalist coined the term 'Flying Saucer'. Arnold became a media sensation and his widely reported experience triggered what came to be known as 'The Year of the Flying Saucer' in 1947. The report was followed just weeks later by, arguably, the most famous UFO encounter of all, which continues to captivate 'UFO buffs' to this day.

On the hot evening of July 2 1947, local Roswell businessman Dan Wilmot was sitting with his wife on their front porch at 105 South Penn, Roswell. It was approximately 10pm when they both noticed a flying object in the southeast coming down with lights flickering. Wilmot described the glowing object as oval in shape and looking like two inverted saucers jammed together. It was travelling at an estimated speed of around 500 miles per hour.

Roswell Daily Record

RECORD PHONES
Business Office 2288
News Department 2287

Established 1888 — Roswell, New Mexico, Tuesday, July 8, 1947 — 5¢ PER COPY

RAAF Captures Flying Saucer On Ranch in Roswell Region

Claims Army Is Stacking Courts Martial

Indiana Senator Lays Protest Before Patterson

Washington, July 8 (AP)—Senator Jenner (R-Ind.) contended today that "the high command in the European theatre is stacking courts against defendants in court martial."

In a letter to Secretary of War Patterson demanding a full investigation of army military trial procedure, Jenner offered what he said was documentary proof that:

1. "Prisoners are not being permitted to employ either civilian or military counsel of their own choice in the preparation and presentation of their defense."

2. "Every effort is being made to prevent attorneys who were connected with the infamous Lichfield prison case to practice in courts martial in the European theatre."

The Indiana senator made public a copy of an informal "routing slip" which he said was signed by Brig. Gen. Cornelius E. Ryan, assistant deputy, military government for Germany, and written by Col. Francis H. Vanderwerker. Jenner told newsmen that the routing slip substantiated his charges.

The slip, addressed to the chief

House Passes Tax Slash by Large Margin

Defeat Amendment By Demos to Remove Many from Rolls

Washington, July 8 (AP) — The house passed today the Republican-backed bill to cut income taxes by $4,000,000,000 annually for 49,000,000 taxpayers, beginning Jan. 1.

It goes to the senate where approval also is forecast.

The vote was 302 to 11, or more than the two-thirds majority needed to override a presidential veto.

The action, which may encounter another presidential veto, came after Speaker Martin (R-Mass.) personally appeal to the house to pass the bill by such a decisive vote— as to persuade the president that the people should have this

Security Council Paves Way to Talks On Arms Reductions

Lake Success, July 8 (AP) — The United Nations security council today approved an American blueprint for the arms reduction discussions despite a Russian warning that the plan would bring about a collapse of arms regulation efforts.

The vote was 9 to 0, with Russia and Poland abstaining.

In view of Russia's first stand against the U.S. plan it had been believed she might invoke the big power veto to block it.

Soviet Deputy Foreign Minister Andrei A. Gromyko gave his warning before the United Nations security council in a new effort to revive the Soviet working plan which already had been rejected by the commission for conventional armaments.

His challenge was taken up promptly by French delegate Alexandre Parodi and U.S. Representative Herschel V. Johnson, who announced their opposition to any

No Details of Flying Disk Are Revealed

Roswell Hardware Man and Wife Report Disk Seen

The intelligence office of the 509th Bombardment group at Roswell Army Air Field announced at noon today, that the field has come into possession of a flying saucer.

According to information released by the department, over authority of Maj. J.A. Marcel, intelligence officer, the disk was recovered on a ranch in the Roswell vicinity, after an unidentified rancher had notified Sheriff Geo. Wilcox, here, that he had found the instrument on his premises.

Major Marcel and a detail from his department went to the ranch and recovered the disk, it was stated.

After the intelligence office here had inspected the instrument it was

Ex-King Carol Weds Mme. Lupescu

Former King Carol of Romania and Mme. Elena Lupescu relax aboard the S. S. America bound for Cuba and Mexico in May, 1941. A member of

The headline in the Roswell local newspaper in July 1947.

Wilmot said the craft was about 5 ft tall and around 20 ft in diameter, flying at a height of about 1,500 ft. It rocked a little bit and swayed from side to side and then managed to steady itself before resuming its flight path. Initially, Wilmot did not report his sighting. In fact, another resident, William Woody, reported a very similar sighting on the same evening, but he believed that what he saw was a meteor.

Wilmot and Woody's sightings were not the only ones, however, in the area. According to researcher David Rudiak, there were more than 110 UFO sightings reported around that time, with about 40 in June (or before) and about 70 during July 1947. Around 70 featured New Mexico or areas immediately adjacent, such as El Paso and SE Arizona.

After a week of hesitation, Wilmot decided to repeat his version of the story to the *Roswell Daily Record* newspaper. Wilmot's sighting was thought to be the beginning of what later became known as the 'Roswell Incident'. The mysterious event became front-page news across the US and it made headlines at radio stations around the world. One of the first people to hear the report on the local Roswell radio station was British actor and entertainer, Hughie Green, who heard it on his car radio as he drove through the area. Soon, though, the whole story was buried and it remained so until American scientist, Stanton Friedman, started talking to a TV producer some 30 years later.

In 1978, Friedman was a renowned 'ufologist' with some big credentials to his name. He was a trained nuclear physicist, who had worked on top-secret Defense Department projects, such as nuclear-powered aircraft, fission and fusion rockets, as well as compact nuclear power plants for spacecraft. Friedman had been invited to take part in a television interview on the subject of UFOs in Louisiana, and while waiting for other guests to arrive, he learned that a friend of the show's producer claimed to have handled parts of a crashed UFO. An excited Friedman tracked down this individual the very next day; he was retired Lieutenant Colonel Jesse Marcel, who had been in the United States Air Force stationed at Roswell Army Air Field Base in New Mexico. By 1947, Roswell was the home of the 509th Bombing Division, which included the combat squadron that dropped the atomic bomb on Hiroshima during the Second World War.

UFO 'wreckage'

Marcel explained to Friedman that in early July 1947 he had handled parts of a crashed UFO. They were recovered by a sheep rancher named William 'Mac' Brazel, who was working at the Foster Ranch, near a small town called Corona about 160 km (100 miles) northwest of Roswell. In late June, Brazel had found debris littered over farmland. Brazel was familiar with high-altitude USAF weather balloons, having found a few over the years, but he was not sure what it was that had crashed on the ranch. Worried that the sheep might eat some of the debris, he started gathering it in bit by bit. By early July, he had recovered a significant amount of debris and took it to the Roswell sheriff's office. The sheriff called Marcel at the Roswell Army Air Field Base.

Marcel went to the ranch with a team of people and managed to retrieve even more material, bringing some of the recovered debris back to his house that evening to show his wife and son. The recovered items consisted mostly of thin, metallic, foil-like material that could not be bent or hammered; it came in the form of lightweight struts and beams that had hieroglyphic symbols in a violet colour displayed along the side. They were impossible to bend. Marcel and his family had never seen anything like this before. They thought they were parts of a crashed flying saucer.

The next day, 8 July 1947, The Roswell Army Air Field (RAAF), under the command of Colonel William Blanchard, released a press statement to the *Roswell Daily Record*, which resulted in the front-page headline: 'RAAF captures Flying Saucer on ranch in Roswell region'. The RAAF's Public Information Officer, Walter Haut, issued the statement that appeared in the press, describing how the RAAF's 509th Bombardment Group had come into possession of a flying disc through a local rancher. It indicated that the disc had landed near Roswell the previous week.

Roswell's two radio stations, KGFL and KSWS Radio, put out the sensational news following briefings from Haut and the story was then released to the Associated Press for wider syndication. This prompted calls from all over the world for more information about the recovered flying disc. In its afternoon printing, the *Roswell Daily Record* reported that the flying saucer wreckage had been sent to Fort Worth Army Air Field for closer inspection. It was then to be flown by cargo plane to Wright Field, Ohio, home of the Air Materiel Command and the USAF's aeronautical research laboratories, for further analysis.

Within hours of KFGL Radio's announcement, lots of other local stations began to run with the story. Lydia Sleppy of Radio KOAT in Albuquerque was one of the recipients of the recovered saucer story and she in turn decided to pass on the news to another station, ABC News, using a teletype machine (like a kind of early email message). However, her story was held up, seemingly by a government agency. Sleppy claimed she heard a bell ring on the teletype machine, which announced a new incoming message from the authorities (probably the FBI). The machine proceeded to automatically type out an instruction that said members of the media must cease all further telecommunications with other news outlets regarding the recovered saucer story. It seemed the FBI wanted to put a lid on it and stop the story from going any farther.

The next day, the RAAF retracted its previous statement and held a press conference to explain that the recovered material was in fact a weather balloon, not a flying disk. Now, Lieutenant Colonel Marcel posed for press photographs holding pieces of a broken Rawin (a device with radar-reflective surfaces that enable it to monitor air currents by tracking weather balloons). He was standing alongside his senior commander, Brigadier General Roger M. Ramey, who was holding what would turn out to be a significant memorandum (see below).

The question is: how could highly trained military experts confidently announce that objects are parts of a large flying saucer, then suddenly decide these were remnants from a weather balloon made of rubber and balsa wood? Marcel would later admit to Friedman that he knew the debris he was photographed holding was not the same as the material he had brought back from the Foster ranch. In fact, he was confident that the latter was not any kind of balloon.

The press appeared to accept the USAF's explanation of a weather balloon and the story faded from memory. However, it's interesting to note that 1st Lt. Walter Haut, the press officer who wrote the initial 'flying disc' recovery story, would later go on to co-found the International UFO Museum and Research Center in Roswell, New Mexico in 1991. This desire to investigate UFOs suggests he could have been party to information that was withheld in 1947.

Haut later explained to the authors of *UFO Crash at Roswell*, Kevin D. Randle & Donald R. Schmitt, that he was asked by Colonel William Blanchard to rewrite the press release concerning the recovered flying disc. When he asked if he could see the actual flying disc concerned, he was told by Blanchard that his 'request was impossible'. He heard more details of this flying disc, however, later on through Jesse Marcel and he 'trusted him on his knowledge'. He later explained that he thought the whole episode was one giant cover-up. He was sure that both Marcel and Blanchard knew what had really happened, which later led him to team up with others to form the International UFO Museum and Research Centre.

The story was mostly forgotten about until Friedman made contact with Marcel in 1978 and later interviewed him in depth about his involvement with the Roswell crash. This became the basis of the book, *The Roswell Incident*, in which Friedman acted as one of the researchers, although it was authored by Charles Berlitz and William Moore. Written in 1980, the book featured the accounts of Bill Brazel, son of rancher 'Mac' Brazel, as well as those from Marcel and his

Brigadier General Roger Ramey and Colonel Thomas DuBose examine the debris from the Roswell crash, 1947.

family. The suggestion was that the crashed saucer was brought down by a lightning strike when it was trying to monitor potential atomic weapons activity over New Mexico. The book contained interviews with 25 witnesses and led to worldwide interest in the story. It also led to a surge in further books on the subject, TV documentaries and even films, such was the interest from the public.

The Ramey memorandum

As time goes on, new technological developments help uncover even more evidence on the Roswell crash. More recently, high-tech scanning equipment and computer software have allowed researchers to closely examine six original photographs of the paper memorandum held by Colonel Ramey at the 1947 press conference. These were taken by press photographer J. Bond Johnson. In 1998, he assembled a team of photographic experts and software developers to do an in-depth analysis of the Ramey papers shown in the photos. By artificially enhancing the image and adjusting the contrast, they claimed that the memo revealed the following text:

> 'AS THE … 4 HRS THE VICTIMS OF THE … AT FORT WORTH, TEX … THE "CRASH" STORY … FOR 0984 ACKNOWLEDGES … EMERGENCY POWERS ARE NEEDED SITE TWO SW OF MAGDALENA, NMEX … SAFE TALK … FOR MEANING OF STORY AND MISSION … WEATHER BALLOONS SENT ON THE … AND LAND.'

If these findings are correct, could a 'crash story' refer to the destruction of an extraterrestrial craft? Would a weather balloon crash involve victims? And why would emergency powers be needed if the crash merely involved a weather-tracking balloon? Could 'site two' near Magdalena relate to another extraterrestrial crash site?

Further analysis carried out some years later suggested other wording in the memo included 'In the disk they will ship'. Many researchers point to the word 'disk' or 'disc' and suggest this could be the alleged flying disc referred to in the initial press release. 'In the disk' might mean objects found in the disk or saucer, possibly bodies? 'They will ship', might indicate the intention of the memo author to send something onwards – maybe, it could be argued, the crashed disc, or the weather balloon. But if a weather balloon came down and broke into many pieces, it was obviously not going to work again. Unless it was of major importance, you would likely just junk it and pick up another weather balloon from your storage unit.

But a flying disc or saucer would be a major find and would certainly be sent on to higher authorities for in-depth investigations to be carried out. Some researchers have suggested that Ramey was handed the memo and was unaware of its contents during the press conference. Interestingly, details that were to feature in later investigations might contradict this idea and suggest that Colonel Ramey was fully briefed. Later tests of enlarged photos of the memo conducted by authors J. Houran and K. D. Randle in 2002 involved three separate groups who assessed the information in controlled conditions. Members of the first group were briefed on the Roswell crash and told it could be connected to that particular incident. The second group was given suggestions that it might contain information about atomic bombs. The third group were not told anything about the memo but asked only to try and read it.

Significantly, the first group came up with words associated with UFOs, crashes and bodies; the second group, looking for associations, made references to atomic bombs; the last group who were told just to look at the documents were a little bit more in the dark. The authors of the study believe that having some previous knowledge of the Roswell incident actually does help when trying to decode the memo. For instance, researcher David Rudiak, mentioned earlier, found letters that could be attributed to officers involved in the incident. In newspapers of the time, journalists mentioned the involvement of General Vandenberg in connection with the alleged recovered craft. When Rudiak studied the header column of the memo, he noticed a word that clearly started with 'VA'. His guess was that this was the beginning of 'Vandenberg'. When this section was blown up further, the name 'Vandenberg' could be seen. That told him that the memo was not intended for Ramey, but was destined for Vandenberg, and could therefore possibly be a typed letter of the kind that would later be teletyped over the wire as in the case of the radio station sending out press releases before the FBI stepped in. A person without that knowledge would possibly see just the two letters and ignore a potentially important clue.

The authors J. Houran and K. D. Randle, who conducted the control group tests on the memo, postulated that further information could be found by using an identical camera to that used to photograph the Ramey memo taken by the original photographer, J. Bond Johnson, using several military messages from that era. New photographs taken of them from various distances at various angles might yield new information. But it's not known if this idea was ever carried forward.

UK researcher and writer David Jones, a former horror novel writer, has spent over a year on the memo. Making use of his background in international logistics, he recognized familiar shipping terms in the memo and managed to crack 77 of the 90 words shown in the photo. He believes much of the text is encrypted with substitute words, which might make sense given that so much of the previous research was reaching dead ends. He believes it was encrypted using a typewriter, by substituting letters with letters or numbers next to the letter or number on the keyboard. In this way, the letter C on a keyboard is next to X. Instead of typing the letter C, the encryption would use the X in place of it.

One sentence decoded by Jones includes the words 'Mystsrous reamnnts og diskb are going'. He translates that to mean 'Mysterious remnants of Disk B are going' and 'Disk B' might indicate then that another disc, 'Disc A', could also have been recovered. What are the mysterious remnants? Well earlier in the memo, he translates another sentence as saying, 'Beings are aliens tacitly "ET" origin in nature.' The speculation and controversy that grew up around his deciphered memo continues, but he believes that ultimately, at some point, AI would be a useful tool to unpack it further.

Crash at Corona

In 1992, Stanton Friedman and aviation author Don Berliner's co-written book, *Crash at Corona*, reignited interest in the Roswell incident and the question of whether a flying saucer had indeed crashed in the New Mexico desert in 1947. The co-authors secured interviews with the original witness, Lt. Col. Jesse Marcel. He had also heard incredible evidence from a local mortician, which is detailed below. In addition, they interviewed Jerry Anderson, who was only seven at the time and out with his family when they claimed to have come across a crashed and damaged flying saucer in the Plains of San Agustin, an area of the New Mexico desert about 240 km (150 miles) west of Corona, where 'Mac' Brazel found the original mysterious debris. This site is also close to the small town of Magdalena – the location possibly identified in the Ramey memorandum. Incredibly, Jerry recounted that the Andersons saw small dead alien bodies that resembled human children, except with small eyes and no ears. He said one of these beings appeared to be alive and was very frightened of the Andersons and the other people there (a small team of archaeologists also happened to discover the crash site too while Jerry and his family were there). There seemed therefore to be two possible crash sites, the one found by 'Mac' Brazel near Magdalena and the other in the Plains of San Austin, discovered by the Andersons and the archaeological team.

For many years, the US Air Force categorically denied anything of significance had happened at Roswell, other than a crashed weather balloon. However, in 1995, the USAF published *The Roswell Report: Fact vs. Fiction in the New Mexico Desert*. This report concluded that the original weather balloon story of 1947 was indeed a fabrication to cover the fact that a top-secret Mogul balloon had crashed and been recovered. Project Mogul was a classified USAF programme that launched microphones attached to balloons into the upper atmosphere to try to detect long-distance sound waves from potential detonations of

Soviet atomic bombs. (At that time, the US was the only country known to have this capability, but it was suspected the Russians were testing their own atomic devices.) The report suggested that the mysterious material recovered from the Foster ranch by Mac Brazel was actually a Mogul balloon. However, it did not mention the eyewitness accounts relating to alien bodies allegedly seen at the time.

Case closed?

Later in 1995, President Clinton spoke openly about Roswell during a visit to Belfast in Northern Ireland. Clinton was known to be very interested in UFOs, including the Roswell Incident, and prior to his visit had received a letter from a 13-year-old boy from Belfast called Ryan, asking him about extraterrestrials. At a press conference, President Clinton revealed, 'that no alien spacecraft, as far as I know, had crashed at Roswell in 1947'. He added, 'If the US Air force have recovered alien bodies, then they didn't tell me about it and I want to know about it!'

Two years later in 1997, under direction from President Clinton, the US Air Force issued a report called *The Roswell Report: Case Closed.* In this final report, it was suggested that witnesses who had allegedly seen dead aliens had probably made a mistake after coming across test dummies that were dropped by the USAF in parachute tests. However, some critics, like Stanton Friedman, pointed out that dummies were never tested in 1947 and were not used until around 1954.

In 2020, President Donald Trump was also asked about Roswell in an interview conducted by his own son. Trump said, 'It's very interesting. I mean, I won't tell you what I know but it is very interesting at Roswell.' Why didn't Trump simply say the real story behind the Roswell Incident was Project Mogul? By this point in time, Project Mogul had been declassified (in 1958) and this was the official line on what happened there in 1947. Trump was hinting in his response that he was privy to some additional information but could not divulge it. Possibly intelligence officials had discovered something more substantial after Clinton's presidency. Could President Trump have been referring to extraterrestrial crash 'victims' supposedly seen by certain witnesses?

A Project Mogul array.

Project Mogul has been discounted by researcher David Rudiak as the official explanation for the Roswell incident, based upon deep analysis of the Ramey memo. He considers the most important word of the entire message is 'VICTIMS' on the third line (taken from part of the phrase 'THE VICTIMS OF THE WRECK'). If there were 'VICTIMS', he says, then this was no Mogul balloon crash as declared by the US Airforce. Going back to the memo, it's interesting that the Airforce stated in their 1994 Roswell report that the CIA's National Photographic Interpretations Center had failed to glean any clear information from a digital scan of the memo as it was of insufficient quality. Yet, ordinary citizens without the CIA budgets managed to get higher-resolution scans of the same memo which made 90 per cent of the words it contains recognizable.

Bringing up the bodies

One of the words that analysts claimed to have identified in the Colonel Ramey memorandum was 'bodies'. During his research, ufologist Stanton Friedman came across a man named W. Glen Dennis, mentioned earlier, who in 1947 had been the contracted mortician for both the locals of Roswell and the USAF staff at the Roswell Army Air Force (RAAF) base. Dennis told Friedman that he had received a telephone call in the afternoon of 7 July from a mortuary officer at the RAAF base asking whether he could supply child-sized coffins that could be hermetically sealed to prevent decomposition. Later, the officer called back to ask for advice on preparing bodies that had been decomposing out in the desert and, in particular, he asked which chemicals would be most effective in preserving these bodies without significantly altering their biology. Dennis offered to come out to the base, but the officer declined, saying this was merely a hypothetical scenario. Dennis assumed there had been a sudden death at the base that the military did not want it made public.

Dennis went on to tell Friedman that, later the same day, a military worker was injured while in town and he drove the injured man back to the RAAF base for further treatment. There, Dennis noticed something unusual: three ambulances were parked outside the base's medical wing with a military policeman standing by each one. The ambulance doors were all open and Dennis observed what he took to be crashed wreckage in each vehicle. He described the debris as consisting of metals burned blue from the heat they had encountered; they were shaped like the front of a canoe. He also noticed writing on the wreckage that to him looked like Egyptian hieroglyphs. Perplexed by this, he walked into the medical wing to find a lieutenant nurse he knew who had recently started working at the RAAF base. He spotted her in a corridor, coming out of one treatment room and about to go into another. Dennis recalled that, when she saw him, she looked very worried and asked, 'How did you get in here? You shouldn't be here. You better get out in a hurry, or you are gonna get in a lot of trouble. Would you please leave?'

Dennis was then confronted by an aggressive officer with red hair who threatened him, telling him not to say anything to anyone about what he had seen. He was then abruptly escorted off the premises by two military policemen. The next day, he met his nurse friend for lunch as he was keen to find out what was going on. The nurse was quite upset during their meeting; she explained that three small bodies had been recovered from a crash and she had been called into one of the rooms where they were being medically examined. Two of the bodies she said were 90 cm to 1.2 m (3 ft to 4 ft) tall and badly mutilated in the crash. However, the doctors appeared to think the third, less mutilated 'child' must have escaped the crash alive and died later.

According to Dennis, the nurse described the victims' fingers as very slender with small suckers at the fingertips. They also had large heads with no ears and a small slit for a mouth, with no lips. It appeared that the bodies had been in the sun for a while, and all three had been partially eaten by wild animals. Despite being someone who regularly dealt with injuries, she told Dennis she had never seen anything so horrific and gruesome in her life, and that when he saw her in the corridor, she had just left the treatment room to be sick because she felt so ill. Other medical staff who were involved in the autopsy examinations had also thrown up. If the nurse's account was accurate, it conflicts with the conclusion of the USAF's *Roswell: Case Closed* report from 1997, which suggested the 'bodies' were actually crash test dummies. How could dummies be eaten by wild animals or, for that matter, horrify trained medical staff?

In a strange twist, Dennis told Stanton Friedman that his nurse friend was abruptly transferred to another army air force base within a day or two of chatting with him, even though she had only been stationed at Roswell for three months. Later, he learned his friend had died in a plane crash in England within two months of leaving the airforce base. Dennis never revealed the name of the nurse that was witness to the alleged alien autopsies. This led to some critics to think he was making it all up. But he maintained his account was the truth until the day he died on 28 April 2015.

Applying extraterrestrial technology

In the same year in which the USAF published its *Roswell: Case Closed* report, a US Army officer, Lieutenant Colonel Philip Corso, detailed his alleged involvement with extraterrestrial technology recovered from the 1947 Roswell crash in his book, *The Day after Roswell*. He claimed that in 1961, while working for the foreign technology desk in the US Army's research and development function in Washington DC, he also wrote about a covert government-backed group known as Majestic 12, operating under the leadership of Admiral Roscoe H. Hillenkoetter, a former director of the Central Intelligence Agency (CIA). UFO researcher and physicist, Stanton Friedman, claimed the group was tasked with secretly gathering information from crashed and recovered UFOs and reverse-engineering it for defence and industrial purposes: for instance, by developing technologies such as accelerated particle beam devices, fibre optics, lasers and integrated circuit chips.

Corso also claimed that private contractors were given some UFO parts with free rein to profit from these if they could 'decode' how they worked and then report back. It's suggested in his book that the craft was possibly controlled by bands that fitted around the heads of the alien pilots and somehow used their thoughts or minds/brains to control the craft, rather than, say, hand controls. Attempts at back engineering other alleged recovered flying saucers often failed, it is claimed, due to the unique interface of the headbands not being compatible with human brains. This may not cover all alleged back-engineered craft, however. Other technological finds within the craft included transparent wires that were able to send information via light. This was apparently the initial starting point of fibre optics, where information is sent through plastic fibre wires or tubes.

Corso also claimed he handled things the size of a quarter dollar, which were later developed into integrated circuits by selected industries. Stanton Friedman also mentioned the covert creation of Majestic 12, even listing the names of purported members.

Corso died in 1998, a year after the publication of his book. He passed away due to a heart attack at the age of 83. Some might speculate that his death was suspicious, since it happened within a year of the publication of his book. But he had already had an operation a few months after his book was published and, if someone was wanting him dead, that would have been the likeliest time that he could have been killed, under the guise of an operation. Yet, he recovered from the operation on his stomach and died about a year later.

As outlined in the next chapter, in 1989 a man named Robert Lazar claimed to have worked on recovered UFO technology (although his scientific credentials and his story have both been challenged). More recently, in 2023 a former intelligence official in the Air Force and National Geospatial Intelligence Agency office named David Grusch, who analysed unidentified anomalous phenomena (UAPs or UFOs) for the US Department of Defense's UAP Task Force, came forward as a 'UFO whistleblower'. After giving interviews to journalists, Grusch testified under oath to a Congressional hearing on UAPs in Washington DC in July 2023 which was viewed on television and live over the internet, stating that the US government operates secret programmes to recover, analyse and reverse-engineer 'non-human spacecraft' and their dead pilots.

At the hearing titled 'Unidentified Anomalous Phenomena: Implications on National Security, Public Safety, and Government Transparency', Grusch informed the Congressional hearing that he was briefed by unidentified insiders of 'a multi-decade UAP crash retrieval and reverse-engineering program' when he began to investigate classified programs. Trying to access those programs proved to be something of a problem for Grusch as he said he was denied access to those specific programs when he requested it. He also publicly accused the military of 'misappropriating funds to hide these operations from congressional oversight'. He later said he had interviewed officials who claimed to have had direct knowledge of aircraft with 'nonhuman' origins, and that so-called 'biologics' were recovered from some craft. 'Aircraft, meaning UAP or UFOs and nonhuman or biologics in typical terms, would be aliens or perhaps extraterrestrials. It caused considerable controversy, which is still unfolding as Grusch has said there is more information to come. The hearings came about due to pressure from the public over a number of years to get the government to come clean on what it knows about UFO phenomena.

The US government seems to have attempted to appear to be offering something with one hand but hiding it with the other. In 2022, it set up the all-domain anomaly resolution officer – AARO – 'to conduct or to coordinate efforts across the Department of Defense and other Federal agents to detect, identify and investigate UAPs'. However, the budget AARO was given remains classified and members of Congress are not able to gain any information from it. On the other hand, NASA, which is responsible for civilian space missions, is also conducting an independent study into UAPs. The hearing recognized though, that there was still a pressing demand 'for government transparency and accountability that cannot be overlooked and that had been a problem that has been around for 50 years'. Interestingly, they did not mention the Roswell incident, which goes back nearly 80 years. One thing that has come about from the hearing is that the Department of Defense no longer denies the existence of UAPs or UFOs. It can no longer say they are mirages, temperature inversions or swamp gas as they used to often state. It may no longer deny them, but the hearings are a unified all-party attempt to gain clarity on the UFO situation. Members stated 'Today, we are not just debating the existence of UAPs. We are deliberating on the principles that define our republic, which is a commitment to transparency and accountability.'

The Department of Defense is just not going to give away too much. The AARO (All-domain Anomaly Resolution Office, part of the Pentagon), in their preliminary report of 2022, called 'Report on the Historical Record of U.S. Government Involvement with Unidentified

Anomalous Phenomena (UAP) Volume I,' stated, 'The goal of this report is not to prove or disprove any particular belief set, but rather to use a rigorous analytic and scientific approach to investigate past USG-sponsored UAP investigation efforts and the claims made by interviewees that the United States Government and various contractors have recovered and are hiding off-world technology and biological material.'

Saying they are not going to prove or disprove any particular belief set suggests that their goal is not actually to try and find hidden UFOs in hangers. Instead, AARO published elements of previous reports that had been compiled over the last 50 years but left out many pertinent government reports from the past. One report critical of them from The Hill said, 'AARO appears to have conducted little investigation beyond superficial interviews.' Robert Powell of the Scientific Coalition for UAP Studies said, 'There is a tendency in the AARO paper to pull the data that supports the AARO position and leave out the data that might argue against it.' Other criticisms of AARO's report point to typographical errors, and getting dates of key UFO sightings wrong, such as Kenneth Arnold's historic sighting from his plane in Washington State. Critics also say that AARO simply reprinted the findings of past official studies on UAP, which were themselves inaccurate. It's therefore hardly rigorous as they claimed it would be. None the less, the Head of AARO, Sean Kirkpatrick, resigned in December 2023, saying he had accomplished what he set out to do.

Alien accident: a timeline?

If some kind of UFO did crash-land in the New Mexico desert on the night of 2 July 1947 – and the US Air Force itself initially stated that it did – how might such an event have played out? Some UFO researchers suggest that the basic Roswell crash scenario appears to suggest that either an unidentified flying object of some kind, maybe a flying disc, came down around the night of July 2 of 1947, or that the Roswell Incident might have been caused by an electrical storm. After crash-landing, the craft might have 'managed to bounce' for a few miles to a new location, at which point the crew could have ejected in pods or gone down with their craft – that's if you accept that there were at least two identified crash sites: the Foster ranch where 'Mac' Brazel found the initial crash debris, and then another 150 miles further west in the Plains of San Augustin, where the final descent occurred, killing all but one of the crew. This was the site discovered by the family of young Jerry Anderson, who claimed he saw three small beings, one still alive.

On the other hand, there's the official version, which says, yes, something unusual did happen, but it wasn't alien. This version of events happened around the Corona crash site and was discovered by the rancher Brazel. It was part of the Mogul balloon experiment, a top-secret government operation designed to monitor Soviet atomic weapon capability, concerning Atomic Detonations in the upper atmosphere. The scientist who broke the Roswell story for the second time, the late Stanton Friedman, said that the incident was the Story of the Millennium. He insisted the truth was that the United States Army Airforce recovered a crashed flying saucer together with alien bodies and was covering this up successfully. Well, maybe not that successfully… People still question the narrative and many do not believe the official line, especially when members of the government spill the beans about incidents that could be indications of the true nature of the Roswell incident.

In a memo from FBI agent, Guy Hottel, to the then head of the FBI, J. Edgar Hoover, in March 1950, he wrote that an Air Force investigator made a report about three recovered flying saucers that had crashed in the New Mexico desert, although the date was not given. He added, 'The saucers were described as being circular in shape with raised centres, approximately 50 feet in diameter. Each one was occupied by three bodies of human shape but only three feet tall, dressed in metallic cloth of a very fine texture. Each body was bandaged in a manner similar to the blackout suits used by speed fliers and test pilots.' The investigator claimed that 'high-powered radar' in the area had interfered with 'the controlling mechanism of the saucers'. And the memo ends simply by saying, 'No further evaluation was attempted', laying the matter to rest as far as the FBI agent was concerned.

The FBI actually released this memo in the late-1970s, but it was rediscovered some time later in an update of the FBI website. The present-day FBI try to downplay the report, saying that it has nothing to do with Roswell. But the fact that it mentions recovered flying saucers and alien bodies in the same area suggests that perhaps Friedman could be right and that Project Mogul, later announced as the basis of the Roswell Incident, could be just another false story designed to obscure the truth.

AREA 51

Around the world, it's not unusual to find military bases located within strategically sensitive areas of each country. In most cases, the wider public is unaware of their existence, unless they happen to live in the local area, work at or supply the base in some civilian capacity… or, of course, they happen to be members of the armed forces serving that facility. However, there is one US Air Force military base that millions around the world do know about: Area 51, the top-secret US Air Force military base at Groom Lake, a dry salt-lake bed in southern Nevada. It is, in fact, probably the most famous 'secret' military base in the world, so deep and widespread is its association in popular culture with extraterrestrial research.

Under constant 24-hour surveillance with no public admittance, all Area 51 employees fly into the base instead of arriving by car or public bus services. Using a restricted terminal at Harry Reid International Airport near Las Vegas, employees travel on one of many unmarked aircraft allowed to fly through the restricted air space to land on the runways there. Only from 2018 did satellite imagery of the installation become available to the public. Why does a military base require such stringent security measures? It's long been associated with highly sensitive spy aircraft, but is Area 51 home to more mysterious, non-human research projects?

The entrance to Area 51

Secret history

The name 'Area 51' derives from the base's map designation. It was established as a Second World War aerial gunnery range for the US Army Air Corps and was also referred to as 'Paradise Ranch' to make it more appealing to those who were working there – other nicknames included 'Watertown' and 'Dreamland'. President Dwight D. Eisenhower approved Area 51 as the test zone (under the codename 'Project Aquatone') for the Lockheed U2 spy plane, a secret high-altitude reconnaissance aircraft made in 1955. Famously, a U2 spy plane, piloted by Gary Powers, was later shot down over the then Soviet Union, a fascinating story in itself. The testing ground was later used for other aircraft, including the A-12 'Oxcart' reconnaissance plane and the F-117A Nighthawk. In 1974, the US space station Skylab inadvertently took photographs of Area 51 without realizing what it was. The images were quickly removed from the rolls of film and stored in a secure vault.

The summer of 2012 finally saw the first official acknowledgement that Area 51 exists as a government facility. This occurred when a Central

A Lockheed U2 spy plane – one of the aircraft tested in Area 51.

Intelligence Agency (CIA) report, written in 1992, was declassified at the request of various journalists and scholars using Freedom of Information laws. Intelligence about other spy planes that had previously been top secret (such as the Lockheed Have Blue, built in 1980) was later declassified. They were designed with radar-invisible capabilities by Lockheed Skunkworks at the Nevada Test Range. This aircraft later developed into the Lockheed F-117A Nighthawk. In this way, it is clear that at least part of Area 51 is designated for secret aircraft development.

'Dennis' lifts the lid

In 1989, an individual named Robert Lazar went in front of a TV camera and told the world about Area 51's more otherworldly activities. Claiming to be a former employee of the US Navy working in an area known as the 'S4' range, which was part of Area 51, he gave an interview to Las Vegas's KLAS-TV reporter, George Knapp, about what he had seen at the secret base during the six months that he worked there.

Lazar was, to say the least, an interesting character. He had previously appeared in the local *Los Alamos Monitor* newspaper in

July 1982 for inventing a jet-powered car that he drove to work every day. The car, a Honda, had been converted to run a kit-supplied jet engine capable of putting out 1,600 pounds of thrust, but this was eventually reduced for safety reasons. The vehicle could travel at up to 200 miles per hour at top speed, although only on desert tracks. Lazar had previously worked for Los Alamos Laboratories, which specialized in nuclear power. It was his ability in the field of engineering and his scientific skill that led to his recruitment to Area 51: specifically to S4, the technical facility located 15 miles south of the Area 51 base. His predecessor in the role had apparently been killed in an accident at the secret military facility.

Using a cover name, 'Dennis', and appearing inside a shaded TV van to protect his face from being recognized in May 1989, Lazar made claims about working on recovered, crashed extraterrestrial 'flying saucers' inside the Area 51 facility. Lazar was in his mid-twenties when he said he was offered the position at S4. (Lazar was named by KLAS-TV in a follow-up series on UFOs broadcast in November 1989.) He explained to Knapp, his interviewer, that he first sighted an actual recovered flying saucer in the secret hangar, which is camouflaged as the side of a mountain. At first, Lazar thought the craft he was working on was manufactured by the United States, but he later found out through a colleague he would only name as 'Barry' that it was extraterrestrial.

Barry showed Lazar components from the strange craft, including a half-sphere on a metal plate about the size of a basketball. This item, said Lazar, had its own gravitational field, which he knew could not be manufactured by human technology. This meant that it counteracted the effect of gravity on Earth by pushing away from it, or defying it, not by using the thrust of rocket or jet exhausts but with a field of what you might call 'anti-gravity'.

Lazar said eventually he learned that he was involved in a project to duplicate alien technology with materials available on Earth. His task was to analyse how the craft was powered, which appeared to be by some kind of reactor technology, and then to reverse-engineer this system. It was, he said, comparable to handing Victorian scientists a small nuclear reactor and asking them to figure out how it might work. While he was excited to be working at the cutting edge of science, it was an enormous responsibility that quickly began to worry him.

In total, Lazar claimed, there were nine craft of varying shapes being examined in the nine adjacent hangars. He added that each team's work was highly compartmentalized and focused on specific areas or components of each individual craft; while his work might occasionally overlap with that of another team, he was only able to examine one craft, which he called the 'Sports Model' due to its sleek design. Photographs of this particular saucer could have been taken in the skies above Europe in 1975 by alleged UFO contactee, Billy Meier, who claimed he was in touch with aliens, who he called the Plejarens. Bob Lazar's saucer sketches were eventually turned into a model plastic kit for the commercial market by the company, Testors.

As part of Lazar's research, he claimed in his original TV interviews from 1989 and 1990 that he was permitted only once to go inside the craft, to check certain things as part of his research. He described its interior as totally smooth across all sections. It appeared as if there were no joins or seams; it had the look of being melted with a dripped candle with no hard edges. He had trouble standing up in the craft, as if it had been envisaged for small beings, much smaller than his stature of 5 ft 10 in. He noticed archways inside, which other scientists were working on, and these could have doubled up as a kind of screen, where images could be projected across the archway gap, beamed out from the inner rim of the arch. Three small seats were situated around the central reactor core, which ran from the base of the craft up to the ceiling. He later learned that this reactor core was part of the propulsion system, using in part a then undiscovered element, which he called Element 115, as part of its power source. He said the reactor core powered three gravity amplifiers in the lower section of the saucer. The wave generated and focused by these amplifiers would then go into gravity-emitters, long tube-like devices in the belly of the saucer that could swing in any direction to enable the craft to fly in space or over land and sea.

However, there were no control panels or switches, or anything resembling a recognizable aircraft cockpit. According to Lazar, the mysterious crafts were round in shape because of the heavy-duty electrical discharge that took place around them. On the top of the craft was what looked like an antenna, but according to Lazar this acted as an extension of the central core reactor. He called this a wave guide because it helped extend the gravity field around the whole of the saucer. The gravity-emitters could be thought of as guns firing out gravity waves, overcoming the gravitational pull of Earth and controlling the rise and fall and changes in direction. In fact, NASA spacecraft also use the gravity of planets to help them swing past other celestial bodies and to change direction.

To Lazar, the materials and components appeared to have capabilities that bordered on the magical. He was able to see that all the craft used some kind of gravity-based propulsion system. Lazar said that, when he asked where the craft came from, he was told 'somewhere else' by Barry his co-worker. He was never told where that 'somewhere else' actually was, but he believed these craft had been in the hangars at Area 51 for quite a while. During his time researching the technology of the saucer he was asked to look into, he learned by reading the available paperwork that it originated from an alien civilization from the third planet in the Zeta Reticuli, a binary star system (double star) in the Reticulum constellation, which can be seen with the naked eye from the southern hemisphere. Supposedly, this was the home of the extraterrestrials who abducted Betty and Barney Hill in 1961 in New Hampshire. Could they be the same alien beings?

Element 115

This chemical element 115 – which was not even part of the Periodic Table back in the 1980s – is a fascinating feature of the Area 51 mystery. Also known as moscovium, this highly radioactive element was synthesized in 2003 by a joint team of Russian and American scientists and it was only officially recognized in 2016 as one of four new elements. Lazar claimed in an interview in 1989 with George Knapp that the craft he studied in Area 51 was, in part, fuelled by Element 115.

On the one occasion when Lazar claimed he was allowed inside the mysterious craft, he noticed other scientists working around the interior archways, which also seemed to operate like a TV screen but one that was not solid. It was not clear from his brief observation, though, what they might be used for. During his six months working at S4 inside Area 51, he was aware of the presence of Russian scientists who seemed to be conducting joint research with the US teams. However, when an important but undisclosed discovery was made, they were soon sent back to the (then) USSR. US military authorities wanted, apparently, to keep the discovery for themselves. Lazar never knew what the discovery was, but perhaps it was Element 115 – the new element is apparently highly unstable as it only lasts less than a second in a lab before it fades away, rather like a bubble popping as soon as you have created it. Remarkably, the Area 51 version used in the saucers was able to remain stable and was therefore very usable.

Video footage

Eventually, Lazar decided he wanted to prove to his friends the truth of what he was telling them in private and started to gather proof that he was working on recovered flying saucers. He knew that flight testing of the UFOs around the base occurred on Wednesday evenings, when the roads were much quieter, so he took them as close as he legally could to the base, using an old desert road. On three successive Wednesday evenings in March 1989, he and four friends, including his then wife and an ex-CIA pilot named John Lear who was already a firm believer in UFOs, took to the perimeter of Area 51 in Tikaboo Valley, southeast of the base.

On each visit, according to Lazar, the group spotted UFOs and managed to film them on video making sharp turns that were not possible for conventional aircraft. The clips were later shown on TV, so presumably the material was not confiscated or was not found. On the third visit, they were detained by security officers, who were monitoring the perimeter. Lazar and his friends were taken to a military installation and interrogated. During this experience, Lazar was informed that his wife was having an affair as her regular phone calls to another man had been uncovered during routine monitoring of employees' home telephones. This was the first time he had been told about it. Lazar knew before he ever went to work there, that his phone calls would be monitored and this he had apparently willingly agreed to.

In later interviews with George Knapp, he alleged that the powers-that-be went on to make his and his friends' lives very difficult. The TV reporter himself claimed that he too was harassed and followed presumably by the security forces. All parties found it hard to progress in their jobs or suddenly had issues with the tax revenue services. Lazar interpreted this as a warning to anyone else who might be considering a security breach and he began to fear for his own safety. It was for these reasons, he claimed, that he decided the best way to protect himself was to go public. For the same reason, in later television interviews he would also choose to show his face and give his real name.

Reaction to Area 51

George Knapp's interview with Robert Lazar in 1989 quickly spread far beyond the local Las Vegas TV station, with excerpts being shown around the world. Within a few days of the KLAS-TV series on UFOs broadcast later in 1989, TV media were flocking to the Nevada desert and UFO enthusiasts and tourists were gathering in droves around the perimeter of the base.

Knapp went on to conduct further television interviews with Lazar. He recalled that during this period both men were followed by unknown individuals who might have been FBI agents, who made their intentions clear. They broke into Lazar's house and wrote warnings on his blackboard and broke into his car, leaving the doors wide open. To Knapp, it seemed as if they were trying to intimidate him and make his life uncomfortable. Knapp was followed and experienced harassing phone calls at his workplace as well.

The truth about the Area 51 mystery obviously rests heavily on the credibility of the main source of information about it – Robert Lazar. TV reporter George Knapp said he thoroughly checked out Lazar's academic and professional background and came up against brick walls. Does this simply mean Lazar was not the highly qualified scientist he claimed to be, or does it indicate the authorities were so uncomfortable with his revelations that they took steps to gaslight the public by obscuring his work record and deleting his academic credentials? Lazar countered that the government and military authorities were trying to undermine him and make him into a 'non-person' by obliterating any records of his education. He was able though to prove to Knapp that he at least did work in some capacity at the Los Alamos Labs, by the simple process of taking him there. He even managed to gain access to the building along with George and a TV crew. He waved hello to former colleagues and knew his way around the place very well, Knapp later said.

Lazar went on to do further interviews with TV stations and radio. At one time, a film was planned of his life at Area 51, but it never materialized. He decided though he did not really want to be known as the UFO guy and set up his own company supplying radioactivity detectors to schools and private business, as well as chemicals for lab professors in educational establishments. He re-emerged in 2018 in film-maker Jeremy Corbell's *Bob Lazar: Area 51 and Flying Saucers*, in which he spoke about his time at the S4 establishment, providing further information on the saucers and how his life had changed since he emerged on to the world stage.

Testing Lazar's claims

Between April and May 1990 Lazar voluntarily agreed to take four polygraph tests, or so-called 'lie-detector' tests. Former policeman, independent security consultant and polygraph expert, Terry Tavernetti concluded that there was no attempt to deceive in any of the tests they did on Lazar. The original polygraph-tester who first wired up Lazar to his machine said the results he obtained indicated a fear behind Lazar's answers. This he thought was because Lazar dreaded consequences from his former employers, so the initial examiner recommended the skills of Tavernetti instead.

When Tavernetti tested Lazar on separate occasions, he said he believed he was telling the truth. Maybe by the second or third test, he was relaxed enough to speak more openly about his experiences. Many years later, during interviews, Lazar admitted he suffered from migraine headaches that affected his long-term memory and ability to focus during interviews. Of course, a sceptic might say this is a convenient get-out should Lazar be challenged on specific details of his claims. However, if Lazar was totally fooling everyone, it was rather strange that Tavernetti found himself in hot water not long after testing Lazar. Firstly, he found his employers were getting calls about him from an unnamed agency, asking why he was getting involved in something that he shouldn't be. The second thing that happened to the tester, was that his own home was broken into two months later – he believed that this was an attempt to steal the charts from Lazar's test. Luckily, he had made back-up copies which he shared with his colleagues, one of whom agreed with his professional opinion on Lazar's test results, while another thought more tests should be conducted.

There are those who are sceptical of Lazar's background and credentials, which obviously affects how they see the whole mystery of Area 51. The late UFO researcher and former nuclear physicist, Stanton Friedman, said Lazar came across to him as a bright individual. However, he could find no record of Lazar attending MIT and earning a Master's Degree in physics or a degree in electronics at CalTec. He also added that he spoke to people at MIT who claimed they never knew him. He also called up his old High School in New Jersey, where they told Friedman that Lazar was in the bottom two-thirds of his science class. Former Intelligence Secretary, Christopher Mellon, went on the Joe Rogan podcast in 2021, claiming that he was friends with Bob's supervisor who was called 'Dennis' at S4. He said that Bob just checked the radiation on people's badges when he worked there. A strange statement to make, when a few years before, they were denying the place existed and now they were almost admitting he did work there but in a lowly capacity.

Lazar has long argued that the authorities have tried to erase him from official records. Going back to the Joe Rogan podcast featuring

Christopher Mellon, Rogan explained to Mellon that Lazar had gone into private details of why his background at MIT was hidden. He said he was sent there by the government to do certain tasks or tests and that these tests for the government were apparently 'horrible' and this is why he can't talk about them too much. Rogan said he would provide Mellon with more details about this away from the studio and certainly off air! We don't know what these 'horrible' experiments might be, but some would argue this is just a bit of back-peddling by Lazar over his claims about MIT. He has never shown paper proofs of his work at MIT or CalTech, but his work at Los Alamos Labs was proven at least to the satisfaction of George Knapp. Other renowned scientists have taken a favourable view of Lazar's claims. One such person, who did actually go to CalTech, was Dr Rudolph Schild, emeritus astronomer at the Harvard and Smithsonian Center for Astrophysics, who researches dark matter, black holes and the cosmic structure of the universe; he has published over 300 peer-reviewed academic articles on astrophysics. While many astronomers reject the existence UFOs for lack of evidence, Dr Schild took a keen interest in Lazar's description of the interior of the UFO craft he claimed to have inspected. During an interview with George Knapp in 2021, Schild said, 'I found Bob Lazar's materials extremely interesting'.

Schild was convinced Lazar was talking about the 'brain' of the UFO, which is essentially its own special computer. He said, 'People who have been on to the craft and have been given a tour,' referring to contactees or abductees, in other words those who have gone on board craft 'and seen the crystal at the top of the central column which is like a sensor of the universe', like perhaps a telescope or map charting the heavens. In layman's terms, Bob had described the navigational instruments, or space navigator on the craft he worked on, and Schild believes others have seen the same type of instruments in crafts they have been on. In his sketches of the craft, Lazar depicted the brain at the top in the dome section, adding that the UFO had two modes of travel, one for travelling through the universe and one for travelling in localized areas such as through Earth's atmosphere.

Schild agrees that there appears to be descriptions out there demonstrating the two modes of travel, citing a lady called Suzy Hansen from New Zealand who claims to have piloted a flying saucer, using the various modes of flight described by Lazar. Starting in 1975, she used manual levers to move the craft forward, but on other occasions she was shown how to move the craft using only her mind. Documentary film-maker Jeremy Corbell, who made the film about Bob Lazar in 2018, also went digging into Lazar's past. Lazar had talked to him about a strange hand-scanner device that was used as part of the entry procedure to the secure S4 facility. He described how it would scan your bones and compare it to a previously accepted record, as apparently our hand bones are as individual as fingerprints.

According to Corbell, when Bob first talked about this in his initial late-80s and early-90s interviews, everyone said he was making it up and there was no such device. However, a contact of Corbell's managed to track down and secure a photograph of the special hand-scanner and put it into the film. No one was more surprised than Lazar when he viewed the film and saw the old hand-scanner that no one had believed existed, so it was apparently true. But could he have made it up anyhow? In the film *2010: The year we make contact*, the 1984 sequel to *2001: A Space Odyssey*, one of the key characters gains access to a secure facility run by the US Government. He places his hand on a special palm-scanner that proceeds to glow as if to scan his hand and then the door opens. Could Lazar have seen this film and deduced that it was probable the government was already doing that kind of thing back in the mid-80s? It is not totally unfeasible.

If the mystery of what happened at Area 51 rests on Robert Lazar's detailed recollections, it can be argued that this was at least indirect support for claims that Area 51 did indeed contain recovered craft from elsewhere in the universe.

Recent developments

Area 51 came under further public scrutiny in the mid-1990s when former employees took the government to court over exposure to hazardous materials that they believed were not being disposed of correctly. The ex-employees alleged violations of the Resource Conservation and Recovery Act 'in the storage, treatment, and disposal of hazardous waste at the operating location near Groom Lake'. A decision in their favour was later overturned when the court decided that the Environmental Protection Agency (EPA) completed its duties satisfactorily. There was no mention, however, of crashed saucers or UFOs being the source of hazardous materials. The government, if they did have anything of that nature, would likely be minded to keep those bits of information away from public courts if they could at that time.

Some have claimed the hazardous waste handled at Area 51 could have been radioactive material. A former security guard who worked at Area 51, Dave Crete, patrolled the perimeter fence as well as other parts of the complex between 1983 to 1987. He has said in TV interviews (in 2023) that he suffers from health issues relating to his work at the installation, where he helped guard Stealth bombers and other secret aircraft. When the site was used as a testing ground for nuclear weapons, the whole area, including the dust Crete later breathed in, became highly radioactive.

The government had apparently told employees that the area was secured off, but this was only with a wire fence, which would have not stopped radioactive particles at all. Crete now suffers from serious health challenges such as tumours and scarring on the lungs caused by breathing in the radioactive dust. He says he and his former colleagues were exposed to Plutonium, Uranium and other such toxic wastes. Crete and his colleagues are now in the process of suing the government and are trying to get them to help with medical benefits. (He may not get very far, however; see below.) Dave Crete said in a *News Nation* interview in 2023 that he was proud to have worked at Area 51 and it was 'unique and incredible'. Could he be referring to secret craft such as UFOs or back-engineered craft made from recovered saucers? It's not clear, but whatever is going on, people are not happy with the way the government has brushed these Area 51 workers to one side.

If materials contained radioactive energy necessary for fuelling alien craft that were highly toxic to humans, it gives another dimension to the decision in September 2003 made by President George W. Bush to exempt the EPA from any litigation issues relating to the Groom Lake region, at that time still not officially recognised as the location of Area 51. This exemption was granted in the wake of the World Trade Center terrorist attack, or '9/11' as it is known, in a climate when the US government was enacting more and more stringent security measures. When considering the question of what might prompt a government to exempt Area 51 in this way, it's not inconceivable that the demand for weapons supremacy and transformative technologies to meet the new threat of global terrorism might lead to free rein for scientists to do whatever is required, regardless of the cost to the environment or humans.

New evidence has also emerged about activities at Area 51. Dr Steven Greer is a physician and 'ufologist', who founded an organization named The Disclosure Project in the early 2000s as a public forum for other UFO researchers and military personnel to share their experiences with UFOs. In July 2016, Dr Greer interviewed a former officer at the US Air Force Office of Special Investigations named Richard Doty, who said he had been based at Area 51 in the 1980s.

Doty confirmed he was based in Area 51 during the 1980s and said there was two different locations in that area. These were named Groom Lake and Dept 3, plus an auxiliary site known as Papoose Lake, a dried salt lake with an underground entrance. He said the Papoose Lake base was supposedly connected underground to other parts of every other sector of Area 51 via a series of tunnels. The main tunnel was shaped like a horseshoe and in theory you could travel all around the base using just these tunnels, including in theory getting to Lazar's S4 facility. Personnel working there had to wear badges indicating their security clearance and these showed whether they had the right to enter certain areas of the complex. While some scientists who were working on both projects shared information, he explained that in general everything was tightly compartmentalized, so each area did not really know much about the other secured areas.

While working at the base, Doty said he saw a 30 m (100 ft) wide, saucer-shaped craft in the underground complex at the Papoose area, and a damaged craft he believed was much older. He also claimed to have seen an alien on a closed-circuit camera being interviewed while he was there, although he did not encounter an extraterrestrial face to face. There were, he said, numerous crashes in the area due to human pilots being unable to fly the recovered alien craft properly. (If true, this could account for the various radiations reported by Area 51 security officers such as Dave Crete.)

Doty also knew of Russian scientists working at the S4 facility while he was there. If true, this means there must have been an agreement between the world's two superpowers to co-operate, despite the ongoing Cold War between them. This was already happening publicly to a degree with the Apollo–Soyuz rendezvous in 1975, when American and Russian space craft docked in space for the first time, paving the way for the construction of the International Space Station. Behind the scenes, however, both sides appeared to be working on spacecraft from an entirely different planet. The USSR may have even had its own version of Area 51, according to some ufologists, in an area known as Kapustin Yar, 100 km (62 miles) east of Volgograd (formerly Stalingrad). This has been confirmed as a site where rockets and missiles are tested, and there are claims that UFOs have also been sighted in the area.

The whistleblower vindicated?

Perhaps most importantly, Doty confirmed that Lazar did indeed work in the S4 division of Area 51. Doty was later criticized, and his testimony was doubted, by some people because his work was in counter-intelligence, which meant to them that he could not be seen as reliable or trustworthy. Others, however, believe he was telling the truth, at least some of the time. In an interview called 'Punk Rock and UFOs', Doty said, 'The only misinformation that is being spread about the UFO phenomenon is from UFO researchers. I have never spread any information that was incorrect.'

A former Air Force Intelligence Officer, Robert M. Collins who co-wrote a book with Doty in 2005 called *Exempt from Disclosure* has said

Rockets at Kapustin Yar, a Russian missile testing site.

about his co-writer, 'What Doty says is true in certain cases and false in others: he has lied or distorted facts in recent interviews but told the truth in other interviews.' So perhaps Collins believes Doty about the Lazar case, maybe because he may have insider knowledge about him too? Collins in the same book provides the reader with 3D maps showing the Area 51 complex, which was later featured in the History Channel show *UFO Files*.

The world's best-known 'unknown' location

Ironically, the top-secret military base has become America's most famous, so much so that on 11 July 2019 over 1.5 million people indicated through Facebook that they would go to an event called 'Storm Area 51, they can't stop us all'. The Facebook event invited people to invade Area 51 on 20 September 2019 at 3am. Around 200 people did turn up outside the gates of Area 51 for the 'raid' on the facility. It turned into something of a party, with nothing sinister really happening. One visitor stepped over the line and was arrested but later released. In

1995, the federal government expanded the area of exclusion around the base to include nearby mountains that had previously provided onlookers with a clear overview of the base, prohibiting access to 3,972 acres (16.07 km2) of land formerly administered by the Bureau of Land Management.

Given that Area 51 has become a victim of its own secrecy, it would also stand to reason that government and military authorities would increase the security there, and also consider whether highly sensitive projects should stay within the complex. It's conceivable then, that like a magician, who tells you to watch his right hand, the left hand is doing all the unseen secret manipulations. Perhaps with Area 51, we have been watching the right hand of the magician so much – including the activity of individuals such as Robert Lazar – that we have completely overlooked the other underhand manoeuvring in the shadows.

It has come to the point now, where the public are so infused with the mystery of Area 51, that the most top-secret base has paradoxically become the most famous. I wonder what other areas of the United States seldom visited by most people, such as Alaska, might contain secret bases. While we are looking at one mystery in Nevada, another one – Area 52? – is probably not even suspected!

THE TUNGUSKA EVENT

When the US dropped two atomic bombs in August 1945 over the Japanese cities of Hiroshima and Nagasaki, the resulting devastation killed between 150,000 and 246,000 people, most of whom were civilians, and led to Japan's surrender six days later, ending the Second World War and forever changing the world.

As horrifically powerful as these bombs were, an event with an explosive energy 1,000 times more powerful than the Hiroshima bomb had already happened decades previously in a remote area of Siberia, a vast and thinly populated region of Russia that is larger than France. What's more, had it occurred just four hours later, the 'Tunguska Event' could itself have changed the course of history. But what exactly was the cause of this enormous blast – was it natural in origin, or the result of human experimentation, or even alien intervention? There is certainly no shortage of theories around this mysterious explosion, from the scientific to the more bizarre.

At around 7.14 am on 30 June 1908 (or June 17 according to the Julian calendar, which was used in imperial Russia before 1918), a huge airborne explosion 5–10 km (15,000–30,000 ft) up in the skies over central Siberia flattened and charred more than 2,150 sq km (830 square miles) of *taiga*, or pine forest, near the Podkamennaya Tunguska River. Also known as the 'Great Siberian Explosion', the Tunguska Event was witnessed by the sparse indigenous population of reindeer herders: the Evenki. Their accounts, passed down through generations, offer the most reliable evidence of what eyewitnesses experienced when the massive explosion occurred.

Some described seeing a very bright bluish light speeding through the sky with a thin trail behind it. One witness, named only as S. Semenov, said it was like two suns were in the sky at the same time. From

Flattened trees after the Tunguska event.

his wooden shelter, he saw a huge cloud forming near the horizon, with a tall plume of fire that cast a red hue across the landscape. The plume then split in two and eventually turned into a black cloud. Semenov recalled wanting to tear off his shirt as an oncoming wave of searing heat engulfed him. Minutes later, there was a cracking sound that he thought could be thunder, and what sounded like rocks smashing together. The earth began to move and shake and the force of what he saw threw him backwards on to the ground. Other witnesses described seeing around four bright explosions in the sky, one after the other. In nearby towns, some people said they saw what appeared to be a bluish-white heavenly body, which for 10 minutes moved downwards from the sky. It was like a pipe or a tube in shape, although too bright to view clearly.

Afterwards, it became clear that this event had flattened thousands of trees and killed many reindeer in its first shattering seconds alone. Scientists now think the blast and its scorching effects may have destroyed as many as 80 million trees. Through Evenki witness accounts, it was estimated that only three people died, either straight away or a short while after the explosion.

Many ran from the terrifying heat and fires, believing that the extreme brightness of the immediate flash meant the end of the world had come. Farther away, people in more populous areas felt the effects of the shockwave, which caused windows to smash and buildings to shake. For the Evenki people, the terrifying blast and its devastation were a sign that their god of thunder, Odgy, was angered by their sins.

Midnight sun around Europe

Around the world, seismic monitors used to measure ground movements resulting from earthquakes recorded the shock wave emerging from Siberia as so powerful that it travelled twice around the world before its energy dissipated.

For a few days, the night sky over Europe was strangely bright, so that even thousands of miles away at an observatory in County Armagh, Northern Ireland the log book recorded a nocturnal glow in the sky throughout the month of July. In 1934, someone added a comment to the same page of the log book attributing this glow to 'the Great Meteor Explosion in Siberia.' In London, a photograph was taken at the Royal Museum in Greenwich around midnight just after the Tunguska Event, and it showed the glare that lit up the sky. In early July, in Godmanchester, Huntingdonshire, England, a resident, Ms Katharine Stephen, described a 'strange light', which made the sky so bright that it was possible to read large print indoors during night-time. The light came from the northeast horizon (looking towards Russia) and was 'a bright flame-colour'. The sky above the light was 'blue as in the daytime' reported a letter to *The Times* newspaper on 2 July 1908.

It was thought that particles thrown up into the atmosphere during the explosion were reflecting the light from the Sun, even though it had already set. Acting rather like a huge mirror, this strange anomaly was reported across several newspapers of the day. In 1966, Soviet astronomer, Vasily Fesenkov, argued, 'The most probable explanation for the anomalously bright nights associated with the Tunguska meteorite fall would be that the meteorite was actually a little comet with a dust tail pointing away from the sun.' He went on to explain that the dust from the comet's tail was dispersed into ice particles in the upper atmosphere. In the 1960s, the most popular theory was that the explosion was caused by a comet with a long tail plume.

However, following the explosion, there appeared to be little serious investigation into the possible causes or consequences by journalists, scientists or government officials, either within Russia or western Europe. The explosion barely made a paragraph in the local Siberian newspaper, even though the estimated death toll of three people, pieced together from eyewitness accounts, could have been significantly higher. As hunters and herders inhabiting a vast area, the Evenki were a migratory people who were unlikely to have been subject to official records. They were left to deal with this terrifying event on their own, fleeing the epicentre to restart their lives. In fact, no one would come from western Russia, where the country's government and key scientific bodies were located, for another 20 years to investigate.

There are vague reports from 1919 of a merchant named Sudzdalev, who is thought to have visited the explosion site and discovered diamonds. It is thought that he did not have the scientific credentials to investigate the possible cause of the explosion, however. That would be left to the first scientist to reach the region some years later.

A scientist asks, 'Why?'

For years, war and the upheaval of the Russian Revolution no doubt hindered any significant investigation into the Tunguska Event, whether or not the Russian, and later Soviet, authorities wanted to understand its origin. The explosion might have been remembered only in the oral histories of the Evenki, if it had not been for one man, Leonid Kulik, a Russian mineralogist known for his research into meteorites.

Kulik was one of the first scientists on the scene of the great explosion, albeit let's admit somewhat belatedly in 1927. He became aware of it after seeing a calendar entry marking the anniversary of the event and persuaded his superiors at the prestigious Soviet Academy of Sciences in St Petersburg, who thought that something of commercial value might be found besides diamonds and that this was worth further investigation. Kulik had read a brief newspaper report describing a bizarre incident on the remote trans-Siberian railway: 'About 8 am, in the middle of June 1908… a huge meteorite is said to have fallen in Tomsk… near Filomonovo Junction. Its fall was accompanied by a frightful roar and a deafening crash… the passengers poured out to examine the fallen object, but they were unable to study the meteorite closely because it was red hot… the meteorite was almost entirely buried in the ground… it was a stone block, whitish in colour, and as much as seven feet in length.' Dazzled by reports like this, he undertook a long and arduous journey to Siberia and started to gather as much information as possible, at first by distributing questionnaires to locals.

Kulik found an area of 15–30 km (10–20 miles) that remained scorched and blackened nearly two decades after the explosion. By marking out the area, he was able to identify the ground-level epicentre underneath the blast, where the uprooted trees had been felled by the

Leonid Kulik led an expedition to investigate what happened at Tunguska.

huge force and were lying in a radial pattern pointing outwards from this central site, which seemed to highlight the direction of the blast. Years later, the atomic bombs over Japan would leave many buildings directly under their drop zones bizarrely intact, much like the epicentre of Tunguska.

Kulik was a specialist in meteorites and, having read the newspaper article about the meteorite that fell near the train in Tomsk, strongly suspected the Tunguska Event was a meteorite impact. Based on this evidence before his eyes, he became convinced that a large meteor strike had caused it. He had also read an article by A. V. Voznesensky in the popular-science magazine *Mirovedeniye* that claimed the Tunguska explosion could be heard over an area of 380,000 square miles. He went on to theorize, 'The body was probably a group of meteorites which "were flying in the same direction and gradually breaking up". A "very considerable mass" fell to earth. Investigators might find "something very similar to the meteorite crater of Arizona", surrounded by a mass of fragments.' This led Kulik to think there would be a meteorite crater somewhere in the epicentre of the impact. (N.B. While a meteor is the 'shooting star' that appears when space rock enters earth's atmosphere and burns up, a meteorite is rock that survives intact and hits the earth's surface.)

Typically, after a meteorite impact, fragments of rock are lodged in the ground and can be seen there. However, Kulik did not find any such remnants. Over the next ten years, he led four expeditions to investigate and excavate the area, with Evenki herdsman acting as guides and assistants. He and his team trawled the bog marshes for meteorite fragments, surveyed the epicentre of the explosion and attempted to locate anything resembling an impact crater.

Kulik's last expedition into the Tunguska region in 1939 succeeded in taking aerial photographs of the devastated area. These photographs illustrated the radial patterns of the shattered forest and they also confirmed the Southern Swamp to be the centre of the explosion. Later photographs taken in 1950 of the 'devastated zone' showed that the blast had descended from a height of several kilometres, felling about

40,000 trees over a radius of 70 km (43 miles). Kulik was planning a fifth trip when the Second World War broke out. Aged 59, he volunteered to serve in the Russian army and sadly died in a German prison camp in 1942.

Despite finding no meteorite, Kulik was hailed in the 1930s as Russia's pre-eminent mineralogist and meteorite man. He was the first scientist to investigate the huge explosion, and years later in the Soviet Union in 1958, on the 50th anniversary of the Tunguska Event, they produced stamps honouring Leonid Kulik's memory and achievements. As the 1960s arrived with no confirmation of a meteorite as the source of the devastation, the Soviet Academy of Sciences decided instead to propose that a comet had caused the explosion and closed the case.

Tesla's intercontinental death ray

In the years following Kulik's investigations, the lack of further research gave rise to some highly unusual theories about the Tunguska explosion. For example, some people blamed famed inventor Nikola Tesla for testing out a death ray on Siberia. This was unlikely to have been true because, in the first years of the 20th century, Tesla was actually too busy developing his hugely ambitious and forward-thinking Wardenclyffe Tower project: a wireless global communications transmitter using the Earth as a conductor.

There was never any evidence suggesting Tesla had designed the tower with a view to creating an intercontinental weapon, and his writings never made mention of anything remotely like this. Given that he was based in the US at the time of the Tunguska Event, had he built such a device then the US military would no doubt have deployed it as a weapon of mass destruction to influence the outcomes of the First and Second World Wars. So far, we know of no such weapon having been developed, let alone used. It is true that Tesla claimed to have developed something like a 'death beam' which he called 'Teleforce' in the 1930s. He claimed to have worked on the 'Teleforce' ray since about 1900, and said that it drew power from the ionosphere, which he described as 'an invisible ball of energy surrounding Earth,' so maybe it could have been in existence by 1908, the time of the explosion at Tunguska. Tesla proposed that, using his death ray, a nation could 'destroy anything approaching within 200 miles', but given that he was based in the US at the time, he would have been too far away to bring about anything like the Tunguska Event in Siberia.

A crashed spaceship

The Tunguska Event inspired many works of fiction. For example, Russian science fiction author Alexander Kazantsev's short story, *Explosion*, published in 1946, postulated that the Tunguska impact was actually caused by an alien spacecraft that had crash-landed in Siberia after a huge on-board nuclear blast. While obviously fictional, such tales – fuelled by the conspicuous lack of official evidence about the explosion – inspired a number of Russian enthusiasts to voluntarily set out on expeditions to Tunguska to investigate this hypothesis for themselves.

In the late-1950s, a young Russian, Gennady Plekhanov, led a group known as The Complex Amateur Expedition, which was firmly focused on the spaceship theory. The group was joined by future Soviet cosmonaut, Georgy Grechko, who was allowed to participate by the Soviet space programme where he worked as an engineer, and who recalled that Kazentsev's story had sparked his ambition to find evidence of a spaceship at the site when he was very young. The group travelled to Tunguska in the hope of finding the remains of a crashed alien spaceship. They theorized that the spacecraft could have been controlled by robots or was even unmanned.

Unfortunately, despite the group's science fiction-based enthusiasm, they found no crashed alien spacecraft in a crater. Instead, they found the same devastation reported by Kulik. Despite discovering no crashed saucers, the group co-operated with mainstream scientists at the Academy of Sciences and supplied extensive amounts of data for astrophysical analysis. New Tunguska hypotheses about the ice core of a comet, geo-tectonic processes and alternative types of asteroids were put forward thanks in part to their efforts. Other visitors to the area, like Russian astronomer Vitaly Romeiko, were firmly of the opinion that the explosion was caused by a comet, not by a meteorite. After 22 expeditions had visited the region, at the 100th anniversary of the Tunguska Event in 2008, Romeiko said, 'These days the main dispute is unfolding between the advocates of the meteor theory and the comet theory, and this one will be extremely hard to resolve. As follows from the latest information we have about the comets' nuclei, they do contain a certain amount of meteoric substance. I can say with certainty that the phenomenon was caused by a comet.'

Space rocks and black holes

During expeditions in the 1960s, researchers such as K. P. Florensky of the Combined Tunguska Meteorite Expedition on behalf of the Vernadsky Institute of the USSR Academy of Sciences discovered tiny silicate and magnetite (iron-based) spheres in the soil around the blast area, which was sifted through intensively; in later years, scientists were able to identify similar spheres in the resin of the fallen trees. They discovered that the spheres had high proportions of nickel relative to iron – a typical feature of meteorites – which led scientists to think they were of extraterrestrial origin. In addition, their location seemed to be consistent with expectations of what the distribution pattern should be after a meteoric explosion above the Earth. It seemed that scientific opinion was moving past the giant explosion and mammoth impact theory to settle on an explosion approximately 8 km (5 miles) above the Earth's surface, which would create a scattering effect, and this too would probably cause the wider flattening of the trees over a larger area.

Even so, another fascinating impact-related hypothesis arose in 1973, when a team of physicists led by A. A. Jackson and Michael P. Ryan Jun., both from the University of Texas at Austin, suggested that a black hole could have punctured the Earth's surface. (According to NASA, even the most microscopic, single-atom black hole has the mass of a large mountain.) This could explain the absence of an impact crater at Tunguska, as well as the blue light witnessed by some of the Evenki people. Since a black hole is a collapsed star that is much smaller than other stars, it could have entered at 30 degrees to the horizon, ripped a hole through the Earth and exited through the northern Atlantic Ocean. The team suggested looking for shock waves and disturbances of the ocean on the opposite side of the world. Despite the availability of undersea mapping technology, scientists do not so far seem to have located any evidence of such an 'exit wound'. This theory, while both cinematic and highly interesting, has been ruled out by scientists simply because the facts we have so far do not match up.

Alien intervention

As scientific arguments developed about the specific kind of planetary object – icy and dusty comet or rocky meteorite – that was the most likely suspect, some 'ufologists' maintained an alien origin.

Eduardo Albert 'Billy' Meier, a Swiss author of UFO books, whom we mentioned in the Area 51 chapter, who lives in the Swiss Alps and claims he has been in contact with humanoid extraterrestrials since he was a child, said an alien being, named Asket, told him on 3 February 1956 near the Jordanian desert that a huge spaceship had become stranded in the Tunguska area in 1908. He added that because these particular aliens were not permitted contact with humans, they decided instead to build a bomb on board their ship to propel their craft into the Earth's atmosphere and then explode it there.

Although Meier claimed to have taken nearly 1,500 photographs of supposed UFOs, including one of the most famous 'flying saucer' images ever – it featured in the *X-Files* television show – many sceptics discount him as a hoaxer. As no parts of spaceships were ever found by Plekhanov and his team, the spaceship theory soon died out. The alien being was supposed to have told Meier, 'From everything only a giant crater remained, which is called erroneously by your scientists a meteor crater.' This is all well and good but for the fact that none of the scientists researching the region ever found a meteor crater up until 1956. Later on, some thought that a nearby lake could be a crater, but this was never mentioned by Meier's alien friend.

Most scientists now believe that the Tunguska explosion occurred in mid-air. On this basis, another much-later contention was that the explosion resulted from an alien interception of an oncoming meteor or comet before it crashed into our planet. In 2004, Yuri Lavbin of the Tunguska Space Phenomenon Foundation also launched an expedition to the region. His group found a curious metal block, which he later announced was from the intercepting alien missile. However, the block was later found to be a part from a farm tractor that Lavbin had found outside the perimeter of the blast area. Sceptical scientists also pointed out that the group announced their theory before making their discoveries – not the approach of reputable scientific research.

Lavbin still displays parts of a meteorite that he claims is the actual Tunguska meteorite, which, he says, is Martian in origin, at his own small museum. He argues that aliens launched the intercepting craft and managed to protect the Earth, for if the incoming meteor had been allowed to continue on its path, it would have resulted in a level of widespread devastation on Earth similar to the meteorite that wiped out the dinosaurs 65 million years ago.

Potential impact crater

In 1999, an Italian scientific team led by Luca Gasparini and Guiseppe Longo from the University of Bologna, Italy began using hi-tech underwater cameras and other geophysical technology to conduct an in-depth examination of Lake Cheko, a small body of water located 8 km (5 miles) from the alleged epicentre of the 1908 Tunguska Event. They made a detailed examination of the lake, which did not appear on maps until 1928. Some eyewitnesses insisted there was no lake there before 1908.

In 2007, Gasparini's team presented their findings. They theorized that Lake Cheko was a lake created either by the impact of a meteorite or it was a remnant left behind after the main rock burned up. They pointed to a funnel-like feature on the lake bottom, which was untypical of other naturally formed lakes nearby.

Using high-tech equipment and underwater cameras, they put forward their conclusions in 2007, with other possible considerations as to what might have created the lake, including the idea that it could have been a volcanic crater that filled with water as a result of a river meandering after the explosion. Other specialists in impact crater science questioned the findings due to the absence of melted rock at the site, which would indicate very high temperatures. Melting permafrost, which is common in the Siberian region landscape, could also account for the existence of the lake, however.

The Chelyabinsk meteor

It's quite possible that, given the huge land mass of the former Soviet Union, many small meteors and asteroids might have struck without alerting the wider population. One recent cosmic visitor was actually captured on thousands of vehicle dashboard cameras in Russia. At 9.20am on 15 February 2013, a meteor entered the atmosphere over Chelyabinsk, Russia and broke apart 22 km (14 miles) above the ground; dashcams recorded the flaming fireball as it blazed across the sky. Like the Tunguska Event in 1908, people described it as being like the sun falling to the ground, while others thought war had broken out. Minutes after the meteor crashed, the shockwaves broke windows and caused factory walls to collapse. Many people were injured by shattered glass or suffered damaged retinas from watching the ultra-bright flash with the naked eye. Fortunately for the local population, the meteor's final resting place was Chebarkul Lake, from which it was raised on 16 October 2013. The largest fragment weighed 654 kg (1,442 lb). Scientists think this meteor was originally part of a bigger asteroid that was sucked into the orbit of Jupiter, the largest planet in the solar system, before probably being ejected into a wider orbit and eventually being caught in Earth's gravitational force.

Could the Tunguska explosion have a similar explanation? Many scientists are coming to this conclusion, although there is no definite proof. The Chelyabinsk meteor offers certain clues as to what the Tunguska explosion might have looked like. Of course, the difference is that the Tunguska Event was the biggest impact event in Earth's recorded history. Fascinatingly, had it occurred around four hours

The Chelyabinsk meteor, February 2013.

later, scientists have estimated it would probably have either struck, or exploded over, the heavily populated city of St Petersburg. As well as mass devastation and death, this would have wiped out the Russian government and economy, most likely changing the course of history. Perhaps there would not have been a Communist revolution in 1917, and maybe no Second World War. Possibly, in this alternative historical timeline, there would have been no need to build the atomic bomb that would be dropped on Japan 37 years later. It could have turned into a mass extinction event that led to the disappearance of humanity itself. Whatever caused this mysterious and mammoth event in Siberia – alien spaceship, black hole, meteorite, or something else – perhaps the biggest question is, if it had occurred further to the west, how much would it have shifted the history of Russia, Europe and the world, and what would our planet look like today?

CHAPTER 2

THE DISAPPEARED AND THE NAMELESS

The ability to disappear without a trace is a particularly unsettling fact of modern life. Indeed, it's an aspect of 21st-century existence that is much harder to accept than it was even a generation ago. That's because we assume that our constant use of computers, mobile phones, satellite navigation, virtual payments and tracking technologies creates a digital footprint that is impossible to eradicate and therefore we are always traceable. Yet, sadly, as their tormented families can confirm, millions of people around the world continue to vanish every year, leaving only ghost-like traces or sometimes none at all. The mysterious disappearances presented here range from those who have literally vanished off the radar altogether, often against their own will, to the case of a protagonist who planned and executed a disappearance with such boldness that it even inspired a fan convention. Of course, the disappearance itself is only the beginning of a long and increasingly complex story, where time, conflicting evidence and the vested interests of those involved – including investigators – serve to further cloak the truth as the years go by.

THE FLANNAN ISLES LIGHTHOUSE MYSTERY

Today, lighthouses around key points of Britain's coastline are all fully automated and controlled remotely by computer, their beams provided by powerful, long-lasting LED lights. You can still visit certain lighthouses and climb the steep staircases to the very top to get a sense of how it must have been for those who worked in these challenging and lonely circumstances. Back in 1900, everything had to be done by lighthouse keepers, from winding the clocks and recording every detail of the weather to manually lighting the oil-powered lamp and keeping watch over it to ensure it never went out, so that ships navigating treacherous coastline in darkness or fog would have a point of reference. Thus, it came as a surprise to a passing vessel when, on 15 December 1900, only a year after it first went into service, the beam from the lighthouse on the highest point of Eilean Mòr, one of a small archipelago of islands known as the Flannan Isles, west of the Outer Hebrides, couldn't be seen. Upon further investigation, the three keepers responsible for this beacon had vanished: more than 120 years on, their fate continues to be a perplexing and compelling mystery.

Blackout

On that December night, the SS *Archtor* out of Philadelphia in the US was sailing around the west coast of Scotland, heading towards Leith in Edinburgh. Captain Holman was concerned at not seeing the light that he expected to be visible from the Eilean Mòr lighthouse, despite being within 10 km (6 miles) of the newly commissioned structure. It was near midnight, the usual time when the lighthouse keepers – James Ducat, Thomas Marshall and Donald McArthur – would change shift, which might have accounted for a brief period of darkness. But no light came on. Nor were there any locals to raise the alarm to authorities because the islands were uninhabited. Captain Holman would report the odd situation upon his arrival, but he was not the only concerned observer of the non-working lighthouse.

On the Isle of Lewis, closer to the Scottish mainland, a gamekeeper named Roderick MacKenzie was paid £8 a year by the Northern Lighthouse Board to observe the lighthouse in Eilean Mòr, some 20 km (12.5 miles) west of his position at Gallan Head. His main task was to watch for communication signals from the lighthouse keepers and

The Flannan Isles lighthouse.

relay them to the Northern Lighthouse Board by telegram. When the weather was poor, he often couldn't see the lighthouse beam, so for a few days he wasn't overly concerned at the absence of a bright beacon casting its light to sea, especially as it wasn't accompanied by any messages of distress. After around eight days, though, MacKenzie had become concerned at not seeing the light. The keepers usually worked on a 28-day rotation, which meant no one would visit the lighthouse for a while, until the fourth member of the team was due to relieve one of his three co-workers on the island.

A sense of foreboding

When Captain Holman managed to send a telegram to the Northern Lighthouse Board headquarters in Edinburgh on 18 December, the board immediately prepared to send the relief lighthouse keeper, Joseph Moore, to the Eilean Mòr lighthouse. Hampered by poor weather around the coast of western Scotland, he was not able to leave Lewis for six days. Moore eventually managed to sail out on the *Hesperus*, reaching the remote island around noon on 26 December.

Moore later said that upon setting foot on the island, and especially as he climbed the steep path towards the lighthouse, he immediately felt that things were not right. The flagstaff would normally be flying a welcome flag, but no flag was up, and the provision boxes that would usually be found at the landing stage for restocking were not there. More worryingly, none of the three keepers had come down to the landing to welcome the visitors ashore. The captain of the *Hesperus*, James Harvie, tried to alert the keepers that visitors had arrived by blowing a loud whistle and firing a flare, but both were equally unsuccessful. The island was deserted.

Moore, being more familiar with the layout of the lighthouse, went to search the compound. The entrance gate to the main building and the main door were both closed. In the living quarters there was no familiar tick of the clocks, as they had not been wound up for some time; Moore also noticed all the beds were unmade but the kitchen area was tidy. Only one of the three heavy oilskin coats worn by the keepers as stormy weather protection was still on its hook – the other two were gone. This indicated that at least two of the men had been wearing their oilskins at the time of their disappearance and the other was not donned for some reason. A search of the rest of the island yielded none of the missing keepers. Moore and two crew members remained at the lighthouse to restart the lamp and resume normal operations as best as they could. On his return to Lewis, Captain Harvie of the *Hesperus* sent a telegram to the Northern Lighthouse Board dated 26 December, saying, 'A dreadful accident has happened at the Flannans. The three keepers, Ducat, Marshall and the Occasional [McArthur], have disappeared from the Island. The clocks were stopped and other signs indicated that the accident must have happened about a week ago. Poor fellows, they must have been blown over the cliffs or drowned trying to secure a crane.'

Meanwhile, Moore and the two *Hesperus* crewmen also continued their investigations around the island. On the east landing side, facing away from the harsh Atlantic Ocean, everything seemed normal and equipment was intact. But on the western landing, there was evidence of damage caused by the recent winter storms. Mooring ropes, landing ropes and crane handles were missing. A wooden box used to store them and kept at around 33 m (110 ft) above sea level, and a lifebuoy that was kept at a similar level, were both gone. Iron railings along the footpath leading up to the lighthouse were bent over; some had been pulled out of their concrete and a rock weighing more than a tonne had been moved from its position. At the very top of the cliff, around 60 m (200 ft) above sea level, grass turf as far as 10 m (33 ft) from the cliff edge had been ripped away.

Official investigation

On 29 December, the Northern Lighthouse Board's Superintendent, Robert Muirhead, arrived on the island to look into the men's disappearance. He knew all three keepers personally, having recruited them himself. His investigation concluded that James Ducat and Thomas Marshall had gone to the western landing stage of the island during a storm and that Donald McArthur had left the lighthouse without his oilskin during this storm, which was against the board's protocol, because he was the less experienced relief keeper. Muirhead wrote in his report that some of the damage found at the island had to be seen to be believed, an interesting statement from someone who lived and worked in the area, knew all about lighthouse conditions, and had seen storm damage on many occasions. Muirhead concluded that, 'From evidence which I was able to procure, I was satisfied that the men had been on duty up till dinner time on Saturday the 15th of December, that they had gone down to secure a box in which the mooring ropes, landing ropes etc. were kept, and which was secured in a crevice in the rock about 110 feet above sea level, and that an extra-large roller or wave had rushed up the face of the rock, had gone above them, and coming down with immense force, had swept them completely away.'

One of the key questions thrown up by this conclusion is that if the men were in fact trying to secure equipment, why were all three doing so at the same time, given that under board regulations one keeper should always be present in the lighthouse? Such uncertainties, and the public interest in the strange story, meant that various theories soon abounded about the fate of the missing men. These ranged from the suggestion that they suddenly decided to begin new lives to more fanciful hypotheses, including abduction by foreign spies or even ghosts from passing ships, or that the men were seized and eaten by mysterious serpents rising up from the watery depths. As happened in other real-life cases of people going missing at sea – most notably the famous *Mary Celeste*, the ship found abandoned and adrift west of Portugal's Atlantic coast in 1872 – some reporters were happy to invent details. Stories about part-eaten meals at the table were invented in periodicals of the time. In fact, the relief keeper, Joseph Moore, made the following observation: 'The kitchen utensils were all very clean, which is a sign that it must be after dinner some time they left.'

Later supposed log-book entries dated around 12 and 15 December blurred the story somewhat when Marshall apparently wrote that a great storm, nothing like he had ever encountered before, had hit the island. He also added that Ducat was very subdued and quiet during this storm. MacArthur, the big burly man, known for his practical approach to things was reported as weeping. Another story emerged that all three men were praying together on the night of the storm. Surely, the men must have survived the storm, people then wondered. However, these particular details later proved to be false, thanks to the investigative efforts of *Fortean Times* journalist, Mike Dash, who found that no such entries were ever made in the log book.

Super waves and blow holes

One potential explanation for the men's actions is that there was a wave so huge that it took even the experienced keepers by surprise. As mentioned by author Keith McCloskey in his book, *The Lighthouse*, published in 2014, the lighthouse was located west of the Outer Hebrides – the Flannan Isles are exposed to the full force of the North Atlantic Ocean. Based on the level of damage to the western side of the island, one theory about the lighthouse keepers' disappearance concerned a giant or 'super' wave. Unlike a tsunami, which is the result of an undersea earthquake, super waves are caused by major storms in an area. Scientists know that storm winds across large expanses of ocean can create massive waves. For example, on 14 February 2011, the *Jason 2* space satellite measured waves in the North Atlantic at up to 20.1 m (66 ft); they were caused by the extra-tropical Storm Quirin. According to the American Meteorological Society, this was the highest recorded wave since satellite-based measuring began in the 1980s. Had the keepers encountered such a monstrous wall of water, it's easy to think they could have been washed away in an instant. After all, the UK's Royal National Lifeboat Institution (RNLI) warns that just 15 cm of water can potentially knock someone off their feet.

A particular geological feature on Eilean Mòr is a blow hole in the rock created over thousands of years; as the sea erodes parts of the rock, this creates a cave in the cliffside from which waves push up and drill through the rocky surface, creating a spout. I have seen this for myself while living in the Orkney Islands, off the north coast of Scotland. At high tide (or a 'swell' as it's also known), waves crashing into the cave can force seawater to burst up and out of these blow holes. Norrie Muir, a former lighthouse keeper on Eilean Mòr in the 1960s, has said that, while he worked there, the keepers could not see the crane mounted on the western side of the island, but if they looked out of the window and saw water shooting out of the blow hole to a height over 30 m (100 ft), then they knew the western landing was taking a battering; this is where the crane, a particularly expensive piece of equipment, was located. With this in mind, is it possible that two of the keepers observed the blow hole and went down to secure the crane and related equipment such as tackle and ropes?

One detail supporting this argument is that Thomas Marshall had already been fined for losing some of his equipment in an earlier storm. Perhaps one of the men succumbed to a giant wave and the other might have run back to get help from the third, who rushed out without his oilskin coat to get a rescue line out to the man in distress. Waves travel in sets and, while it's often said the seventh wave will be the biggest, in fact this depends on specific conditions (the RNLI notes that the middle wave of a set is often the biggest). On 15 December, winds in the area were around 'near gale' force at 7 at 8am, rising to 'strong gale' force 9 by around 6pm; that is, up to 88 km (54 miles) per hour. Reports indicated that the sea was very disturbed around the Flannan Isles leading up to the last known log entry on 15 December. Keith McCloskey's excellent book, *The Lighthouse*, about the Flannan Isles mystery contained interviews with several retired lighthouse keepers and most of them emphasized that they would never have ventured out into a storm. A likely explanation, therefore, is that the three men ventured out as the storm winds abated but were still taken by a freak wave – possibly a huge middle wave they were not expecting.

Murder in the lighthouse

It has been suggested that one of the keepers killed his two colleagues and either left the island to escape punishment or, unable to stand the guilt, committed suicide by throwing himself off the rocky cliff into the sea. It's not entirely clear where this idea came about, but a poem, 'The Flannan Isle', by Wilfrid Wilson Gibson in 1912 made mention of overturned chairs and how one of the keepers had 'fallen dead by the lighthouse wall', suggesting with the overturned chair that some kind of argument or scuffle might have broken out.

While this may sound unlikely, violence has occurred at lighthouses, including the Flannan Isles lighthouse itself. Author McCloskey recalls an interesting occurrence in his 2014 book about the doomed lighthouse. Donald John Macleod, a former keeper, who worked there during the Second World War, recalled that one keeper had a mental breakdown. Macleod and the third keeper were both suffering from flu at the time and were not fit enough to perform their usual duties. With the relief keeper not due to arrive for another four days, the pressure of trying to do all the work on his own led the third keeper to break down and threaten violence.

For their own safety, Macleod and his sick colleague had to physically restrain the man and tie him up until help arrived. Macleod thought that something similar could have happened in 1900; the monotony of the work and the isolation took their toll and, in those days, little or no consideration was given to workers' mental health and their ability to cope with stress. Studies into the effects of long-term space missions on astronauts have revealed that a mix of close confinement and over-proximity to colleagues can lead to psychological problems such as depression.

In northern parts of Europe, research has also found a link between long dark winters and depression, heavy drinking and mood swings. In 2018, Dr Peter McCann of Pittsburgh Liver Research Centre used data from 193 countries, including those in the Northern Hemisphere, to provide evidence that darker climates contributed to a higher incidence of binge drinking. It is possible that one of the keepers had a sudden mental breakdown and felt he had to get away from the confined lighthouse, and the other two put on their oilskins to go out and find him in dreadful conditions, with all three being blown or swept by water off the rocks. Or he may have had some kind of psychotic episode and attacked his colleagues, then either full of remorse or wishing to harm himself, too, jumped into the sea. No note was found, although the log indicated the weather was probably taking a great toll on them, as it was getting worse from that morning of 15 December right up until 6-7pm when it was just below storm force. No one can say for sure whether the men were praying for the storm to cease, however, in the Western Isles, many if not all the population are very religious, so it would not be surprising for this to be true. Donald McArthur, the 'occasional' or relief keeper, was reported to have had a volatile temper, which may have led to arguments that possibly erupted into violence.

Deadly bread

An unexpected but fascinating suspect in the Flannan Isles lighthouse mystery is, strangely, bread. It was a staple of the lighthouse keepers' diet and in the cold and wet winter months, when it was harder to keep food supplies dry, it would often go mouldy. In 1976, *Science magazine* published an article by Linnda R. Caporeal suggesting that the 1692 Salem witchcraft trials mentioned visions of ghosts and painful physical sensations described by the girls who claimed to be bewitched. These might have been caused by eating mouldy bread made with flour contaminated by ergot, a naturally occurring fungal hallucinogen that grows on rye and wheat grain. When it was consumed as bread or beer, it could cause convulsions, hallucinations and other strange behaviours.

The lighthouse keepers could have been consuming mouldy bread spores regularly in the winter of 1900. If so, could this have caused hallucinations and irrational behaviour, making one or more of the men lash out at each other? There was, however, no evidence of any violence or unusual activity found inside the lighthouse – as mentioned, the kitchen was tidied and witnesses mentioned that oil lamps were prepared and water canteens were filled, exactly as normal. It could be that only one of the men suffered from ergot effects and ran outside without his oilskin; his unaffected colleagues may have followed, pausing to put on their oilskins first, but a chaotic scuffle in high winds led to their deaths. No arguments or disagreements were officially logged in the lighthouse records, but the keepers would probably have only been required to log weather patterns and technical issues. Keith McCloskey also ventured in his book that perhaps mercury might have been a possible source of keepers going mad. Some of the Flannan Lighthouse lens apparatus floated in a special bath of mercury to help it turn, rather than being placed on rollers. A theory he discovered was that one of the keepers could have been poisoned partly by the mercury vapours coming from the lens apparatus over a period of time and was eventually driven insane by this. He might have run out of the lighthouse in the stormy weather followed by the two, who would have tried to calm him down.

Deep-sea creatures

Many tales have surfaced of sea monsters snatching the men away. But how likely is this? The northern and western islands of Scotland are cultures replete with legends of mermaids and selkies (shape-shifting human–seal hybrids), as well as creatures of the deep sea, including enormous whales and giant squid. Not all of these are folk stories or fishermen's tales; live specimens of incredible ocean inhabitants have been captured on camera as recently as 2007 in Antarctica.

In wartime 1942, the British Navy ship HMS *Britannia* was returning to England when it was sunk in the South Atlantic. Twelve men survived the sinking and Lieutenant Raymond Edmund Grimani Cox recalled how they clung to a raft for five days. At first there were shark attacks, then on the fifth day a giant squid attacked the raft. It dragged one of the men away and returned a few minutes later. Although it was hard to see in the darkness, Lt. Cox could make out its massive shape against the stars as one of its tentacles reached over the side of the raft and tried to pull him to his death. Fortunately, his shipmates managed to hold on to him and eventually the squid withdrew, but not before it had pulled lumps of flesh from Lt. Cox's legs and body. Based on the size of his scars, the squid was estimated to be 7 m (23 ft) long.

Reported squid attacks have occurred in the deeper parts of the oceans, therefore it's highly unlikely that such a creature would be able to approach the steep, rocky cliffs of an island in stormy weather without endangering itself and being smashed against the rocks. It's hard to imagine any squid could be big enough to scoop men from the cliff top. Being eaten by sharks after drowning and floating into deeper waters would be a stronger possibility, which may explain why the men's bodies were never found. Sharks have been known to eat the bodies of victims of airliner crashes in the Atlantic Ocean, which has hampered recovery of remains. On 23 June 1985, Air India Flight 182 blew up over the Atlantic Ocean after a terrorist bomb exploded. Eventually, 132 bodies were recovered, but the operation was hampered by the fact that many of them were partly eaten by sharks swimming off the Irish coast, where the plane sank after disintegrating in the air.

Sadly, the fate of the three lighthouse keepers remains unsolved to this day. Most probably, they met their deaths either in, or because of, the stormy ocean that surrounded them. The bigger mystery is why they went out into the storm in the first place, knowing as they did that it was an extremely dangerous thing to do. Ducat, Marshall and McArthur have inspired poems, books, songs and films, even a *Dr Who* story and at least some of these honour the bravery required to do their arduous and isolated work. More importantly, even though the keepers themselves were lost, their legacy is the lives of all those who were safeguarded by the Flannan Isles lighthouse and their many descendants.

D. B. COOPER, THE PARACHUTING HIJACKER

Since the '9/11' terrorist attacks in New York in 2001, when four airliners were hijacked and crashed into the World Trade Center, the Pentagon and the Pennsylvania countryside, the airline industry has taken significant steps to reduce the incidence of aircraft being hijacked, or 'skyjacked'. This has involved a combination of locked cockpits, tracking technology, X-ray scans, additional passenger searches and the presence of on-board air marshals.

The first reported skyjacking occurred in Peru in 1931; since then, many have been carried out, mostly by organized crime groups in search of money, by extremists wanting to draw attention to their cause or by protestors aiming to achieve a specific objective like prisoner releases. Their increasing frequency in the late-1960s led the US government to introduce air marshals on some domestic flights.

Among the many, one hijacking stands out from the rest, because it was ingenious, extremely risky and successfully executed by a lone skyjacker – above all, it has never been solved, a fact that has intrigued professional and amateur detectives for decades. Despite threats, no one on the plane was physically harmed and the ingenuity and bravery of the plan captured many imaginations. As a result 'D. B. Cooper' became a heroic anti-establishment figure, a 'sky pirate' who frustrated the FBI for over 50 years and got away with it. Or did he?

On 24 November 1971, the eve of America's Thanksgiving holiday, a rather nondescript forty-something man calling himself Dan Cooper paid $20 cash for a ticket on Northwest Orient Airlines' 30-minute flight from Portland, Oregon to Seattle, Washington State. (Later, a journalist would mistakenly report his name as 'D. B. Cooper', a detail that would stick.) Portland was a fairly quiet regional airport, rather than a major

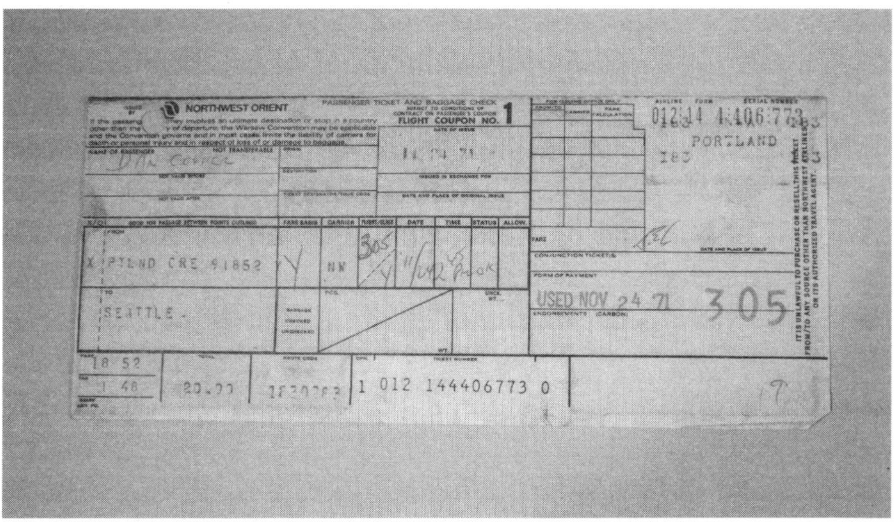

D. B. Cooper's plane ticket.

hub, although on that day it was busy with travellers making their way home for Thanksgiving. Cooper appeared to want to hide his face, wearing sunglasses in addition to the typical businessman's attire of a suit and tie plus briefcase. He sat at the back of Flight 305, a Boeing 727, and Northwest Orient flight attendant, Florence Schaffner, settled him in with a drink. The plane departed Portland at around 2.58pm.

'Miss, I have a bomb here'

After serving drinks, Schaffner sat in her own seat, a few feet from Cooper. He handed her an envelope and, looking serious, insisted she read the contents straight away. She was shocked to read the words, 'Miss, I have a bomb here and I would like you to sit by me.' She did so, asking if he was serious: 'Deadly serious,' he replied. Schaffner called over her colleague, Tina Mucklow, and Cooper opened his briefcase to show them what appeared to be a home-made bomb inside it, with wires, battery, detonator and dynamite. There were also two bare wires: Cooper said he only needed to touch these together to detonate the bomb and blow up the plane.

Schaffner explained the situation to Captain William Scott and he informed the airline, which in turn alerted the Federal Bureau of Investigations (FBI). Meanwhile, Cooper calmly explained to Schaffner that he wanted $200,000 (worth $1.5 million today). He told her to go to the cockpit and stay there for the rest of the flight, while Mucklow would carry messages between him and Captain Scott. Later, Mucklow recalled that Cooper was not nervous at all; in fact, she added, 'He seemed rather nice and he was not cruel or nasty', even offering her a cigarette. She also noted that Cooper seemed very familiar with the terrain, recognizing certain towns as they looked out of the window together.

Cooper also requested four parachutes: two back-fitting and two front-fitting. This was a clever move because it could indicate he would force a hostage to jump too, which would have then discouraged the authorities from supplying non-functional equipment. The captain told passengers, who were unaware of the danger they were in, that the plane would need to divert due to technical problems. Cooper also told Mucklow to return the notes he had written to the captain to him, which also indicated careful planning.

Northwest Orient Airlines' president authorized full payment of the ransom and ordered all employees to co-operate fully with Cooper. Flight 305 flew around the Puget Sound area for approximately two hours, while the airline, the FBI and the Seattle police organized the ransom money and parachutes. However, the seemingly meticulous 'pirate' appears to have overlooked key details. The FBI asked a Seattle bank to provide the ransom money and to record all the serial numbers via microfilm, so that they would be able, hopefully, to trace it later on. He also failed to specify the bill denominations.

Safe landing

At around 5.46pm, the aircraft landed safely at Seattle's Tacoma Airport and, as Cooper instructed, taxied to a quiet part of the runway. The parachutes and cash were loaded on to the plane in a cloth bag – but as the ransom was made up entirely of $20 bills, the bag weighed a hefty 10 kg (23 lb). All 36 passengers, still unaware of the hijacking, were allowed to leave the aircraft, along with all the flight attendants except Tina Mucklow. The flight crew also stayed on board. Cooper transferred the cash to a parachute bag, which he improvised into a kind of holdall.

Once the plane was refuelled and cleared for take-off, Cooper instructed Captain Scott to fly at the lower-than-normal altitude of 3,050 m (10,000 ft), where oxygen would be available, and with the landing gear down and the wing flaps at around 15 degrees (their down position), which would slow the aircraft considerably. Again, Cooper's knowledge of such details is notable and could even suggest he himself was a pilot. By now, it was dark outside, making any landmarks harder to see, and while the plane was travelling slowly, it was still flying at 320 km (200 miles) per hour. Cooper demanded they fly to Mexico City, but the captain informed him this was impossible due to the amount of fuel in the plane's tanks. On Captain Scott's advice, Cooper agreed to

An FBI sketch of D. B. Cooper.

fly to Reno, saying it was a nice place to visit. Could he have even hailed from Reno himself?

A jump from 10,000 feet

As the plane slowed to 320 km (200 miles) per hour, it was escorted to Reno by US Air Force jets. At 7.42pm, Cooper told Mucklow to join the captain in the cockpit. As she headed there, she glanced back briefly and saw Cooper strapping the money bag to himself. At 8.02pm, an alarm sounded in the cockpit that the aft (back) stairway door was open. At that time, the Boeing 727 was the only commercial airliner with such a door, which could only be opened by someone familiar with its workings – further signs that Cooper had some kind of insider knowledge. The plane's crew realized Cooper was about to make the incredible jump, but would he detonate the bomb? Luckily, the answer was negative. At around 8.10pm, the co-pilot noticed the cabin was now losing pressure because the aft door was wide open. In the next few moments, Cooper jumped into the darkness, with $200,000 in cash. He was never seen or heard from again.

Looking for clues

The FBI had opened its investigation, code-named 'NORJAK', while the plane was still in flight. When it finally touched down in Reno, dozens of FBI agents boarded to examine it for clues. They found Cooper's tie on a seat, presumably removed before he jumped to stop it flapping as he parachuted down. Agents also retrieved cigarette butts but unfortunately not his drinking glass, which had been mixed up with the other passengers' glasses during the flight. (At this time, DNA testing was still a long way off in the future.) Cooper took the ransom notes he had written, so that his handwriting could not provide any clues. Based upon eyewitness statements, the FBI quickly had the now-notorious sketch drawn up that showed Cooper in his sunglasses.

As the plane was on autopilot and its route known, aviation experts were able to work out a potential drop zone in which Cooper landed with his parachute. The FBI would later calculate that Cooper probably jumped at around 8.13pm, shortly after opening the aft door; the pilots noticed that the aircraft's tail section suddenly pitched upward, probably due to the sudden weight shift as Cooper jumped out. Given the strong westerly winds in the area that night, the FBI estimated a drop zone of approximately 73 sq km (28 sq miles) to search for where he landed.

The next morning, the largest manhunt in US history up to that point began. FBI agents and National Guardsmen swooped down on the area, near Ariel in Washington State, and helicopters and spotter planes surveyed the terrain. The search found no trace of a parachute or Cooper – not one footprint or broken branch to indicate that he had been in the area. He had seemingly vanished into thin air. The FBI searched through records for pilots and skydivers, given Cooper's knowledge of parachuting, the aft plane door and the landscape, but found nothing that connected with him.

Copycat heist

A few months later, there was another skyjacking that closely matched Cooper's crime. On 7 April, in Denver, Colorado, a man calling himself James Johnson hijacked a Boeing 727, demanded $500,000 and four parachutes, and also leaped from the lowered steps at the plane's aft end, in this case as it flew over Utah. He might have got away with his crime as well, if not for boasting to a friend that, if he had hijacked a plane, he would have asked for $500,000, not $200,000 like Cooper. The friend tipped off the FBI and they raided the man's home. He was Richard McCoy, an ex-Vietnam pilot who was actually involved in the helicopter search for the hijacker! Federal agents also found a jumpsuit and duffle bag filled with the ransom cash. McCoy was arrested in connection with both hijackings, but the FBI could not connect him to Cooper and realized they were two different men when eyewitnesses could not identify him from the previous incident. McCoy was sentenced to 45 years in a state penitentiary.

The McCoy skyjack proved it was possible to survive a jump in a parachute from the back of an airliner and his background also reinforced the likelihood that Cooper was knowledgeable about aviation. (Also, the parachutes that were supplied to Cooper for his jump were delivered with instructions, but Cooper told Tina Mucklow that he would not need to read them.) The FBI interviewed more than 800 suspects in the first five years of its investigation, but even so the trail grew cold until nearly a decade later.

Follow the money

In February 1980, Dwayne Ingram and his son Brian were collecting firewood from the banks of the Columbia River, Clarke County, about nine miles downstream from Vancouver, Washington State, when Brian was raking over the dry river bed sand, so his dad could make a small fire. As he did so, he found something rough below the surface, slightly protruding upwards, which he pulled at. He found three bundles of worn, mouldy cash, secured with rubber bands, with the inner notes in much better condition. The FBI matched the legible serial numbers of the cash, totalling $5,800, to the Cooper ransom money. Investigators noted, however, that the money was found more than 32 km (20 miles) south of the estimated drop zone. Could this mean that Cooper jumped out of the plane much later than previously thought, or that he travelled down the river towards Portland, where he began his journey?

FBI geologists initially thought that the level where the cash was found in 1980, just a few inches from the surface of the sand, was significant because the river had been dredged in 1974. (Dredging is used by water authorities to remove sediment and debris from the bottom of lakes, rivers and harbours to ensure that waterways stay open.) This meant that the disposed cash was put there three years after the hijacking, because the dredging process would have likely buried the cash deeper in the sand and not left it near the surface. Alternatively, the banknotes could simply have floated downstream from the estimated drop zone sometime during a three-year period. Some people speculated that Cooper buried a small amount of the money at that spot specifically to confuse the FBI, although this seems unlikely because he would have had to hope that someone would discover it, which might never have happened. Another insight came during a documentary film about the D. B. Cooper case called *The Skyjacker That Got Away* made in 2009. A palaeontologist from the Burke Museum, Tom Kaye, featured in the documentary. He helped the FBI as part of a team of volunteers and discovered that the actual 1974 river dredge stopped 150 feet short of where the cash was found in 1980. He therefore believed the dredging operation had no impact on the original burial and calculated that the money arrived there not long after Cooper's jump.

Initially, in the 1970s, FBI investigators believed that Cooper parachuted out of the plane while it was over the Lewis River in Washington State, based upon the time the aft door opened. They suspected the makeshift holdall cash bag could have become detached before he opened his chute, fallen into the river and split open, causing some of the cash to float downstream from the Lewis River to join with the larger Columbia River and be found later in 1980.

Retired FBI agent, Richard Tosaw, has theorized that the bundles of cash discovered in 1980 by the Columbia River could have been the actual cash offered by Cooper to flight attendant Tina Mucklow during the flight. He was acting quite relaxed during the flight, offering bundles of the ransom cash to Mucklow. After she jokingly asked for some of the cash to try and break the tension, he handed her a few bundles, but she gave them back, insisting company policy was not to accept tips from passengers. In hindsight, it could have actually been beneficial in the search later had she accepted a few banknotes – they could have checked to see if the cash had any fingerprints left by Cooper. When she refused to accept them, Cooper just took them back and put them in his pocket instead of the holdall bag. It seems reasonable to think they would be more likely to have fallen out of his pocket during the descent or on landing.

Apart from the cash found by the river, no other records show that the ransom money delivered to Cooper was ever spent. However, even if the banks and law enforcement agencies had been able to trace the cash, it seems they might not have done so in practice. Seattle FBI agent, Larry Carr, reportedly said in a CNN radio interview in 2008 that, in fact, most banks abandoned the search for the ransom cash within three months of the hijacking – and virtually all of them gave up within six months. The US Treasury Bureau of Printing and Engraving in Washington DC, where used notes are eventually recycled, received 'truckloads' of used and damaged bills each week. If such a search for the Cooper cash was conducted there, it would have gone on for no more than a few days, and a week at most. So maybe all Cooper had to do was wait a few months, then test out small amounts of cash here and there, to check he was in the clear.

Leap of faith

Due to the fact that the ransom money came in small denominations, Cooper would have had the added burden of around 10 kg (23 lb) extra weight when he jumped, which might have affected his centre of balance during the short free fall. The type of military parachute he was given could not be steered, so he was at the mercy of the wind direction. As the FBI notes in its own case summary, he was jumping into a heavily wooded area in the dark, a dangerous proposition for a veteran parachutist. The other problem he faced, even if he got his chute open in the dark, was landing at night in unfamiliar territory. He would not be able to see if he was going to come down in a clearing or on a tree, which could have caused serious injury, or even death. Yet no body was found.

Alternatively, with a westerly wind he might have landed either in the Lewis River, or perhaps nearby Lake Merwin, depending on how quickly he opened his chute. The water at that time of year would have been icy cold. If he succumbed and either drowned or froze to death in the water, what would have happened to his body?

Cold shock

GP Dr Nisa Aslam, speaking to Nottinghamshire Live in Dec 2023, said 'Cold water shock can happen in water 15 degrees Celsius or below. It can cause drowning due to panic and involuntary gasping for breath. The first stage following full immersion is known as 'cold shock'. In the first few seconds, your lungs contract. This can be followed by uncontrollable rapid or deep breathing – hyperventilation – and loss of breathing control,' continued Dr Aslam. If Cooper died in the water, he might not have washed ashore.

He could have been caught in the flow of the river with his parachute and bag and some researchers think his body might have got caught in the propellers of the large vessels in the shipping lanes of the Lewis and Columbia rivers, leading out to the Pacific Ocean, and eventually been tugged out to sea, never to be seen again. However, wouldn't a tangled parachute in the propeller shaft of a ship have been found during a regular inspection? No shipping companies came forward with any subsequent information.

There was also speculation that, as the plane touched down with the aft doors open, Cooper could have jumped off the back of the plane and run off into the darkness. However, the landing speed of the plane would be about 240 kph (149 mph), and it would have to slow somewhat to enable someone to jump off the back steps safely. Police and FBI were waiting to board the plane and would likely have seen Cooper had he run off into the night from the tail section stairs.

Hunting high and low

The next day, 25 November 1971, law enforcement agencies, search-and-rescue units and the county sheriff's mounted police station launched a grid search of the target area around the Lewis River, near the town of Ariel where Cooper was thought to have come down. Nothing relating to Cooper was ever found, and even five flights on 6 December 1971, made by the famed SR-71 Blackbird plane over the area, which took detailed photographs, resulted in nothing. Previously, the Blackbird was used by the US Airforce in secret spying missions and was developed at none other than Area 51 (see page 51). It became famous as the fastest and highest-flying jet aircraft in history. Lone researcher, John Banks, was convinced that Cooper landed and drowned in Lake Merwin, and consequently spent two years and $15,000 exploring the bottom of the 61 m (200 ft) lake in a mini submarine. Unfortunately, he, too, found nothing. Later in March 1972, a skeleton was discovered by two women in an abandoned building in Clark County, just north of Portland, but this was later identified as the remains of teenager, Barbara Ann Derry, who had been kidnapped and murdered.

As the investigation stretched from months into years and then decades, the authorities made a number of adjustments to their estimates about where Cooper probably made his jump. As early as March 1972, following a joint investigation with Northwest Orient Airlines and the US Air Force, the FBI estimated that Cooper probably jumped out over the town of La Center, Washington State, which is about 16 miles southwest of the Lewis River and the town of Ariel. Still, they couldn't find what they were looking for. A new theory developed that the eruption of Mount St Helens volcano in 1980 could have obliterated any traces of Cooper's jump.

DNA and newer science

Scientific advances opened up new investigative possibilities to the FBI from the 1990s onwards, although some were thwarted by basic procedural mistakes. In 1998, agents tried to begin the process of extracting DNA from the cigarette butts found in the ashtray of Cooper's seat, only to find these had been destroyed by the Las Vegas field office. In 2002, agents also found that hair samples retrieved from the back of Cooper's headrest had been lost. A 2020 analysis of plankton on the dollar bills found in 1980 did at least suggest the bills were not present in the river at the time of the hijacking in November 1971. Only plankton that blossomed in the spring were discovered, indicating the cash was first present in the river location a few months after the hijacking. Unfortunately, this knowledge brought Cooper no closer to the FBI's grasp.

Cooper's tie has also been analysed, with interesting results. It was found to contain small amounts of unique titanium metal particles, which were traced back to a titanium research laboratory in Pennsylvania, part of the US conglomerate Crucible Steel. Eric Ulis, an author who has long researched the Cooper hijacking, noted that Crucible also supplied parts for Boeing aircraft, so its employees often travelled to Seattle, where the Boeing plant was based in 1971. In his opinion, 'D. B. Cooper' was actually a Crucible research engineer named Vince Peterson, who died in 2002. Peterson's family do not accept that he was the mysterious Cooper and have offered an old letter that Peterson wrote in 1961 as a source of DNA to test against Cooper's tie, which is held by the FBI. Ulis was hoping to achieve a breakthrough, providing he could get access to that tie. So far, permission has not been granted by the FBI, but Ulis still contends that, even if Peterson wasn't Cooper, he would have rubbed shoulders with him.

More Cooper suspects

Over the years since 1971, many names have been put forward as the possible hijacker, including army and navy veterans, skydivers and Boeing workers, as well as some transgender people, while numerous other 'Coopers' have also offered up supposed death-bed confessions. But though it seems none of these tip-offs or confessions were significant enough for the FBI to make a convincing case, some interesting potential suspects have emerged.

In 2007, a New York private investigator, Skipp Portious, was called by a man who claimed that Cooper was his brother, Kenneth Christiansen, who worked as a flight attendant for Northwest Orient Airlines in 1971. According to his brother, Christiansen had a grievance against the airline over pay cuts and redundancies. Around a year after the hijacking, he managed to purchase a house in Washington State in cash, even though his weekly salary was only $150.

Although Kenneth Christiansen would have known about planes, flight schedules and staff rotas, it seems unlikely that he would hijack a plane from his own company and risk being recognized by colleagues. However, flight attendant Florence Schaffner, who spent time with Cooper at the back of the plane, is said to have remarked that a photo of Christiansen bore a very strong resemblance to the hijacker, when author Geoffrey Gray showed it to her during an interview in 2007.

Cooper drank Bourbon and appeared to be a regular smoker, both of which also applied to Christiansen. The FBI, however, did not act on Portious's tip-off because the man not only never admitted to being Cooper, but didn't resemble him in any way. FBI agent, Larry Carr, said in December 2007 that the FBI have a very good physical descriptions that ruled out Ken Christiansen. 'I can say there's no way these stewardesses, who spent hours with this individual, this guy who was pale, five-eight tall with blue eyes and get him confused with a 6 foot Mediterranean with brown eyes.'

One of the most intriguing potential sightings of Cooper came from a young guitarist driving his work truck to a gig on the same night in 1971 that Cooper jumped from the plane. Jeff Osiadacz came forward in 2016 and recalled that he was taking a coffee break in a diner near Highway 10, when he saw a man entering the diner within an hour of the parachute jump. The man was smartly dressed in a suit but was soaking wet and not wearing a tie. He had no weather protection from the heavy rain and seemed to be travelling alone on foot. Osiadacz said he had seen him earlier trying to hitchhike, but did not stop to offer him a lift because that was against his work regulations. Strangely, the man came over to Osiadacz and asked where this place was; Osiadacz replied they were four miles east of Cle Ellum, near Highway 10.

The suited 'hiker' then made a call and got Osiadacz to take the receiver and give directions to someone on the other end of the line, who agreed to collect the stranger. Osiadacz told the man it would take his friend about an hour and a half to get there and the grateful stranger paid Osiadacz's coffee bill. Osiadacz only found out about the hijacking the next day and his sighting, if accurate, is possibly the strongest indication that Cooper did survive the jump.

If the mystery man was Cooper, he would probably have settled Osiadacz's tab from his own money rather than the ransom cash, to prevent it being traced back to him. Maybe by this point, Cooper understood his mistake in not asking for bigger bills, and knew he would have to spend money slowly and only in small amounts.

Sky pirate or failed skyjacker?

It does seem odd that Cooper planned his crime so meticulously yet overlooked the detail about the bill denominations. Also, it's arguable that the very fact he made such a dangerous jump into the darkness indicates he was not an experienced parachutist or criminal. Whether this modern-day sky pirate got away with it, or died either in the attempt or soon afterwards, taking his money with him, what is certain is that many admire Cooper for taking on the system. Indeed, CooperCon is an annual convention held every year since 2018 in Seattle, Washington. Founded by the mystery researcher Eric Ulis, it is attended by enthusiasts from around the US to celebrate and discuss the infamous hijacker.

Maybe in the future, their convention might announce the breakthrough they have all been waiting for: the real identity of 'D. B' or 'Dan Cooper'. While the FBI officially closed the case in 2016, they appear to remain open-minded about it being re-opened should the right information come through. Retired FBI agent Carr said in 2024, that he thought 'it very much a conceivable possibility' that the FBI will follow up on new leads, especially with a focus on any possible DNA evidence from Cooper's neck-tie left on the plane after he jumped. Meanwhile, it's ironic that his act made air travel safer for passengers and less so for would-be hijackers and terrorists. Whoever he was, the hijacking hi-jinks of Dan Cooper are unlikely to be repeated in the future.

MISSING FLIGHT MH370

On 8 March 2014, at 12.41am local time, a Boeing 777 aircraft carrying 227 passengers and 12 crew took off from Kuala Lumpur International Airport but never reached its destination, Beijing Capital International Airport. After flying for an hour over the South China Sea, Malaysia Airlines Flight MH370 vanished suddenly off the radar, becoming the most infamous aviation mystery on record. Many theories have been put forward to explain what caused MH370 to veer so far off course, but until the aircraft's 'black box' flight recorder device is located, it will remain an especially baffling mystery, particularly since it happened in our modern age of global satellite tracking.

Statistically speaking, flying is one of the safest forms of travel. According to United Nations data, around 1.35 million people die in road or traffic accidents each year; by contrast, there were 176 deaths as a result of air travel in 2021. Even so, aircraft accidents are highly publicized because often multiple lives are lost at the same time. The myriad questions surrounding what happened to Flight MH370 and the 239 people on board make this event all the more unsettling. It is essential to understand why it happened, primarily to give family and friends the answers they need to help them come to terms with the tragedy of losing loved ones, and so safety experts can work out how to prevent something similar in future. But also because it's simply part of our human nature to want to *know*, especially when it's something that could also happen to any one of us.

Before the flight

Flight MH370 was captained by 52-year-old Zaharie Ahmad Shah from Penang, Malaysia. Since joining Malaysia Airlines as a cadet pilot in 1982, Captain Zaharie had accumulated a total of 18,365 hours of flying experience. His co-pilot was 26-year-old First Officer Fariq Abdul Hamid. By the time of Flight MHA370 in 2014, he had accumulated 2,763 hours of flying experience, including 39 hours in the Boeing 777. Flight MH370 was his final training flight.

The range of the Boeing 777 (Extended Range Version) was around 14,305 km (8,889 miles), so it was eminently suitable for long distance flights from one country to another. This model of airliner had a near-perfect safety record by the time Malaysia Airlines took it on, acquiring it in 2002. It was delivered new to Malaysia Airlines on 31 May 2002, with a total 53,471.6 hours flown by the time of its ill-fated last flight.

With most airliners expected to last between 20 and 30 years, there was still a good amount of flight time potential left on the clock. The plane itself had only been involved in a few previous mishaps, the most notable being a small minor collision on the tarmac at Shanghai International

Airport in August 2012, when its wing tip was shaved off by another aircraft. This was repaired and the plane went on to fly successfully for another few years before it went missing. Other very minor defects were noted in the aircraft maintenance log but were not deemed critical for flying; such things included a bathroom light being cracked and the entertainment system not displaying flight information for passengers, neither of which were critical to the plane's ability to fly safely.

Captain Zaharie reported for duty at 10.50pm on 7 March 2014 and was joined by First Officer Fariq at 11.15pm. Zaharie arrived earlier than usual to complete paperwork relating to Fariq as this flight was part of his final examination. (Fariq had reportedly passed all his other exams with excellent scores.) They began their pre-flight checks and discussions, including confirmation of their flight path, altitude, the relevant flight duties for each officer and general-maintenance log checks. This also involved informing Air Traffic Control (ATC) about their intended flight path and calculations for how much fuel they would need to reach two pre-selected airports closer to their designated airport, Beijing Capital, should an unscheduled incident

The aircraft from Flight MH370 that went missing.

stop them from landing there. On this occasion, it was logged that the pilots had agreed to take on 49,100 kg of aviation fuel, sufficient to allow the Boeing 777 to fly for around 7.5 hours with around 6 hours and 20 minutes being the expected flight duration to Beijing.

The weather was clear and calm at both airports, with forecasts of brief, minor turbulence on the way, not untypical for this particular journey. Once loaded up with crew and passengers, many returning to China, the plane was given permission to push back from the terminal building at 12.27am on 8 March. It took off at 12:41am without incident and 11 minutes later had climbed to a 35,000-ft (10,668-m) cruising altitude, which is normal for an aircraft of this type.

'Goodnight, Malaysian 370'

The aircraft would continue to maintain contact with ATC at Kuala Lumpur. At around 1.19am, Kuala Lumpur ATC informed MH370 that it would soon leave Malaysian air space and to contact Ho Chi Minh ATC in Vietnam. The plane's on-board aircraft communication, addressing and reporting system (ACARS), which transmitted data about its performance, sent its last piece of information at 1.07am and then went silent. As the flight passed into Vietnamese air space at 1.19am, Captain Zaharie signed off from Kuala Lumpur ATC with the words, 'Goodnight, Malaysian 370' – the final words from the flight crew. At 1.21am, the plane's transponder, the device that tells ATC about a plane's specific location and altitude, also appeared to be switched off.

Initially, Kuala Lumpur ATC was unconcerned that no further flight data was coming from MH370, assuming it had gone out of radar range. However, when nothing appeared on Ho Chi Minh ATC's radar, controllers tried to contact MH370 for 18 minutes but heard only static in return – the plane seemed to have vanished. Eventually, a call was put out for other planes in the immediate area to call MH370 and report back, but nothing was forthcoming. After 19 minutes, Ho Chi Minh ATC finally notified Kuala Lumpur ATC that there had been no contact from the plane. (Ho Chi Minh should have done this after five minutes of no contact, but controllers were busy trying to locate contacts between MH370 and other aircraft.)

Kuala Lumpur ATC contacted the Malaysia Airlines operations centre at 02:03 to relay the news and were told the flight was showing up in Cambodian air space, well away from its designated flight path. However, they did this – which seems to us now to have been rather unconventional — by going on to an aviation radar website, which would not have provided absolutely accurate information and was 'based on flight projection and not reliable for aircraft positioning' because it used only secondary data rather than primary data from ATC. These websites are publicly available and can sometimes make up information about planes if the plane's transponder, effectively a 'beacon' that transmits an automatic response to radio contacts, is switched off and giving a false impression of the aircraft's whereabouts.

At 2.39am, frantic staff at Malaysia Airlines tried to make a direct phone call to MH370 using a satellite phone. Although there was no answer, the satellite call did lock on to the plane, indicating it was still airborne. While no firm data on its exact location was given, there were suggestions from the Australian government who were helping with the search for the missing plane, that it had in fact turned south sooner than was originally thought. At this point, it is possible that the plane could have been flying purely on autopilot: for instance, if the pressurization unit that keeps oxygen flowing around the cabin was no longer activated, this would have led to unconsciousness within minutes. In 2005, this happened on a Helios Airways flight, which flew for hours in autopilot mode until the fuel ran out and it crashed, killing all on board.

Code red

At 3am local Malaysian time, the situation was referred to Malaysia Airlines' Crisis Director, Mohd Fuad Sharuji, who declared it a 'code red emergency', the highest level of aviation emergency. By 5.30am, Malaysia Airlines had notified the Malaysian government about the unfolding crisis. The 'Watch Supervisor' at Malaysian Air Traffic Control contacted the Kuala Lumpur Aeronautical Rescue Coordination Centre (ARCC). Rescuers were immediately dispatched to locate the missing plane to the area in the South China Sea where it was last recorded on radar before moving out of Kuala Lumpur ATC's radar range. Air Traffic Control made another unsuccessful call by satellite phone to the plane, which had been due to land at Beijing at 6.30am local time. The plane had been airborne for over four hours by now without contact from the pilot. Later, on the morning of 8 March, Malaysia Airlines made a public statement that it believed the plane had crashed.

MH370's strange flight path

The following day, 9 March, the Malaysian Air Force announced that it had tracked MH370 using primary radar, which does not require a beacon from the plane, between 1.30am and 2.22am on 8 March. According to this data, just after the plane entered Vietnamese air space it suddenly turned sharply left back towards Malaysia, flying southwest over the coast of the Malay Peninsula and passing just south of the island of Penang. It then turned northwest and flew across the Strait of Malacca. By the time military radar lost contact with the plane at 2:22am, it was over the Andaman Sea. Based on this new evidence, search teams widened their area of operation.

The fact that the Malaysian Air Force tracked the flight but appeared not to raise the alarm was concerning to some reporters. But responding to criticism that Malaysian fighter jets should have been scrambled to investigate the unidentified flight passing through Malaysian air space, Defence Minister, Hishammuddin Hussein, said in an interview with the Australian Broadcasting Corporation's *Four Corners* programmme in May 2014 that the plane was deemed commercial and not hostile. Neighbouring Indonesia and Thailand, however, reported that their military radars detected no sign of any unusual aircraft in their air space.

Tracking MH370

By 7:24am, Malaysia Airlines issued an announcement to the press and TV that Flight 370 was officially missing after contact was lost with

Malaysian Air Traffic Control. The search began soon afterwards and the Malaysian government mobilized its civil aviation department, air force, navy and Maritime Enforcement Agency. Under the Five Power Defence Arrangements, which consists of the five Commonwealth powers of Australia, Malaysia, New Zealand, Singapore and the United Kingdom, a search and rescue mission was mounted in the region's waters. Within two days of the plane going missing, the countries had sent more than 34 aircraft and 40 ships to the area of the Andaman Sea, northwest of Malaysia.

The search radius was increased from the original 20 nmi (37 km; 23 mi) from the plane's last known position, south of Thổ Chu Island, Thailand to 100 nmi (190 km; 120 mi), which then extended to the Strait of Malacca along the west coast of the Malaysian Peninsula. On 13 March, the British satellite manufacturer, Inmarsat, notified the Malaysian government that it had received routine communications from the plane via its Indian Ocean Region satellite. If the satellite's ground station (in Australia) did not hear from an aircraft, it would automatically send an hourly log-on-log-off message, known as a 'ping', to the satellite, and if it was still logged into the system the plane would automatically send back a short message. This interaction was known as a 'handshake'. Inmarsat initially recorded six complete handshakes after the plane's own ACARS communications system had stopped sending messages.

Investigators discovered that there was a further seventh handshake attempt, around an hour after the last one, when the aircraft transmitted a ping to the satellite. The log-on message was sent from the aircraft at 8.19am and aviation experts say that there were only a few reasons that the SDU or Satellite Data Unit (a communication device between the aircraft and satellite) would transmit a log-on message, including for instance a brief loss of power or software failure. Eventually, unless it landed, the plane would run out of fuel, and the fuel that powered the electrical systems would fail However, the plane still had a vital but small back-up system in place to enable a pilot in distress, with no fuel left, to help glide the plane with some navigational assistance. The

APU, or Auxiliary Power Unit, which is based in the tail section of the 777, taps into the very last drops of the aircraft's fuel, which is reserved specifically for this unit. It provides the plane with limited electrical and hydraulic power. One of the systems that came back on was the Satellite Data Unit and it was this that sent a seventh ping up to the satellite at around 08.19 in the morning.

The company made calculations, using the automatic 'pings' or signals sent to Inmarsat's ground station in Australia, about the distance of the aircraft from the satellite, and the duration it took for each 'ping' to be sent and received. This produced two possible positions: a northern pathway from Vietnam across Asia, and a southern pathway from Java over the Indian Ocean southwest of Australia. The very last seventh ping produced a slight difference in the calculations in that it showed that the aircraft was lower in the air than during previous pings. This meant that the fuel was most certainly out and the plane was now gliding downwards. Shortly afterwards, Malaysia's Prime Minister, Najib Razak, confirmed that MH370 was deliberately diverted and flew for another six hours after losing contact with air traffic controllers.

As stated, Australia, the UK, Singapore and New Zealand were the first countries to offer assistance in searching for the missing flight. Australia now led the search on 17 March, when Inmarsat's satellite communications network determined that the plane flew on into the southern Indian Ocean until at least 8.19am. On 24 March, the Malaysian government announced that it believed Flight MH370 ended somewhere in the southern Indian Ocean.

Although the search for MH370 continued over the following weeks, no physical trace of the plane was found. At first, there was much confusion, with little information forthcoming from either the airline or the Malaysian government, simply because they had none at that time.

Understandably, this lack of information attracted angry criticism from people in China, as many of the passengers on board MH370 were of Chinese origin. Relatives and friends of the missing passengers in China grew increasingly angry with the Malaysian government saying, 'It lacked being transparent and there were too many delays in passing on information to them', and so they staged protests that gained wide publicity. Anti-Malaysian sentiment also flared on Chinese social media along with the Chinese state media also voicing criticism. Protests were made outside the Malaysian embassy in Beijing.

Debris discovered

In 2015 and 2016, several pieces of debris floated ashore in the western Indian Ocean, some of which were confirmed to have come from MH370. One piece of the plane was a wing flap found on France's Reunion Island, east of Madagascar. This was about 3,700km (2,300 miles) away from the main search site in the southern Indian Ocean. French authorities began an aerial search for possible marine debris around the island, followed by a later foot search on 7 August 2015, covering an area 120 km (75 mi) by 40 km (25 mi) along the east coast of Reunion. This discovery was a major lead in the search for the missing plane, which at least provided some kind of closure for the families of the people on board.

Reunion Island oceanographer, Dr Roland Trouadec, told the BBC in August 2015 that the direction of the powerful Southern Equatorial Current was influenced by many things, including water temperature, salinity, wind speed, water density and also the Earth's rotation, which determined the direction of travel. 'If you look at Reunion on a map, it is only a pinpoint in the ocean. For the piece of the plane to arrive on this island is remarkable,' Dr Trouadec said. Later analysis of the flap by the French Army suggested that it had floated in the water for over a year and four months, but it gave no real clues as to where the actual plane might have crashed.

The Maldives authorities also searched their beaches when islanders found aircraft parts washed ashore, but unfortunately, in that particular case, they did not turn out to be connected with the missing plane. In March 2016, more parts of the plane washed up on the East African coastline. Darren Chester, the Australian minister for infrastructure and transport, said after the discovery of debris located in Mozambique that it was 'consistent with drift modelling'. Six months later in September 2016, a piece of debris, a large outboard flap, was discovered off the coast of Tanzania and was later confirmed as being from MH370.

By December 2016, families of those lost aboard MH370 also joined the search on Madagascan beaches in the hope of finding more debris from the plane, resulting in a small piece being discovered. By January 2017, the underwater search for MH370 came to an end with the Australian Transport Safety Bureau abandoning the quest after searching a massive 120,000 sq km (46,000 sq mi) area in the southern Indian Ocean west of Perth for nearly two-and-a-half years without success. A year later, in January 2018, a US seabed exploration company called Ocean Infinity, chartered a Norwegian ship under a 'no find, no fee' agreement with the Malaysian Government, expanding its search in May of that year, after finding nothing in a 25,000 sq km (10,000 sq mi) 'priority area' previously identified by Australian experts as MH370's most likely resting place.

By July that year, the official investigation report was released in Malaysia, concluding that the plane was manually turned around in mid-air, rather than being under the control of autopilot. However, they also said that 'unlawful interference by a third party' could not be ruled out. Theories that suggested the pilot and first officer deliberately crashed the plane in a suicide mission were quickly dismissed and no mechanical or structural failure of the plane was uncovered. In June that year, the Australians authorities also released a preliminary report, in which their theories suggested that the plane continued in autopilot mode after a possible catastrophe caused the crew to become incapacitated due to oxygen starvation.

By 28 January 2015, the Malaysian government officially declared the disappearance of MH370 to be an accident, with all passengers and crew presumed dead 327 days after it vanished. The aircraft, they said, had exhausted its fuel 'over a defined area of the southern Indian Ocean'. With no searches resulting in the finding of the plane, things remained quiet for about six years. Then, suddenly, in December 2024, the Malaysian government agreed with the help of Ocean Infinity to resume their efforts to locate the remains of Flight MH370. A new area would be searched in a 15,000 sq km (6,000 sq mi) patch in the southern Indian Ocean, based on new data that Kuala Lumpur found to be 'credible', the country's transport minister, Anthony Loke, said.

Was MH370 hijacked?

Since Flight MH370 disappeared, many theories have emerged to explain the disappearance of the plane. Among the more outlandish explanations were that North Korea somehow took control of the plane, or that juice from mangoes in the hold escaped and ignited, and even that a black hole appeared over the Earth and MH370 was sucked into it. There were also suggestions that a meteor struck it, UFOs abducted everyone on board, or that it landed at the US base of Diego Garcia in the Indian Ocean. Numerous amateur sleuths around the world reported possible debris from the missing plane and some thought they had found parts of the plane off the coast of Vietnam, contradicting the Inmarsat data that suggested it flew south over the Indian ocean.

A somewhat more plausible solution is that Flight MH370 was hijacked, based on the loss of signals from on board. As mentioned earlier, the plane was fitted with ACARS, a paid-for automated digital system for transmitting 'health check' messages between the plane and ground stations via airband radio or satellite. This system stopped working just before the plane crossed over the Malay Peninsula. Not long after, the aircraft's transponder also ceased transmitting along the border area between Malaysian and Vietnamese air space. It seemed likely that these systems had been deliberately turned off, which, together with the absence of any further voice communication, could suggest hijacking.

However, in a 'typical' skyjacking communication would normally remain open, so pilots can pass on the hijackers' demands to authorities. No such demands were received from the MH370 cockpit. Also arguing against hijack was the lack of any group coming forward to claim responsibility, and the fact that the plane appeared to fly over the remote Indian Ocean rather than landing at an airport, where hijackers could use the passengers more effectively as a bargaining chip.

Did the captain crash the plane on purpose?

Shortly after the plane had disappeared, in March 2014 an unnamed Malaysian government official said he was convinced that the plane had been hijacked. The official, who spoke to the Associated Press on condition of remaining anonymous because he was not authorized to brief the media, said that hijacking was no longer a theory. 'It is conclusive,' he said. 'The plane's communication instruments that dealt with data about the flight path were switched off deliberately and showed that the plane was steered in a way to avoid detection by radar.'

A joint suicide mission was ruled out, though, as both pilots had not requested to work together that night. Not long after, the aircraft's transponder ceased transmitting along the border area between Malaysian and Vietnamese air space. First Officer Fariq had previously broken strict aviation rules by inviting two female passengers into the cockpit during a flight from Kuala Lumpur to the island of Phuket. Malaysia Airlines only became aware of this fact when one of the female passengers came forward after MH370 went missing. In a statement, Malaysia Airlines said it was 'shocked by these allegations'. South African Teenager, Jonti Roos, joined Fariq in the cockpit of a flight she took in 2011 and had her photo taken with him. In the US, such practices are illegal, but elsewhere around the world such things are at the discretion of the pilot. Perhaps something similar may have happened on MH370 and both pilots were overcome by passengers in the cockpit.

Captain Zaharie's last spoken radio message, using the phrase 'Good night', raised suspicion that he may have been suicidal and decided to deliberately crash the plane. Among aviation experts, appearing on Australia's 60 minutes programme *MH370: The Situation Room* in 2018, was Larry Vance, veteran air crash investigator from Canada, who said that Captain Zaharie flew the plane on for another six hours to deliberately make it disappear. All the experts on the programme agreed that the plane was under the control of someone, rather than experiencing mechanical failure. They pointed the finger at Zaharie as being the most experienced and, therefore, the obvious choice.

He was in their eyes, the likely candidate to take the plane off course and switch off the ACARS and the transponder, since he clearly knew the aircraft very well and even had a flight simulator at his home. According to a magazine report in 2016, he had simulated a flight over the Indian Ocean a few weeks before MH370 was lost. But how would he have overcome the objections of his younger co-pilot? Perhaps he could have suggested the co-pilot Fariq should leave the cockpit momentarily, maybe to fetch them both a coffee, and then locked the door. He might then have switched off the electronics, making the plane invisible to air traffic controllers at the pivotal point between two different air jurisdictions.

Larry Vance said that, as the plane turned back to Malaysia, it was at this point the captain could have depressurized the cabin; passenger emergency drop-down masks, deployed in the event of a depressurization, would work for around 20 minutes, and the captain's for a few hours longer. In fact, the oxygen supply in his tank had been fully replenished earlier in the day by ground crew technicians. In this case, the co-pilot might have been trying desperately to get back into the cockpit but would eventually have succumbed due to the lack of oxygen in the cabin unless he had managed to secure an emergency oxygen tank and mask situated in the forward cabin section for crew to use. If the captain had locked him out of the cabin, he would certainly have tried to gain access to it via an entry code on the door panel. But if he was locked out, this would not have opened the door. He could have then used an emergency entry code, which would cause a buzzer alarm to go off in the cockpit. This would buzz for around 30 seconds and the captain could have, if he wanted to, unlocked it. This probably didn't happen, however, if Zaharie was deliberately locking his co-pilot out. Could it also be feasible that the pilots were themselves incapacitated by a sudden fire or depressurization and tried to turn the plane back towards home, only to be overcome by fumes or hypoxia, leading to the unusual flight pattern? Being overcome by fumes or lack of oxygen, a condition known as hypoxia, a confused Zaharie or Fariq might then have accidentally turned off all comms equipment. The plane would still fly but would then have continued in what is known as a 'ghost flight', in which its occupants are dead but the aircraft continues on autopilot, eventually crashing into the sea after the fuel runs out. Although the data implies that the comms were switched off at certain key points along the flight path, this could surely only have been done deliberately.

MH370 appeared to weave in and out in the last part of its flight, possibly to avoid radar detection and other air traffic paths, which only an experienced pilot would know about. As the aircraft began to run out of fuel, some experts believe it flew in a strange figure-of-eight pattern, which is something that could only be imposed manually. If, as suggested by signals mentioned earlier, the plane was last in the air at about 8.19am, it would have been daylight in that part of the Indian Ocean. If the captain was intending to crash the plane, he might have wanted to check to see whether there were any ships in the area to avoid possible eyewitnesses.

Russian involvement?

Just a few months after MH370 vanished, in July 2014 another Malaysia Airlines Boeing 777 crashed. All 300 people on board Flight MH17 from Amsterdam to Kuala Lumpur were killed when it came down in Ukraine. In this case, the plane was shot down by a surface-to-air missile fired by a Russian-backed militia unit. Was there a link between the two planes? Although debris found washed up on the coast of Madagascar and nearby islands has apparently been confirmed as belonging to MH370, if the aircraft was shot down it was still somehow recorded as flying for another six hours out towards the Indian Ocean, with certain communications instruments switched off at certain points.

Existing recordings of the flight do not match up with the idea of an air missile suddenly shooting the plane down. Besides, there would be also a lot more wreckage floating on the surface of the water after the plane broke up. For instance, Siberia Airlines Flight 1812 was shot down by the Ukrainian Air Force over the Black Sea on 4 October 2001, en route from Tel Aviv, Israel, to Novosibirsk, Russia. The aircraft carried 66 passengers and 12 crew members, all of whom died. The crash site is about 190 km (118 mi) westsouthwest of the Black Sea resort of Sochi. There was plenty of debris floating on the surface and the Black Box flight recorder was detected at the bottom of the sea at a depth of approximately 1,000 m (3,300 ft), which was too great a depth for retrieval.

As this showed, a mid-air explosion would have caused instant decompression with internal objects dispersed by the explosion over a wide area as it was still in forward momentum – all the wreckage would have spread out, making it easier to locate from the air. From the satellite data, it's believed that the MH370 777 might have gone though two possible scenarios. One was a steep death dive at maximum speed, and the second was a more controlled descent, landing the aircraft on the ocean, where it slowly sank. Both ideas were tested out in a flight simulator by Boeing 777 pilot, Simon Hardy, for the Australian *60 Minutes* programme in 2018. In the first scenario, Hardy turned off one engine and the plane turned itself to the right and began to descend, struggling for power. With Hardy barely touching the controls further, in this first scenario the fuel ran out and the second engine stopped working as the plane entered a steep dive. Hardy believed that, in the first scenario, the plane might have reached supersonic speeds as it came down. From cruising altitude to the death dive into the ocean, it took just two minutes. Hardy didn't think this particular scenario actually occurred, however.

In the second scenario, Hardy once again, switched off one of the engines to simulate a loss of fuel to that engine. The plane would once again bank to one side as the remaining engine tried to compensate, but it still descended at a rapid speed at around 5,000 ft per minute. In this second display however, Hardy then took the steering column of the plane and pulled up slightly to level off. The plane was no longer diving. Instead, it glided under control, but with no engine power. Turning the plane into a silent glider, the journey to the surface of the sea from cruising altitude of around 35,000 ft took around nine minutes and increased the journey by about 100 nautical miles. Hardy concluded that this second test would have put the plane outside the current search area.

American aviation writer, Jeff Wise, thinks the flight headed north instead of south. He contends that the plane's satellite data unit (SDU), was turned off and then back on again three minutes after the plane left primary radar coverage, which disguised its flight path, so that anyone tracking it would think the plane headed south, when instead it flew north. Pilots who fly the Boeing 777 are not trained in switching the SDU back on, and Wise believes it could not have come on again accidentally. Something – or someone – did switch on the SDU, and he claims that the three Russian passengers listed on the plane were intelligence agents, who could have created a distraction to climb unseen into the base of the aircraft, take over the major electronics of the plane and fly it remotely from there. They could also have triggered decompression of the cabin at the same time, so that they would not be further disturbed in their mission. Wise believes the plane was then flown north to Kazakhstan, where it was either landed or crashed, to deflect international attention away from Russia's annexation of Crimea, which is part of Ukraine.

US security and intelligence

It has been alleged by French author, Florence de Changy, that France's intelligence services informed a French relative of one of the passengers on MH370 that they believed two US Airborne Control and Warning (AWACs) planes were present in the area that night. These military planes are fitted with long-range radar systems capable of monitoring the air space within a radius of more than 400 km (250 miles). De Changy suggested that the MH370 communications system was jammed, possibly by the two US AWACs. She claims this may have been done to force the plane to land at, say, Diego Garcia, in order to pick up a highly sensitive cargo, which American intelligence services didn't want to fall into Chinese hands. Supposedly, a 2.5-tonne cargo consignment was placed inside the plane under tight escort and was not X-rayed.

Author Jeff Wise has voiced concerns that the data provided by Inmarsat may not have been totally reliable. The company was initially reluctant to publish its findings and, when these were eventually made public, important details necessary to understand the calculations were missing. Wise interviewed cybersecurity professionals, Ken Munroe and Todd Humphries, who suggested that there really was reason to think that MH370 could have been hacked. According to Wise, once the Inmarsat engineers figured out what the BFO data was telling them, they were very confident that they had figured out where the plane went. He said the 'calculations were complicated, but their significance could not have been plainer. They had figured out where the plane had gone, they just needed to go, look there and find it.'

Nonetheless, the plane still wasn't in the search area. The data could have been hacked to provide false breadcrumbs, so to speak, for searchers. The drawback to this theory is that the unit that has to be hacked is in a rack above the heads of passengers and behind a panel. This panel can only be reached with a stepladder, according to Ken Munro of the Pen Test Partners in the UK, who test out vulnerabilities of cybersecurity. This makes the hacking theory slightly more implausible, unless you can decompress the cabin air and render everyone on board unconscious, so that this procedure can be done without interference.

The late John Lear, an experienced pilot and son of the private jet manufacturer who flew many different planes, suggested that as the engine manufacturer, Rolls-Royce, provided engines for the Boeing 777, it would be able to track the plane via technology built into the engines. Yet, according to Lear, Rolls Royce did not come forward with any information about the location of the missing plane. He also claimed Boeing would know the whereabouts of their own planes, again with similar tracking abilities. Supposedly, this data would still be transmitting even if circuit-breakers were pulled in the cockpit to prevent it. According to Lear, information on the plane's whereabouts could have been suppressed under anti-terrorism legislation that effectively gags companies from releasing information to the public.

Another theory proposed, somewhat incredibly, that MH370 was downed in retribution for Malaysia's attempts from 2007 onwards to establish war crimes tribunals to try former US President George W. Bush, former British Prime Minister Tony Blair and other senior figures in both administrations for the invasion of Iraq. In 2014, Malaysia Airlines flights represented around half a per cent of all flights, yet more than half of air-crash deaths were because of MH370 and MH17.

Could the washed-up wreckage actually have been deliberately placed to deceive people into thinking that Flight MH370 plummeted into the southern Indian Ocean? Or could the plane somehow have been escorted to a military base in the Indian Ocean or remotely flown northwards into Kazakhstan? It could be the case that certain governments know more about its final position than the wider public. After all, the less we actually know, the more speculation tends to spread online and further muddy the waters. Even if MH370's 'black box' flight recorder was found at the bottom of the Indian Ocean, it might still not tell the full story of how the plane ended up there because the pilot could have disabled it by pulling the circuit-breaker, pulling the plug as it were.

One of the many haunting elements of the MH370 tragedy supposedly occurred in the hotel where all the relatives of the passengers were assembled shortly after it went missing. Naturally, many were dialling loved ones on their mobile phones and leaving voice messages, desperately hoping to hear they were still alive. However, some sources reported that one passenger did receive a call back from their relative on the missing plane, but for some reason did not answer. This story is not verified, but if it were to be true it suggests that if, for example, everyone else on the plane had passed out through hypoxia, then at least one poor soul might still have been conscious. If nothing else, this serves to remind all of us who simply want to know what happened that Flight MH370's disappearance caused devastation for many families, and will continue to do so until those who were bereaved find some answers.

SOMERTON MAN

In 1949, *The Advertiser*, an Australian newspaper, described it as 'one of Australia's most profound mysteries' and the story of so-called 'Somerton Man' continues to intrigue, even though many journalists declared it to be solved in 2022. While, sadly, many people are found dead in public places, this case presented a compelling mix of conflicting evidence and lack of identifying detail that, taken together, baffled the police and other expert investigators for decades. After nearly 80 years though, could we soon find out once and for all who this mysterious man really was?

This strange story occurred during the early Cold War years just after the Second World War, when the world was still recovering from the conflict, political boundaries were shifting and the Soviet Union was strengthening its grip across eastern Europe, making its relationship with its former wartime allies, the US and Britain, increasingly uneasy. In addition, millions of people were displaced and on the move, which helped to fuel rising suspicions that Communist spies were operating all around the 'free' world, including in British Commonwealth countries like Australia.

Slumped on the beach

It was in this climate of tension that on the early morning of 1 December 1948, two trainee jockeys exercising their horses along Somerton Park Beach in a suburb of Adelaide, South Australia, came across the body of a man slumped against the sea wall. The dead man was smartly dressed in a white shirt with a red, white and blue tie, brown trousers, socks and smart shoes, along with a brown knitted pullover and fashionable grey-and-brown, double-breasted jacket, which suggested 'American' tailoring. Later, he was considered to be British in appearance and thought to be aged between 40 and 45 and in 'top physical condition'. He was lying on his back in the sand with his head resting against the seawall, legs extended and feet crossed – almost as if he died in his sleep, which is what some initially assumed. In addition, a cigarette stub was found near his coat collar.

The corpse had no identification on him and, oddly, all the labels seemed to have been removed from his clothes. Nor were local police able to find a match to a missing person report. When they examined his body further, they discovered an unusual clue tucked away in a 'secret' fob (watch) pocket: a rolled-up scrap of paper seemingly torn out from a book, with the words *tamám shud* printed on it. This turned out to be a Farsi (Persian) phrase meaning 'it's over' or 'the end'.

Adelaide police were able to identify the words. They came from the final page of a 12th-century book of Persian poetry, the *Rubaiyat of Omar Khayyám*. They appealed to the public for help in locating a copy with the same (final) page missing. A member of the public, named Ronald Francis, came forward and produced a copy minus its last page; while it's unclear if Francis owned the book, according to a *Guardian* report from 2022, he claimed it had been thrown into the back seat of his car, which at the time was in Glenelg, another beachside suburb of Adelaide.

Police detectives noticed indentations inside the book's back cover, as if it had been leant on while someone was writing notes on a piece of paper, and from this they were able to identify a local telephone number, another unknown number and lines of random letters that they thought resembled a coded message of some kind. This puzzled the police back in 1948, and to this day these 'codes' have not been deciphered to anyone's satisfaction.

Witnesses later told the police they had observed a man who may have been the Somerton Man late on the evening of 30 November, lying on his back in the very same spot where the body was discovered the next morning. Some thought they had observed him earlier that evening: at around 7pm, a couple said they saw a man in the same place by the beach wall, stretch his right arm fully out and then relax it. Others said they saw a man lying in the same position, at the same place at some time between 7.30pm and 8pm that evening, illuminated by streetlights, although he did not seem to move at all during this time. Wondering why he wasn't reacting to the mosquitoes that had landed on him, they assumed he was either drunk or in a deep sleep.

Not a natural death

Following his post-mortem examination of Somerton Man, pathologist John Burton Cleland reported that he was 1.8 m (5 ft 11 in) tall and estimated he was around 40 to 45 years old and possibly British. Cleland also noted that he was in 'top physical condition'. As mentioned, although he was smartly dressed, his clothing had no labels and there was no wallet to help identify him. Of course, the wallet could simply have been stolen if he had been attacked.

The autopsy of the body revealed his estimated time of death was around 2am on 1 December 1948. According to the pathologist, John Dwyer, some of the autopsy findings suggest that Somerton Man could have ingested poison before his death. In particular, it noted, 'The stomach was deeply congested… There was congestion in the second half of the duodenum. There was blood mixed with the food in the stomach. Both kidneys were congested, and the liver contained a great excess of blood in its vessels… The spleen was strikingly large… about 3 times normal size… there was destruction of the centre of the liver lobules revealed under the microscope. [There was]… acute gastritis haemorrhage, extensive congestion of the liver and spleen, and the congestion to the brain.'

The pathologist went on to tell the coroner (the official who rules on cause of death and decides if an inquest is required) that it was very likely the death was not natural. In fact, he suggested the deceased had possibly been poisoned with a barbiturate or a soluble hypnotic. However, the coroner was unable to reach any firm conclusions about Somerton Man's identity or the cause of his death. The inquest was adjourned because the evidence was too inconclusive to reach a finding. The inquest was adjourned until June 1949.

In his evidence to the inquest, Dr Robert Cowan, Deputy Government Analyst, said he was unaware of any poison that can cause death,

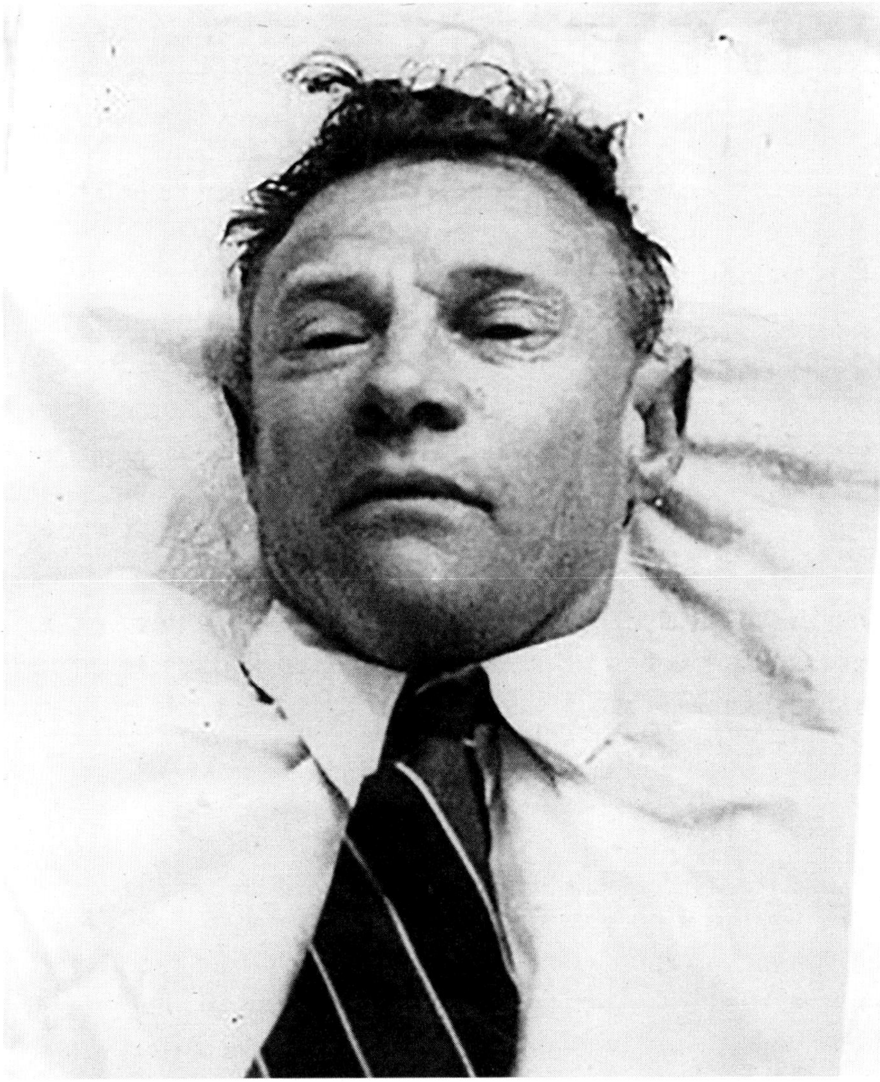

A police photo of the corpse of Somerton man.

then 'disappear' from the body, so that it can't be identified by post-mortem analysis. He stated, 'I feel quite satisfied that if death were caused by any common poison, my examination would have revealed its nature. If he did die from poison, I think it would be a very rare poison.'

At the inquest, Cleland had speculated that as none of the witnesses could conclusively identify the man they saw the previous night of 30 November as the same person discovered the next morning dead against the beach wall, there was the possibility the man had died at another location and been brought to Somerton beach by persons unknown and dumped there. Cleland added this was purely speculation as all the witnesses believed it was 'definitely the same person' since the body was in the same place and lying in the same distinctive position.

After the coroner officially announced that they were unable to identify Somerton Man, his body was embalmed on 10 December 1948. This was the first time, according to the police, this procedure was performed for a specific reason: this procedure gave police extra time to find out more information, perhaps through more tests at another autopsy. A plaster cast was made of his head, which later proved very useful. The mystery man was later buried in Adelaide cemetery on 14 June 1949, with a tombstone reading, 'Here lies the unknown man who was found at Somerton Beach.' The ceremony was taken by Salvation Army Captain, Em Webb, who led the prayers, and it was attended by reporters and police.

Strange belongings

There was a new twist in the case early the following year, in January 1949, when a suitcase was found by staff in a locker at Adelaide's railway station. This contained items thought to belong to 'Somerton Man'. As well as smart clothes and shaving equipment, there were some unusual items that seemed unsuited to a business or leisure trip: a table knife modified into a short, sharp instrument, an electrician's screwdriver, scissors with sharpened ends and a stencilling brush typically used to stencil cargo ships. The only new clue that police could come up with as far as the suitcase was concerned was that the stitching on a coat found inside the case suggested that it had come from America at some point, so they postulated that the missing man had at one time visited America.

The inquest into Somerton Man's death was reconvened on 17 June 1949. Cleland, as the investigating pathologist, decided to re-examine the Somerton body and made a number of findings. He discovered that the man's shoes were extremely clean and looked to have been recently polished, which did not fit with someone who had arrived in town and wandered around on the day before he died. (The police thought it likely he arrived by train into Adelaide on the morning of 30 November.) In addition, there was no evidence of vomiting and convulsions at the spot where the dead man was found on the beach, suggesting he had reacted to the toxins elsewhere. This supported the theory that Somerton Man's body might have been brought to the beach wall after his death.

Did the unknown man die at another location, his body then being dumped at Somerton Park Beach? Cleland stressed that this was a purely speculative proposition. Nor was there any new evidence that helped the inquest to identify the body.

However, based on items found in his clothing, the inquest was able to establish that, on 30 November, Somerton Man bought a train ticket but for some reason decided not to take the train, because he then bought a bus ticket from the railway station to the beach. Early in the case, police thought they had managed to identify the dead man as Mr E. C. Johnson, but on 3 December 1948, Mr Johnson himself walked into police headquarters and let officials know he was alive and well. Other unknown members of the public who had viewed the dead body of the man at the local morgue came forward with possible identities, with one man believing the victim to be a former Prospect resident named Jack Thomas McLean. The man who viewed the body told Adelaide police that he had last seen Jack McLean about three or four years previously around 1945, when he was working on coastal ships. He did not know whether McLean was married or where he lived but believed he had resided at one point in the town of Prospect.

After the inquest was unable to rule on a definite cause of death, the requested plaster cast that was made of the mystery man's head and shoulders was eventually passed to the care of the South Australian Police Historical Society. According to the *Adelaide Advertiser* in April 1949, this was an 'unparalleled mystery'.

A new witness

The case took a mysterious turn around a decade later when another eyewitness came forward. On 5 December 1959, Adelaide police detective, Don O'Doherty, reported that this witness said he and three others had seen a respectable-looking man carrying another man on his shoulders the length of Somerton Park Beach the same night as other witnesses had seen the slumped or sleeping man. Could this man have been the body discovered later on the beach – either already dead or so sick or injured he couldn't walk?

Deciphering a 'code'

Many people were convinced that the key to unlock the mystery of Somerton Man's identity, and to explain why he may have been killed, lay in the book, *The Rubaiyat of Omar Khayyám*. The strange handwritten lines of capital letters indented into the back cover of the book were as follows:

> 'WRGOABABD
> ~~MLIAOI~~
> WTBIMPANETP
> MLIABOAIAQC
> ITTMTSAMSTGAB'

As shown, the second line had been crossed out, which could indicate a mistake, while a similar, but not identical, sequence of capital letters was written on the fourth line.

Some letters in these lines were not clearly written, leading to additional confusion about what they may indicate. For example, the police speculated about whether the first line began with 'M' or 'W'; many observers thought W was more likely, because it looks different to the crossed-out 'M'. In 1978, cryptographers acting for ABC Televisions's Stuart Littlemore, a barrister and TV presenter, analysed the letters in detail. Unfortunately, they were not able to decipher them, and suggested that rather than a code, the text could be the 'meaningless' product of a 'disturbed mind'.

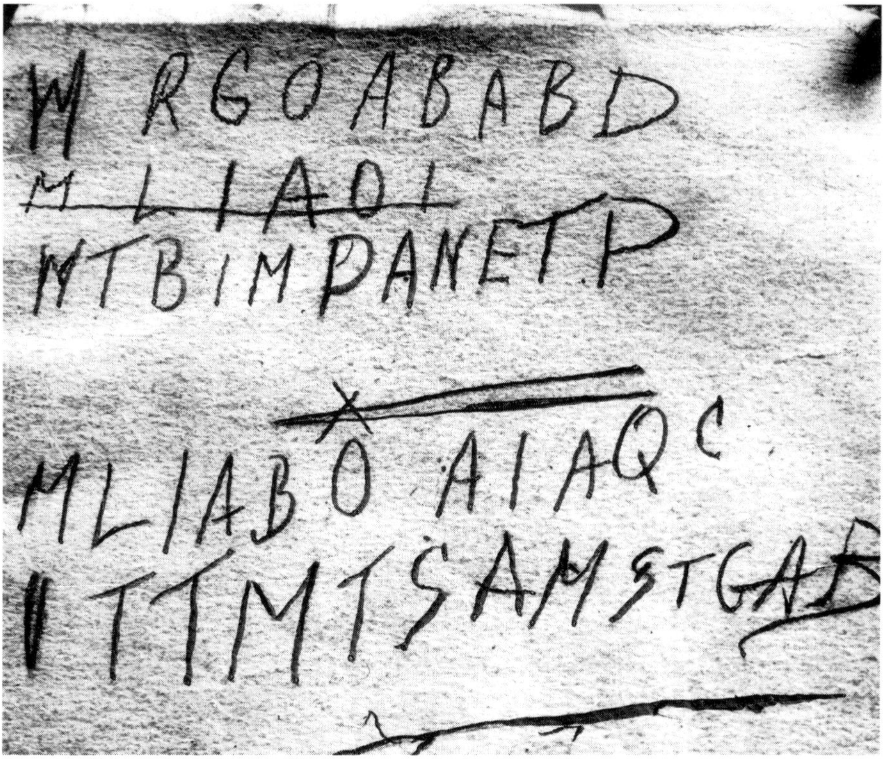

The code found in the *Rubaiyat of Omar Khayyam* found with Somerton Man.

More recently, in 2014, an examination by an expert in language modelling and analysis, John Rehling, suggested that the letters formed the initials of words making up phrases in English. However, after conducting a widespread study of phrases, he found no matches and said it was more likely the lines were a personal shorthand rather than a code. Perhaps Somerton Man had paranoid tendencies and used a personal system to prevent anyone finding out his thoughts and motives. Of course, these 'codes' could simply have been written by someone else entirely, and Somerton Man may have only been interested in obtaining the scrap of Persian text to carry with him. Retired Detective, Gerry Feltus, contributing to a *Sunday Mail* article in 2004, however suggested that the first part of the final line 'ITTMTSAMSTGAB' could stand for the initials of 'It's Time To Move To South Australia Moseley Street'. Moseley Street is where another Somerton Man link had materialized.

The nurse who knew something?

Another baffling aspect of the Somerton Man story involved someone linked to one of the telephone numbers that police identified from the book's cover: a nurse named Jessica Ellen Thomson. When police traced her in 1948, Thomson denied knowing either the deceased man or why he would even have her phone number. Intriguingly though, at the time she lived in Moseley Street, Glenelg – see earlier – which was only around 400 m (1,300 ft) north of Somerton Park Beach, where his body was found. What's more, Thomson was interviewed by police and told them that a stranger had attempted to visit her in late 1948 and questioned her next-door neighbour about where she could be found.

Gerry Feltus, the retired police detective who interviewed Thomson in 2002 (five years before her death in 2007) for a book on the case, thought she seemed quite evasive and reluctant to talk about the case. In his book, *The Unknown Man* (2010), Feltus concluded that Thomson probably knew the Somerton Man's identity. In 1949, Thomson was shown the plaster cast of Somerton Man's head by Detective Leane of Adelaide Police, who was leading the investigation. He recalled that she appeared to almost faint at the sight and was 'completely taken aback'. Thomson claimed that she couldn't identify the man. Later, in 2009, the technician who created the plaster cast came forward and said in a Youtube interview that, as it was shown to Thomson, she immediately turned away and would not look at it again. It appears that seeing this man made the nurse extremely uncomfortable.

In a later television interview in 2013 for Australia's *60 Minutes* programme, Thomson's daughter, Kate, said that she thought her mother did in fact know Somerton Man but was reluctant to let that be known. She revealed that her mother also told her she had lied to the police.

Kate was convinced both that her mother knew his identity, and that this was also 'known to a level higher than the police force'. In her opinion, both her mother and Somerton Man were likely to have been spies: Jessica Thomson expressed interest in Communism and spoke fluent Russian, but never explained to Kate where she learned it or why.

Could Somerton Man have been some kind of foreign agent, trying to make contact with the Russian-speaking nurse and, if so, why?

It's quite possible that Russian spies were operating in Australia at that time. It has been found in the US that Russian operatives were also operating under cover. In 2000, the FBI learned through 'Operation Ghost Stories', one of the largest FBI counter-intelligence investigations, that spies trained in Russia were told to assimilate into everyday American life. They did this by getting married, working in normal everyday jobs and even raising families, while simultaneously also sending encoded messages back home.

A DNA breakthrough

It would be nearly 70 years before a potential breakthrough on Somerton Man's identity occurred as a result of developments in DNA analysis. In March 2009, University of Adelaide physicist and engineering professor, Derek Abbott, began a fresh investigation into the case. As part of this, Professor Abbott proposed exhuming the body to test for DNA samples; initially, the authorities refused, but eventually he was given permission and, in December 2017, he managed to retrieve three 'excellent' hairs from the plaster cast head. Test results indicated that Somerton Man's DNA 'haplogroup' was found in only 1 per cent of Europeans. He worked with American forensic expert Colleen Fitzpatrick to create a 'family' of thousands, then narrowed it down to one person, using DNA testing.

On 26 July 2022, Professor Abbott published his team's headline discovery, that Somerton Man was Carl 'Charles' Webb, an electrical engineer born in 1905 in Footscray, a suburb of Victoria's state capital, Melbourne. The youngest of six children, his father was Richard August Webb, who emigrated to Australia from Germany and eventually opened a bakery business in Victoria. Carl Webb's wife, Dorothy, described him as moody and often threatening; he had few friends and Dorothy said theirs was not a harmonious marriage. Webb was said to be fond of poetry and wrote his own poems, too, mostly on the subject of death. It's interesting that the *Rubaiyat* often muses on death and the afterlife, which may indicate the book with the scrap of printed text removed could have been his own copy. Information gleaned from public records on Webb showed he liked to bet on horse racing, so perhaps the lines of letters simply corresponded to the names of horses running in specific races.

In a divorce statement, Dorothy reportedly said that her husband had attempted suicide with an overdose of ether. She found him in time and nursed him back to health, although he only became more abusive and violent, and eventually she left him in September 1946. She was granted a divorce in 1952, at which point she was living around 90 miles from Adelaide. Webb left the house they shared in April 1947, leaving no paper trail of where he went. There was speculation that he might have come to Adelaide to find Dorothy in 1948. If he did suffer from poor mental health, as Dorothy claimed, this could explain a potential connection with the nurse, Jessica Thomson, who could have treated him at some point. While it's not the only explanation, it is feasible that Webb had Nurse Thomson's phone number because he was in personal contact with her.

A nuclear twist

Many news sources reported the Somerton Man case as solved in 2022. However, a few months before Professor Abbott announced an identity for Somerton Man, an alternative individual was proposed. In January 2022, former Adelaide lawyer, Sophie Holsman, claimed to have solid evidence that he was really Carl or Charles Josef Halban, an Austrian milliner and Communist spy, who was related to an individual involved in development work on the atomic bomb in Britain.

She claimed that hair samples taken from the body of Somerton Man showed his connections to atomic research. Paul Lawson, the man who created the plaster bust of the Somerton Man, secretly took samples of his hair in 1949 as he revealed in an interview in 2023. Lawson said he gave the hair samples to a specialist who analysed them. Lawson was startled by the results he got back because they indicated that the dead man had been poisoned and that there were traces of arsenic present in the retrieved samples. Lawson also said there were also additional traces of Strontium 90. This indicated that the man had possibly been near an atomic explosion of some kind. Lawson was also of the opinion that the man had been heavily sedated and that the police knew that. Holsman believed that high levels of Strontium-90 – a radioactive isotope of strontium produced by nuclear fission – is only found at atomic testing sites. Carl Webb never travelled overseas and therefore could not have got the material in his hair.

Lawson went further in his interview with Gordon Cramer, suggesting the origins of the man's identity. He said that the man was Russian-born with a Russian name, and he had heard that from others (unnamed) involved in the case. He said the man had at one point visited Odessa and the rocket range that was not far from that city (Kapustin Yar). The man had then been transported to Kangaroo Island for his own safety and it was from there that he was able to return to Adelaide.

In 2024, the South Australian Police issued a media statement saying, 'Since the exhumation of the remains of Somerton Man two years ago, SAPOL (South Australia Police) in partnership with the AFP (Australian Federal Police) and FSSA (The Australian Federal Scientific Agency) have engaged with forensic specialists here, interstate and overseas to assist in the identification process. The DNA work on the Somerton Man's remains was recently completed, with analysis of these results to be reported to the State Coroner in the final report along with completed Forensic Anthropology and Forensic Odontology reports, and results of some outstanding forensic analysis that will be completed soon. It is anticipated that the final report will be made available to the State Coroner in 2024 or early 2025.'

At time of writing, this final report has not yet been submitted to the coroner and/or made public. It may confirm the match made by Professor Abbott to Carl Webb, or it may suggest another person entirely. Even if we learn the final truth about Somerton Man's identity, it may not provide all the answers about how he died, where he was killed (and who may have carried him to the beach and why) and the possible reasons for his connection to the Russian-speaking Nurse Thomson.

Was Somerton Man a spy trying to forge local connections for some purpose, or a man who was suffering mental trauma? In September 2023, the family of an Austrian man, Carl Josef Halban, left a birthday message on a sculpture that marks the Somerton Man's place of death. Whoever the smartly dressed man with clean shoes and no form of identification was, it's hard to ignore the feeling that the case of Australia's most mysterious unknown person is likely to yield more surprising twists and turns in the future.

THE INCIDENT AT DYATLOV PASS

The bizarre deaths of nine Russian skiers in the remote Ural Mountains in 1959 has long been a source of curiosity for mystery buffs. This unsettling story remained hidden from western eyes until the Soviet Union collapsed and information, including details of this frankly odd occurrence, began to seep out to media outlets in the west. The combination of the sheer number of deaths, the grisly details of how the bodies were found and, probably most of all, the fact that the case files seemed to have been marked 'top secret' for many years have made this a compelling modern-day mystery. In fact, it was not until 2019 that the case was officially re-opened and officials reconsidered how nine experienced skiers and hikers, eight of whom were only just into their twenties and looking forward to an enjoyable hike with comrades, could have suffered such unusual injuries and died so inexplicably.

The group of college friends, eight men and two women, were all experienced hikers with ski tour experience; they were working towards a Grade 3 level in skiing and hiking, the highest certification in the Soviet Union. They were intending to ski and hike in the remote northern regions of the Sverdlovsk Oblast and the Lozva River, deep in the Ural mountains and on the border with Siberia. They set off on 23 January 1959, travelling by train to Ivdel and then by truck to Vizhai, the last inhabited settlement on their journey.

On 28 January, which was five days into the journey, one of the group, Yuri Yudin, decided that due to ill health he would turn back and wished his comrades well for the rest of the trek. He would become the only survivor. The remaining hikers were led by 23-year-old Igor Dyatlov, who was studying engineering at the Ural Polytechnical Institute (now the Ural State Technical University) in Yekaterinburg, Sverdlovsk Oblast. The rest of the young group consisted of Zinaida Kolmogorova, 22, from the same faculty, Yuri Doroshenko, 21, who was studying power economics, Alexander Kolevatov, 24, studying nuclear physics, Rustem Slobodin, 23 and Nicolas Thibeaux-Brignolle 23 – both enginering students. Lyudmila Dubinina, 20, was studying economics, while Semyon Zolotaryov was a 38-year-old sports instructor and veteran of World War Two. At some point, they made the fateful decision to set up camp at Kholat Syakl, a mountain whose name can be translated from the local Mansi language, via Russian, to 'Death Mountain'.

Through diaries and photographs found at the site of the camp it was possible to piece together an approximate timeline for the group's trek. The group boarded the sleeper train heading north to the town of Serov on the evening of 23 January 1959, from Sverdlovsk, just east of the Ural Mountains. Their overnight journey took them to Serov station, arriving early at 7.39am after covering a distance of 388 km (241 mi). Lyudmila wrote fatefully in her diary that evening, 'I wonder what awaits us in this trip? What will we encounter?' They left Serov around 6.30pm and took another late train further north to Ivdel, some 75 miles away. The group kept themselves entertained most evenings by singing songs that kept their spirits high. During the day at Serov, the students paid a visit to a local school and they told the young children there about the upcoming trip. Lyudmila wrote a poignant entry in her diary concerning the school visit, saying, 'We went and talked to the schoolchildren, then they all saw us off, even burst into tears, didn't want to let us go.'

Perhaps some of the children sensed something in the not-too-distant future that might befall their new friends. The group took a crowded bus for a day visit to Vizhay, nearly 800 miles east of Moscow, arriving at about 2pm on 24 January. Their journey was briefly held up, with four of the group taking a short walk to sightsee a power station. Unfortunately, they missed the bus, and because of this had to hike to try and catch up with it. Fortunately, or maybe not so fortunately, a girl who was also hiking managed to stop the bus to allow the others to catch up with it. Their group diary mentioned this incident, citing their good fortune at catching up with the bus, commenting that 'fate was merciful'.

Their diary for 26 January noted their last day in Vishay, and the Dyatlov group left on the back of a GAZ-63 truck heading for the 41st logging site. Their diary marked it as follows: 'Today is the last day of civilization', as the group sent out postcards to family indicating they would return around 5 March. Comradeship seemed to develop in the group as Zinaida Kolmogorova wrote in her diary for that day, 'Today I wore Yuri's mittens,' but she did so reluctantly out of politeness it seems, because she did not really want to wear them. A feature of members of the group wearing other member's clothes was to prove to have significance later on.

On 27 January, the first ski-led part of the expedition, the group wrote in their diary about Yuri Yudin departing from the group due to health issues. 'Yuri is leaving us today. His sciatic nerves are inflamed again and he is leaving. Such a pity.' He may have been upset to cut short his trip with his friends, but he may well have been grateful for his decision in hindsight. In the event, due to his health issues, he did not actually leave the group until 28 January. Outside temperatures were around -17°C and trying to make a tea took about six hours of warming the water on damp wood that would not heat up very well. They left District 4 on this day with the goal of reaching the 2nd North, which was an abandoned village consisting mostly of huts that had been empty since 1952. They met people along the way and learned some of the local dialect from what were known as the Mansi people, friendly indigenous people living in the Urals. Suspicions would later fall on these people when the students went missing.

On 28 January, they reached the river Lozva at around 5.30pm and they set up their tent and spent the night there. The mood was light and jovial with the singing of songs and talk of love. After bidding farewell to Yuri, the group collected minerals, with the weather now slightly warmer. The next day, they set out for the next leg of their trek, further north by10 km (6 mi) from their starting point in 2nd Northern and 7 km (4 mi) to the Auspiya river. The group found a Mansi ski trail and soon began seeing Mansi signs on trees, left probably as guideposts for other tribes people to follow. The group set up their tent and spent the night at the river Hoysipulsos. They also celebrated Yuri Doroshenko's birthday. He had just turned 21.

On 30 January, they spent their third cold night by the river, with temperatures dropping at night to -26°C. Their diary reported, 'The wind is strong, southwest, snow begins to fall, heavy clouds, drop in temperature. The temperature is normal for Northern Ural.' By this point, the group had encountered lots of trees in their pathway, many with further Mansi signs on them. By January 31, things were starting to look tough for the students. Zinaida wrote in one of her last diary entries, 'All day long, we followed the river. At night, we'll camp on a Mansi trail. I burned my mittens and Yura's jacket at the camp fire – he cursed me a lot!'

With the weather beginning to worsen, the group complained how difficult it was to navigate the trail. 'We can't see the trail, have to grope our way through at times. Can't do more than 1.52 km (1 mile) per hour.' Dyatlov and the others in his group left food supplies at strategic points along the valley, so that they could camp there on the way back.

They headed uphill in the Auspiya valley and set up their tent with the howling wind outside in the deepest snow and they reported they were 'hundreds of kilometres away from human settlements'. By 1 February, the group started out late on their trek and, due to poor weather, only covered 2 km (1.2 mi) before deciding to pitch a tent on the open ridge for a 'cold' overnight, i.e. without firewood, before their planned ascent up to Mount Otorten – or 'don't go there' in the language of the Mansi. The group had been instructed by their superiors to prepare a note for the ascent to Mount Otorten for publication in their university newsletter, but instead they changed it to a humorous 'Evening Otorten No 1', or a satirical propaganda leaflet which read, 'From now on, we know the Snowmen exist. They can be found in the Northern Ural, next to Mt Otorten.' By 'Snowmen', they were referring to Yeti, the Russian version of Bigfoot. Later, photographs found at the campsite would show a mysterious figure in the woods, which some people suggested was the 'Yeti'.

It was thought that the group then had a 'warmer' overnight on 2 February at lake Lunthusaptur near the base of Mount Otorten, where the source of the river Lozva begins. On 3 February, after lunchtime, Dyatlov took the fateful decision to lead the group up the next mountain, Kholat Syakhl, the so-called Mountain of Death.

As a result of particularly heavy snowfall and high winds, the group wanted to gain higher footing and stay on the ridge of the mountain for another 'cold' overnight. They went a further 2 km and about 3pm set up a campsite for the night on the side of Kholat Syakhl, 300 metres from the top, in thick snow and exposed to harsh winds. Further down the valley from their tent was the ravine, where presumably the group planned to get water from. This was probably their last night together. Ever since, this mysterious point in time has become known as 'the incident'.

A search begins

Before beginning their hike, Dyatlov told staff at the Ural Polytechnical Institute that he thought the hikers would be in a position to send a telegram letting them know all was well by around 12 February. When Yuri Yudin left, Dyatlov told him that their journey might take longer because the weather was taking a turn for the worse. As a result, there was no alarm when 12 February came and went with no communication from Dyatlov's party. It was simply assumed they were behind schedule, as indicated by Yudin. (The group had no radio with them to communicate with.) After the students' families still hadn't heard from them in the next few days, on 20 February the university sent out a search and rescue team; police officers, army helicopters and planes were despatched to locate the missing hikers.

By 25 February, the search teams had managed to locate some ski tracks and followed their trail. The next day, 26 February, one of the search party, Mikhail Sharavin, came across the group's tent, which was torn and partly buried under snow. One tent pole was just sticking up above the snow and there was a torch lying on top of the canvas, which still worked when it was switched on. However, they didn't find any of the hikers. Strangely all their provisions, including clothes, food, cameras and journals, were still inside their tent.

No time to dress

The search team identified tracks coming from the tent that suggested the students were either barefoot or in socks, as there were no tread marks in these footprints. The footprints led to a nearby tree line; the next day, the search team found remains of an old fire under a cedar tree and, not long after that, the bodies of Yuri (Georgiy) Krivonishenko, aged 23, and Yuri Nikolayevich Doroshenko, aged 21. Both men were dressed only in their underwear and were shoeless; Krivonishenko was missing his socks as well. Branches of the cedar tree standing over their bodies were broken at a height of around 5 m (16 ft), suggesting that one of them had climbed up the tree, possibly trying to locate the others or to escape from something. Krivonischenko had, it seemed, bitten off a piece of his own knuckle!

The bodies of the group's leader, Igor Dyatlov, and those of Zinaida Kolmogorova, a woman aged 22, and Rustem Slobodin, aged 23, were found just a little further up between the pine and the camp, at the edge of the tree line, closer to the tent. Dyatlov, found by a tree, was dressed with socks but no shoes on and was found lying face down in the snow, arm draped over a birch branch. Dyatlov and Slobodin were found to have bruising in the knuckle joints on both hands, which is a common symptom found in hand-to-hand combat. Dyatlov was also missing a tooth as well as having bloody lips, while Slobodin had frozen blood coming from his nose. His body fell when still warm and there was a

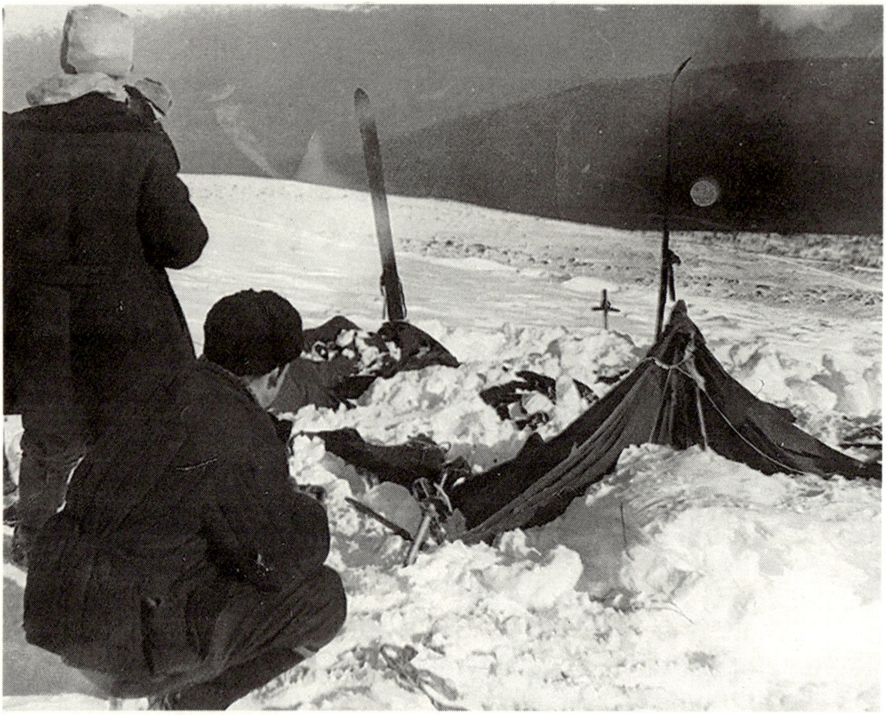

The tent found by the rescue party, 26 February 1959.

noticeable heat exchange into the environment causing an icy layer to form below him. His body heat had melted the snow, which later froze into ice. It was not reported if this happened to the others, or perhaps it was a fact that was just overlooked.

Kolmogorova was clothed and lay near Slobodin and her position suggested to the search party that she had been desperately trying to scramble back uphill towards the tent. On the right-hand side of her torso there was a long bright red bruise as if she had been struck by a baton. All three were in a single-file row, one behind the other, as if they might have been following each other in bad weather. Both Kolmogorova and Slobodin were initially found to have livor mortis spots on the top surface of the body. This led to speculation that their bodies were moved – turned over – after their deaths. Livor mortis occurs when blood settles in the lower parts of the body following death, causing a discolouration of the skin. However, some researchers, like M. I. Rayski, suggest that the medical examiner, Vozrozhdenniy, mistook frostbite erythema for livor mortis since bodies tend to change colour in a warm room. The hikers' bodies were found at distances of 300, 480, and 630 m (980, 1,570, and 2,070 ft) from the tree line.

The search for the five remaining students continued and was led by prosecutor Lev Ivanov (forensic prosecutor of the Sverdlovsk region). He ordered that the tent, which searchers noted had been cut, should be removed and taken back to the police station at the Polunochnoe village by helicopter for forensic analysis.

Cut from the inside

On closer examination by a seamstress, it became apparent that the tent had been cut from the inside, suggesting that those inside could not get out through the normal opening. This discovery raised several possibilities. Deep snow may have been blocking the tent opening. If you had found your tent was blocked by snow at the entrance, would you not have cut a hole in the side of the tent to escape? Or would you just open the tent door and dig the snow away to make a clearing? Alternatively, was the tent cut open in a panic? The students left the tent in only their socks and were partially clothed, which certainly suggests they wanted to escape, and quickly. Perhaps wild animals had found the tent; however, even the youngest of the Russians were experienced hikers and knew they could scare predators away with fire if need be, as during previous trips Yuri Doroshenko had chased bears away with hammers. Or was an avalanche imminent, causing the group to quickly seek the protection of the trees?

Hypothermia and mutilation

Autopsies on the recovered corpses suggested that they probably died from exposure to the cold. They were dressed only in underwear and their feet were bare or in socks at temperatures of around -25 to -30°C (-13 to -22°F). However, it was also noted that the corpses displayed other injuries, including bruises, scratches, burnt hair, burnt fingers and damaged skulls.

On 4 May 1959, the last four bodies were finally discovered in a ravine under 4 m (13 ft) of snow, near a stream of running water. Nikolai Thibeaux-Brignolles, aged 23, had a fatal skull injury that had resulted in pieces of bone being driven into his brain. Semyon Zolotaryov, an instructor and the oldest member of the group at 38, was found with severe chest injuries, including multiple broken ribs. Alexander Kolevatov, aged 24, had been found with lack of soft tissues around the eyes. His eyebrows were missing and his skull was exposed. The bridge of his nose was straight; the nose cartilage was soft when palpated and had unusual mobility; the base of the nose was flattened with the nostrils compressed. There was also an open wound behind one ear, 3 x 1.5 cm in size, and his neck was deformed. Diffused bleeding was found in the underlying tissues of his left knee. His skin was softened and there was a whitened (maceration) of the fingers and feet consistent with putrefaction in a wet environment.

The second woman in the group, 20-year-old Lyudmila Dubinina, had also suffered major chest injuries, again with broken ribs, as well as a major haemorrhage in the right side of her heart. However, there were no signs of injuries on the outside of the hikers' chests; this suggests they had experienced extremely high-impact pressure, similar to the impact of a car crash or falling from a great height. Dubinina's autopsy report and photographs proved to be harrowing for investigators, with mentions of 'soft tissues missing around eyes, eyebrows and nose bridge, and the left cheek bone is partially exposed.'

A particularly disturbing detail was the fact that Dubinina's body was partially mutilated. Her tongue, eyes and part of her upper lip were missing, as well as the skin on her face and a fragment of skull bone. Zolotaryov, was mutilated in a similar way and his eyeballs were also missing, while Kolevatov's eyebrows were nowhere to be found. Teodora Hadjiyska and Igor Pavlov, who wrote the book *1079: The overwhelming force of Dyatlov Pass* in 2015, suggested that broken noses along with open wounds behind the ears and deformed necks might indicate that fights could have broken out either among the group or with unknown assailants and could be the cause of deaths. However, they also counter that possibility by suggesting that injuries might also have partly been caused by the natural environment since the bodies were exposed to the elements for a whole three whole months with weighted snow bearing down on top of them. They point out that autopsy report by the doctor ignored this matter and it doesn't try to explain the reason for these strange injuries. They also add that snapped necks and blows behind the ear are a common sign of killing performed by military special forces. However, they can't be sure about that point because the autopsy report didn't give any further details about the bodies.

The final group of bodies was found with the clothes of the two victims under the cedar tree camp. For example, Dubinina's left foot and shin were wrapped in a torn sweater that belonged to Krivonischenko. It appeared that the last four had attempted to survive the harsh cold by removing the clothes from their dead comrades at some point. According to authors Hadjiyska and Pavlov, the bodies of Doroshenko and Krivonischenko had frozen to death and their clothes were removed by their friends. Survival of the remaining group was only prolonged by taking the clothes of their dead comrades and it must have been a harrowing experience but a necessary one. Different bits of clothing were simply cut or taken from their dead friends and then used by surviving members of the group. The first two bodies appeared to be laid out respectfully side by side, one facing downwards and one facing upwards. Their possessions were divided and distributed among the survivors

The investigative timeline

One of the most perplexing elements of this story was the discovery of radiation on some of the clothes found on the final group. According to reports, the levels of radioactivity on the clothing may have been significantly higher earlier on but could then have been reduced by the stream running over the bodies. Whatever the truth of this, as soon as radiation was discovered on the victims' clothing, the investigation was shut down. The reason given was that homicide was not suspected but there could have been more to it than that.

The first part of the investigation began on 26 February 1959 with attorney, Ivdel Tempalov, opening proceedings, along with prosecutor,

Lev Ivanov, overseeing it. They decided that the group of hikers had come across an overwhelming natural force, which they had not been able to overcome. This was, to say the least, a rather strange and cryptic conclusion that did not really explain much at all. The inquest concluded in May 1959 as a result of the absence of a guilty party, with the files being sent off to a secret archive, according to the *St Petersburg Times* writer, Svetlana Osadchuk, and with the result that skiers and 'other adventurers were barred from the area for three years'.

In 1974, the case was transferred to the State Archive of the Sverdlovsk Region from the secret archive of the prosecutor's office. After the Iron Curtain came down in 1989, state secrets started to be leaked to Western journalists, including details of the Soviet Space Programme, information about the 1986 Ukrainian Chernobyl nuclear disaster and also stories, which were vaguely known through rumours circulated by students at the Ural Polytechnical Institute, such as the Dyatlov Pass incident. In 1997, it was revealed, perhaps by prosecutor Ivanov's daughter, that the negatives from Krivonishenko's camera were secretly kept in his private archive. Journalists had already visited him in the early 1990s, but they were not told about the negatives. The film material was donated by Ivanov's daughter to the Dyatlov Foundation, while the diaries of the hiking party fell into Russia's public domain in 2009. As the years passed, a further Dyatlov investigation was prompted by public and media pressure on the Russian authorities, with many believing something was being hidden.

The original 1959 Soviet authorities' explanation was not considered a plausible one, with many holes or gaps in their conclusions that led to the spread of conspiracy theories, some of which I cover here. Beginning in 2015, the Investigative Committee of the Russian Federation (ICRF) decided to re-open the investigation and concluded in 2019 that a snow avalanche was the most likely cause of the accident. The investigators narrowed this down from an official list of 75 theories, ranging from government conspiracy to supernatural events, to arrive at their final explanation, suggesting the incident was a slab avalanche of snow sliding out from the slope above the hikers' tent. This could have caused the hikers to flee from their tent, cutting a hole in the side to escape and the snow den dug out by the remaining four could have collapsed on them.

Murder on the mountain?

Given the opaque conclusion of the initial investigation, and the secrecy and the plethora of unusual information that surrounded the incident at what is now called Dyatlov Pass, it's hardly surprising that it generated a range of fascinating – albeit conflicting – theories about what actually happened to the unfortunate Russian hikers in 1959. Initially, there was speculation that the indigenous Mansi people, who subsisted through reindeer herding, were responsible for their deaths, but this was later ruled out after the authorities had conducted interviews with them. In fact, it was local Mansi people that helped search teams locate some of the bodies. They also reported intriguing details to team members; notably about seeing strange orange lights or fireballs in the sky in the same period of time as the students went missing. An animal attack was also an early suggestion, although this was deemed unlikely because no animal tracks were found near the hikers' tents.

Another early suspect was Yuri Yudin. If you recall, this was a tenth member of the group who turned back early in the trek across the Urals because of the pain he was enduring. As he was the last known person to see the hikers before they died, he became a person of interest to the local police investigating. They suspected he had perhaps killed all his fellow hikers in some strange outburst. However, when police took him to the locations of the bodies, it was Yudin who noticed that some of the corpses were wearing their fellow hikers' clothes. He had spotted that they had clothed themselves in their deceased comrades' clothes in an effort to keep warm. He was visibly upset at the sight of his dead friends and was ruled out of investigations after it was confirmed that he was with his family on 1 and 2 February, the estimated time of death of the hikers. He was eventually dropped as a major suspect.

Dangerous weather

The investigation into the incident that occurred in 2019 concluded that a sudden 'slab avalanche' caused the hikers to leave their tents in a panic, which led to their deaths from hypothermia. Andrei Kuryakov, the prosecutor who led the new investigation, proposed it was still possible for a slab of snow to slide out over a tent. He based his decision on research conducted by E. V. Baranov at the federal budgetary institution, the 'Ural Regional Center for Forensic Expertise of the Ministry of Justice of the Russian Federation'.

He suggested this might have caused a panic, which led the hikers to fear that a larger avalanche was on its way. This might explain why they cut their way out of the tent and ran away in a hurry without grabbing their boots. Escaping to what they thought was a safe distance from the tent, they then started a fire to try to keep warm and dug a snow den. Kuryakov explained that then the snow den could have collapsed on the hikers who were sheltering inside. The collapse might have caused the severe injuries found on the bodies. Later, scavenging animals could have eaten the missing eyes and tongues. Those outside the tent would've died from hyperthermia.

During the search for the dead hikers made by Vladislav Karelin in 2020, a close examination of the slope by the tent showed that even if there had been an avalanche, its path would have gone past the tent. The tent had collapsed from the side but not been flattened in a way that would be typically seen after an avalanche. It could also have collapsed because it was weakened when cut from the inside, then battered further by heavy snowfall and high winds. It's also likely that Dyatlov, a highly experienced skier and hiker, and the older Zolotaryov would have known not to erect a tent near a potential avalanche site.

The weather on the night of the tragedy was extremely severe, with wind speeds of between 72 and 108 kph (45–67 mph), a snowstorm and temperatures of -40°C (-40°F). It has also been suggested that a 'katabatic' wind could have injured or killed the hikers by causing a violent blast against their tent. This type of wind 'tumbles' downhill when gravity forces heavier, higher-density air down a slope towards lower-density air. In 2019, Richard Holmgren and Andreas Liljegren, both Swedish adventurers, visited the route taken by the Dyatlov skiers. During their night on the mountain, the adventurers encountered a strong katabatic wind that reduced the temperature of their camp to well below -30°C (-22°F). Their experience of these winds on that night is what helped Holmgren to form the foundation for his theory. Holmgren, investigating the incident, suggested that an instant katabatic wind would have forced the hikers to seek shelter behind the tree line, because it would make sleeping in a tent impossible. However, this does not explain the presence of radiation on the victims' clothing, or their injuries.

A different angle on weather-related causes was put forward in 2013 by American film producer, director and author, Donnie Eichar, in his book *Dead Mountain.* He pointed out that infrasound is an audible sound caused by the strong winds as it whistles over the tops of mountains; it can cause discomfort and mental distress to mountaineers and could have caused the Russian hikers to become disoriented.

Eichar has suggested this distress was so bad it caused them to panic, cut their way out of their tent and run down the slope. Eventually, they would have moved out of the infrasound's range and recovered their senses. But affected by the darkness, heavy weather and the after-effects of disorientation, they would have been unable to return to their tent. In his view, the mutilation injuries found on three of the bodies occurred later as a result of accidentally falling into the ravine and smashing against rocks at the bottom. This would not explain Dubinina's missing tongue or other victims' missing eyeballs.

If the bodies were in the river, covered in snow, it would have been more difficult for animals to locate them. Vets and farmers advise that dead animals like pets, or farm stock, should be buried at least three to four feet down to stop predators from digging them up. They also recommend additional wood to cover the corpse before soil is laid over it. The Dyatlov bodies found in the ravine were buried under approximately 13 feet (or 4 metres) of snow. If animals had dug down through 13 feet of snow, there would have been animal tracks and yet none were found.

Plus, it would have been easier for any animal to eat the bodies of those found by the cedar tree who were covered in a few feet of snow only. Yet their eyes, tongues were still present when discovered.

Weapons testing

Other non-natural explanations have been offered for the tragic death of the nine Russians, including the fact that they were unfortunate enough to set up camp during a Soviet parachute mine exercise. Parachute mines were bombs dropped by parachute and often detonated above ground level to maximize the blast's effects across a wider area. The most vocal proponent of the parachute mine theory was Yuri Yudin, the only surviving member at the time, who turned back when he became ill. Until he died in 2013, Yuri insisted his friends were accidentally killed by these powerful weapons that could cause major internal injuries like those found on the corpses.

It was confirmed that testing of these weapons was going on at the time. There are records of Soviet parachute mines being dropped in the area at that time, according to author Keith McCloskey (*Mountain of the Dead*, 2013). Also, as mentioned previously, the local Mansi people had described seeing glowing orange orbs or spheres in the region in the previous days, which could have been the mines falling from parachutes and being detonated in the air. In 1959, Sergey Sogrin was a young student helping in the search for the missing hikers. In the 1970s, he claimed he met in Pamir with a certain I. D. Bogachev, a 'master of sports in mountaineering'. He told Sogrin that, in the 1950s and 1960s, he was working in Moscow at a secret research institute. In the evening, when they were gathered around the campfire at Iskander-Kul lake, Sogrin told Bogachev about his connection to the Dyatlov group, to which Bogachey replied, 'In those years, we dropped the spent rocket launchers into the uninhabited regions of the Northern Urals, and Dyatlov was the victim.'

If true, it seems feasible that as the bombs were dropped, the noise of the explosions might well have terrified the hikers enough for them to flee without putting on their shoes and outer clothes first. After some froze to death while seeking protection underneath the trees, their clothes would have been removed by the surviving members of the group seeking to stay warm. The remaining hikers could have been injured by the exploding mines, causing the chest injuries and terrible wounds mentioned in reports, and eventually freezing to death. Parachute mines are said to produce injuries very similar to those found on the hikers, namely brutal internal damage with little or no external signs of injury.

In a tantalising additional clue, one of the photographs from cameras found in the camp that were later developed may have captured an image of military aircraft; unfortunately, the image is too dark to see this clearly. It was not the only photograph to raise questions about the hikers' fate.

Yeti attack

One of the last photographs taken by the Dyatlov group appeared to show a slightly blurred figure at a distance and looking at the photographer from behind a tree. In the dark, the figure had no clearly visible features but was human-like in shape. This sparked the incredible suggestion that a Yeti, nicknamed the 'Abominable Snowman', had attacked the hikers.

There have been numerous sightings reported across the Ural mountains of huge, ape-like hominid creatures covered in hair. If it exists, could a Yeti had come into contact with the hikers and attacked and killed them? The photo shows no one recognizable from the group of hikers. Maybe more sad than strange, a few weeks before embarking on their tragic hike, the young hikers joked about encountering a Yeti in their college newsletter. There was absolutely no evidence of large footprints in the deep snow, although arguably such prints could have been covered by later snowfalls. This would not be the only bizarre hypothesis for the shocking tragedy of nine deaths.

Otherworldly attack

After the 'Iron Curtain' lifted and the Soviet regime crumbled at the start of the 1990s, Russians began to speak more freely about the Dyatlov Pass incident. In 1990, Ivanov who led the original investigation, spoke to *Uralskiy Rabochy*, a Russian state-owned magazine, saying, 'We found that some young trees on the forest tree line have traces of burning, but they are not in concentric shape or any other system. There was no epicentre. This once again confirmed a source of heat ray or completely unknown to us energy acting selectively – the snow was not melted; the trees were not damaged. It seemed like when the hikers walked on their feet more than 500 metres down from the mountain, someone dealt with some of them as direct targets.' In his opinion, the hikers were killed by 'a heat ray or a force unknown' from an unidentified flying object (UFO). Ivanov claimed he was ordered not to talk about this to anyone by his superiors. He continued, 'I reported the initial data to the first secretary of the regional party committee, L. P. Kirilenko, and he gave a clear command – all the work should be classified and not a single word of information should be leaked. Kirilenko then ordered the hikers to be buried in closed coffins and the relatives were to be told that they died from hypothermia.'

Could the orange orbs reported in the area be UFOs or might the flares caught on the hikers' photographs actually be UFOs? During the initial investigation, a small article appeared in the *Soviet Tagil Worker* newspaper stating that, during the period when the hikers were on Mount Otorten where they had set up their tent, 'a fireball was seen in the sky over Nizhniy Tagil'. Apparently, this luminous object flew silently towards the northern peaks of the Ural Mountains. The author of the article was puzzled and asked, 'What could it be?' For publishing this information, the editor of the newspaper was penalized.

For his part, Ivanov said they knew little about unidentified flying objects at that time, adding, 'We did not know about radiation either.' A witness, G. Atamanaki, who was working in the region at the time, also saw objects, or fire balls as he called them. He said, 'I saw this ball over Otorten on the night of 1 February.' Ivanov duly reported his findings to Yeshtokin as ordered and the response was clear. '[He wanted] to classify everything, to seal everything up, to hand it over to the special unit and forget about it.'

What kind of special unit was it that Ivanov was ordered to hand over his findings to? While this sounds a little crazy at first, it's worth considering further discoveries by subsequent investigations. Keith McCloskey, who has researched the Dyatlov Pass incident for many years, travelled there in 2015 with Yuri Kuntsevich, president of the Dyatlov Group Memorial Foundation, an organization set up in 2000 to honour the memory of the lost hikers. They discovered that the location of the tent was too close to the spur of the ridge for any significant accumulation of snow to cause an avalanche. In addition, the continuous wind blowing over the area would also have cleared snow away from the edge of the ridge on the side where the tent was, so perhaps the idea of drifting parachute mines, or overflying fireballs may not be so far-fetched after all. Kuntsevich, though, is convinced that a Soviet secret missile launch of some kind went disastrously wrong, severely injuring some of the skiers and forcing the rest of the group to flee their tent, at which point they either froze to death or were later killed by military observers, which might explain some of the injuries found, like the bruising found on their bodies or teeth being knocked out.

In an interview with authors Teodora Hadjiyska and Igor Pavlov in 2015, Evgeny Okishev, deputy head of the Investigative Department of Sverdlovsk Oblast Prosecutor's Office, working under the authority of Ivanov on the investigation into the deaths, spoke out. He said he was about to visit the Dyatlov Pass in 1959 when Deputy Prosecutor General Urakov arrived from Moscow and ordered the case to be shut down.

Okishev also revealed that Klinov, head of the Sverdlovsk Prosecutor's Office, was present at the first post-mortems and spent three days there, which was highly unusual and the only time he had ever known it to happen. Why would law officers be acting in such a manner, if not to cover something up? Could there have been a UFO connection?

UFO researcher David Cayton has investigated numerous cases of animal mutilations in Britain linked to UFO sightings. Where a number of animals have been killed at once, he often found they were discovered laid out neatly side by side, ruling out wild predators. While acknowledging the absence of detailed autopsy reports, he noted that the Dyatlov Pass victims bore similar injuries to those seen in both mutilated animals and human bodies found in locations where UFO sightings had been reported. There have been cases in the US of cattle found with tongues and eyes removed, and injuries consistent with being dropped from a great height into heavily indented earth. The late Tony Todd, a British policeman, was one of the early researchers into the British mutilations, which allegedly happened in the 1970s and 1980s. Presumably because of his police connections, he was able to delve deeper and found cases of teenagers in Staffordshire who had reportedly died from these mutilations. These cases were never reported openly in the media and Todd said that the relatives of those

The grave of those who died in the Dyatlov Pass.

that had died were told they were missing. Similar cover-ups perhaps to the Dyatlov incident were at play.

In one online report from 2008, an anonymous source, claiming to be a former member of a NATO 'Black Ops' team, said it was his job to retrieve victims who were mutilated by aliens and dropped from UFOs to cover up such occurrences. He said he had worked around the world, including on Russian territory, and throughout his career had recovered around 30 mutilated human bodies allegedly dropped by UFOs. The bodies at Dyatlov Pass, however, were neither secretly retrieved nor cleared away. And no one has ever come up with an explanation for the radiation on their clothing. But remember, as this was in 1959, the investigators had not encountered this type of incident before. Perhaps in later years, the military developed covert practices to keep news of such events away from the public and out of the news. The thing is, could this incident really have come from an alien source? Surely the cause is more likely to have been human.

A known force?

In 2021, British documentary filmmaker, Liam Le Guillout, travelled to the Dyatlov Pass, including the spot where the hikers pitched their tent, for his film *An Unknown Compelling Force*. He spoke to a Russian criminologist named Natalia Sakharova, who suggested the cut marks on the hiker's tent, originally thought to be cut from the inside, were actually made from the outside. If this is correct, it places a different perspective on the case, suggesting that someone or something was trying to get into the tent. Sakharova also claimed the cuts and injuries sustained by the students were done to them by other people.

Also interviewed were retired FBI agent Mick Fennerty and Ken Holmes, formerly the coroner of Marin County in California. Based on the nature of the injuries, both men suggested that the deaths were the result of homicide. In their view, the head injuries found on some of the Russians were not the result of simply falling, but of the use of severe force. In addition, according to Le Guillou, the radiation traces found on some of the dead skiers' clothes were there because some members of the group had previously worked at nuclear plants, one of which suffered a disaster which was hushed up by Soviet authorities. As evidenced by other nuclear disasters, this is unlikely to be something that the Russian authorities would be keen to discuss publicly, even today.

Unfortunately, short of some new revelation that has so far been kept quiet, the incident at Dyatlov Pass is likely to remain an unsolved cold case for the foreseeable future. Meanwhile, the exposed spot on 'Dead Mountain' where eight young people and their instructor perished has become a popular place for hikers and amateur detectives from around the world to visit. Here, they can consider what happened for themselves.

CHAPTER 3

IMPOSSIBLE OCCURRENCES

There is a centuries-old theoretical principle called 'Occam's Razor', which, at its most basic, says the simplest explanation is also the most likely to be true. In this chapter, we consider experiences and accounts that are called impossible by many sceptics, even though these non-believers are not able to provide a simpler explanation that really explains them fully. While it can seem hard to believe that such events actually happen, some are backed up by official documents and eyewitness accounts from people who are absolutely certain of what they saw. Some are denied outright at the highest levels, but there are those who maintain these mysterious events occurred, pointing to small details that suggest the truth has been told. Other occurrences are very 'out there'. And once again, if we apply Occam's razor, does this automatically mean they didn't actually happen? Is a sole eyewitness, who appears perfectly rational and maintains the truth of what they experienced until their dying day, enough to convince? The simplest explanation might just be 'it's possible', but is it true? That is for each reader to decide.

THE OAKVILLE BLOBS

Before August 1994, the small 'timber town' of Oakville had one rather minor claim to fame as the home of the last-ever bank in Washington

State to have been robbed on horseback. That was all to change one rainy night. Due to its location in the USA's Pacific Northwest, the townsfolk were used to wet weather, with rain falling for 150 days per year on average. However, the torrent of weird gelatinous blobs that suddenly fell from the sky on to the unsuspecting community of around 700 people is an unexplained mystery, which came to be known as the 'Oakville Blobs'.

At 3am on 7 August 1994, police officer David Lacey was on patrol in his car when the downpour began. Believing it was merely heavy rain, he turned his windscreen wipers on, but instead of wiping the drops away the wiper blades smeared the 'rain' all over the windscreen, reducing his visibility. To be on the safe side, he decided to stop and pulled over into a local petrol station to wash the clear, petroleum jelly-like substance off the screen. He was cautious enough to put on latex gloves before doing so. In a later interview, Officer Lacey described the clear substance as 'very mushy', almost like jelly pudding. He realized that whatever was on the car, it was not normal and definitely not rain. But he had absolutely no idea what it could be.

As it got lighter, a local farmer, Dotty Hearn, and her daughter also noticed that small translucent blobs or globules, approximately half the size of a grain of rice, had appeared all around their farm, situated on the edge of Oakville. Hearn described the blobs as being everywhere – on the truck, the grass, the trees and bushes. From a distance, she initially thought they were hailstones, but when she touched one of the blobs, she, too, found it was actually a strange, gelatinous substance. As the day went on, many other residents of the town began to report the same kind of blobs appearing all around their homes and land.

Oakville citizens get sick

In the late afternoon of 7 August, officer Lacey began to feel unwell. He suddenly experienced extreme vomiting, found it very difficult to breathe and was rendered unable to do anything. It occurred to him that the blob-like substance could have been the cause of his sickness as he had never felt ill like this before. Later on the same day, Dotty

Hearn was found by her daughter on the ground, suffering from extreme dizziness, fatigue and nausea. She too had touched the blobs, but without gloves. Her vision was so blurred that she could not make out figures clearly, and she also began to vomit.

After examining her at the local hospital, the doctor initially diagnosed Hearn with Ménière's disease, an inner-ear condition that can cause sudden attacks of vertigo and nausea. During an attack, sufferers feel like everything around them is spinning, as if they are on a merry-go-round. However, Hearn also had a high fever and symptoms of infection. She was to spend four days in hospital, although doctors were still at a loss to explain what had caused her sickness. While Ménière's is a chronic (recurring) condition, Hearn's symptoms eventually cleared up and never returned. Meanwhile, other disconcerting events were occurring.

Hearn's daughter, Sunny Barclift, who worked as a lab technician, decided to collect some samples of the blobs. Barclift's kitten had died within three days of the blobs falling, and the family's dogs suddenly began suffering vomiting and diarrhoea. It was never proven, however, that this widespread illness was caused by the blobs themselves.

More local residents also began to fall ill over the next few days despite taking measures to protect themselves by handling the blobs with latex gloves. The symptoms varied across Oakville: some people suffered extreme nausea, while others had severe flu-type symptoms. For some, the symptoms lasted up to three months. In addition, after the blobs first came down, family pets and wildlife, including birds and frogs, were found dead near blob clumps, reportedly with green slime dripping from their mouths.

Even some larger farm animals, such as horses and cows, were not sturdy enough to withstand the mystery illness that struck them after the blobs fell on to farmland around Oakville. On 20 August 1994, the local *Oakville Observer Reporter* said that rumours of flying jelly fish were being spread around the town. One local resident later told a television documentary about the mystery that she knew of 12 animals that had died after the blobs appeared. The blobs caught the attention of newspapers and TV from around the country, including the *New York Times*, the National Geographic Channel and the television show, *Unsolved Mysteries*.

More strange 'rain'

The mysterious blobs did not rain down just once. After the initial fall on 7 August, there were five more downfalls during what remained of August 1994. After each downfall of gelatinous drops, more people fell ill, again reporting the same set of symptoms. Then, the weird 'rain' simply stopped falling from the skies, and blobs already on the ground either dissolved or evaporated in the warmer sunny spells, making it harder to pinpoint their location.

Strange stories began to circulate concerning strange things falling from the sky. The *Casper Star Tribune* published an interesting report from a weather service in the area, saying they had received a call from an unidentified man in early August describing hot, metallic particles from the sky that burned holes in his children's trampoline.

Suspecting the strange blobs could have caused their mother's illness, Barclift and her brother, an ambulance driver, gave the frozen blob sample she had collected to the doctor at the Providence St Peter Hospital in nearby Lacy who had treated their mother. Dr David Little agreed to send the sample to the hospital's research laboratory for further analysis. After examining the substance, a laboratory technician concluded that the blobs contained cells that looked similar to human white blood cells.

Analysing the blobs

About three weeks later, further testing by a scientist, Mike Osweiler, at the Hazardous-Material Spill Response Unit for Southwest Washington, part of the Department of Ecology, refuted these results after tests showed that there were no nuclei present. This was significant in that it disproved the previous lab's claim that the blobs contained human white blood cells, which have nuclei. Osweiler stated the blob samples were very uniform and added, 'There's a number of cells of various sizes,' and that no clear structure could be seen with a microscope. He also found that the blob sample contained two types of bacteria, both of which are found in the human digestive tract. The first, *Pseduomomas fluorescens*, causes infections in people with compromised immune systems, with symptoms including high fever, chills, nausea, vomiting, confused thinking and a racing heartbeat. Strains of the second bacteria, *Enterobacter cloacae*, are associated with infections of the urinary tract, chest and respiratory system, bones, heart lining and other soft tissue.

Another scientist came to a different conclusion. Later in August, Mike McDowell, microbiologist at the Department of Health, told the local *Observer-Reporter* newspaper that the blobs contained 'a number of cells of various sizes'. More importantly, he was certain that the cells originated from something that had once been alive but was not human. He concluded the blobs contained two types of bacteria but was unable to match them up with known strains. McDowell also confirmed that the blobs did not contain human white blood cells because those cells have nuclei, which contain the organism's genetic material, while the blob cells he examined were missing their nuclei.

Oddly, the samples in McDowell's care were later found to have gone missing. McDowell arrived back at the lab the next day to find the samples had mysteriously disappeared. He went to his manager to ask if they had any idea what happened to the sample blobs and his manager allegedly replied, 'Do not ask!'

Some suspect that the toxic samples were deliberately 'lost'. Maybe the blobs' appearance might point to some environmental accident that had taken place elsewhere and, as such, needed to disappear to deter investigators. The samples maybe provided clear evidence of some kind of biological hazard and so were deliberately 'lost' to obstruct further investigations. This of course raises the question, what kind of environmental accident happens six times over the course of three weeks? Alternatively, this could simply be an unfortunate case of poor processing and care of the samples, with someone mistakenly putting them into the wrong storage container or mislabelling them.

Given the similarity between the symptoms mentioned by government scientists and the experiences of townsfolk in Oakville, Sunny Barclift wondered whether the blobs could have been human waste dropped from airliners passing overhead. Two weeks after the first appearance of the strange blobs, Sunny managed to put this theory to Dick Meyer, spokesman for the Federal Aviation Administration in Seattle, who told *The Lewistone Tribune*, 'We don't know what it is or where it came from, it's a puzzle.' The Federal Aviation Administration explained that human waste is typically dyed blue as it goes through aircraft waste disposal systems, so that waste leaks from aircraft can be tracked and traced. The Oakville blobs were clear, not blue.

Live rain

In 1995, the year after the blobs fell over Oakville, Barclift gave more frozen samples of the blobs to a private research laboratory, Amtest Laboratories, for further analysis. The microbiologist who examined them, Tim Davis, said he thought he identified a eukaryotic cell within the sample. A eukaryote has a clearly defined nucleus and is a type of cell that is found in most mammals. In effect, this would mean the blobs were living organisms of some kind.

The scientists' conflicting findings led to a spate of different theories about the origin of the mysterious blobs. The FAA investigator decided to ask the military if there had been any flights over Oakville and surrounding areas that might explain the blobs. 'This is where the jellyfish theory came in,' Meyer said.

One hypothesis, which rests on the presence of eukaryotic cells in the blobs, is that while the US military was conducting bombing raids at sea, it accidentally blew up jellyfish, dispersing fragments that travelled around 80 km (50 miles) from the coast, falling over the inland town of Oakville.

It was reported at the time that the 354th Fighter Squadron of the US Air Force was dropping live bombs over the Pacific Ocean off the coast of Washington State around the same time the blobs fell over Oakville. How likely was it, though, that the same accident would have happened six times in a row, with particles falling over the same small town? And if the jellyfish were bombed only once, could the particles have stayed in the air long enough to come down over a period of weeks?

'They were conducting bombing runs using live ordnance,' said Master Sergeant Thaddeus Hosley. Hosley, a spokesman at McChord Air Force Base. He said that 354th Fighter Squadron flew over two consecutive weeks, dropping bombs about 16 to 32 km (10 to 20 miles) west of Ocean Shores, which is about 80 km (50 miles) to the west of Oakville. At the time, Hosley was reported as trying but failing to stifle a laugh, but then said he could not comment on the jellyfish theory. Barclift herself found the jellyfish theory '*somewhat preposterous*'.

Star jelly

Another theory put forward to explain the Oakville blobs is that they are 'star jelly', a substance often found in trees and on grass as if it had fallen there from above. The term was first recorded in the 17th century and is thought to come from the belief that this clear, gooey substance fell from the sky when meteors, or shooting stars, appeared. Back then, the droplets were called *stella terrae* and the substance they were made of was believed to have medicinal, possibly heaven-sent or holy, properties. While there is disagreement about what star jelly actually is, the Natural History Museum analysed some samples and found they were frog spawn (eggs), probably expelled by frog-eating birds. This would make it hard to explain how the Oakville blobs fell in torrents, like heavy rainfall, and had to be wiped off windscreens.

Industrial or military origin

How many toxic chemicals fall from the skies besides those suspected at Oakville? Over the years, there have been reports from around the world of industrial chemicals dropping out of the sky. For instance, in April 2024 the European Environmental Agency published a report indicating heavy metals, including mercury, cadmium, lead and nickel, that have been released into the atmosphere in recent years; although their recorded levels in the environment have dropped over the last 15 years, they are still considered a hazard to human health. From 2012 to 2021, the total health costs related to industrial emissions of heavy metals were estimated to be around 120 billion euros (£100 billion/$130 billion).

Another strange material fell to the ground in 2012, this time in the English seaside town of Bournemouth in Dorset. According to local resident, Steve Hornsby, an aircraft engineer, the sky above his house turned dark, then took on a yellowish tone. This was not the Aurora Borealis, or Northern Lights, which have been spotted as far south as Dorset. After the sky turned dark-yellow, there was a strong blustery wind and afterwards Hornsby found small gel-like blue balls in his garden. He kept some samples of these crystals and later these were analysed by the School of Applied Sciences at Bournemouth University.

Rather than a life form, as some believe the Oakville blobs to be, these strange balls were found to be a chemical called sodium polyacrylate, often used in gardening products or agriculture to improve soil texture as well as in disposable nappies. How, though, did the crystals end up in his garden? Perhaps they were already present, from previous use of garden fertilizers or because they were thrown over the garden fence by a passing fly-tipper or carried and deposited there during windy weather. Heavy rain could then have turned invisible dry crystals into the gel-like blue balls that Hornsby later found. Given Bournemouth's seaside location, another culprit could be seagulls, which are known to raid household rubbish bags on the street. A discarded nappy could have been pecked at by gulls, which then distributed tiny pieces of the material into gardens as they flew over.

Oakville is approximately 80 km (50 miles) inland from the Pacific Ocean however, so any seagulls carrying waste would have a long flight to drop it over Oakville residents. While the blobs for examination were still in the care of research technician, Mike Osweiler, he thought they appeared to be man-made in origin. Further support for this line of thought was provided by Dotty Hearn, who said she had noticed the US Air Force was conducting flights overhead in the weeks and days prior to the blobs suddenly appearing. Helicopters and slow-flying bombers, all black in colour, were seen at low altitude near Oakville. She postulated that the mystery blobs might originate from these aircraft. Holidaymakers on the coast also spotted military flights out at sea.

It may seem outlandish to suggest that the US government would sanction chemical or biological experiments on its own citizens. However, between 1949 and 1969, the US military did conduct multiple biowarfare test-run operations that dropped supposedly harmless agents on the unsuspecting populations of New York, Minneapolis and San Francisco. For example, in September 1950, 'Operation Seaspray' saw US Navy ships secretly spray a bright-red agent called *Serratia marcescens* over the San Francisco Bay Area, simulating a chemical attack to assess how a real-life germ warfare might impact the city and its population. It was designed, so nearly all 800,000 inhabitants would inhale at least 5,000 particles, thought to be sufficient for infection with an Anthrax virus. To track its spread, samples were taken at 43 locations around the city of San Francisco. While *Serratia marcescens* was thought to be harmless to humans, by October numerous locals were in hospital suffering from serious pneumonia and urinary tract infections. The US military denied any connection between its actions and the resulting illnesses to the US Senate Subcommittee on Health and Scientific Research hearings on these operations in 1977, claiming that the health conditions arising after Seaspray were coincidental.

So far at least, there has been no serious suggestion, and certainly no official confirmation, of any military origin for the Oakville blobs. As mentioned earlier, practice bombing raids were reported at sea. The *Palm Beach Post* on 21 August 1994 said that a couple, Jim and Kathy Belanger, reported seeing dead crabs every few feet along the Washington State coastline on a camping trip around the time the Oakville blobs first appeared. They also saw a clear, globular substance nearby. At first, the couple thought the gooey substance might be dead jellyfish. Kathy and her dog touched the substance on the beach, and both became very ill the next day. They also reported hearing loud

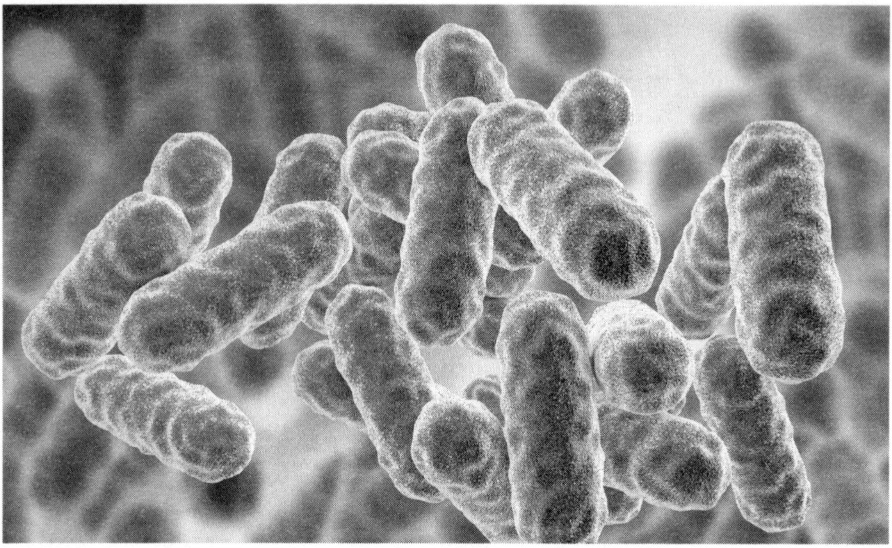

In Operation Sea-Spray, the US Navy sprayed *Serratia marcescens* across San Francisco Bay to simulate a chemical attack.

explosions out at sea. Jim and Kathy were unaware of the connection to the Oakville blobs until they read about them sometime later, which makes their evidence compelling.

The cause of the mysterious blobs at Oakville remains unknown. Could these have been some completely freak event, a random one-off occurrence where substances rained down on one town over a month? Or was it the result of some kind of military operation or even a wargame that somehow went awry, with the authorities remaining tight-lipped? Although we still cannot know for certain what the blobs were actually made of, the evidence seems to point to something organized. Unless an amateur detective makes a breakthrough, or a whistleblower comes forward with new evidence, this mystery is likely to fade from memory, just as the last remnants of the Oakville blobs faded away or, as some suspect, were deliberately destroyed.

THE ALDEBURGH PLATFORM

The late-1940s saw an explosion of media and public interest in what were initially called 'flying saucers', particularly after American pilot Kenneth Arnold reported seeing nine unusual, saucer-like craft speeding past Mount Rainier in Washington State in June 1947. In his book, *Flying Saucers Are Real*, published in 1950, Major Donald Keyhoe would first bring the term 'unidentified flying object' (UFO) to wide public attention. Major Keyhoe believed that UFOs had been spotted for around 200 years. Early in the 20th century, in the small, quiet seaside coastal town of Aldeburgh, in the English county of Suffolk, a possible UFO sighting occurred that did not generate any national newspaper headlines. In fact, it did not make any newspapers at all until the late-1960s, when the case was reported by the witness's son who recounted her story in a letter to the *Daily Mirror*, in an attempt to encourage other possible witnesses to come forward.

On a sunny day in the summer of 1916, or 1917 – the actual year is unclear because this strange tale was only recounted to family members – a woman named Agnes Whiteland was cleaning her house on Leighton Road. While she was upstairs making the beds, she looked out of the window to see if anyone she knew was walking down the road. Most residents in this quiet town worked in agriculture, fishing in nearby Aldeburgh-on-Sea or for the railway. Agnes Whiteland was hoping to see a familiar face who would be able to stop for a chat. She didn't see anyone, but a few minutes later something prompted her to look again. 'It was one of those things… you look again, hoping just to see someone or something moving,' she said in her letter to UFO researcher, Carl Grove. That second glance changed her forever.

Taking a second look, she was shocked to see a large object fly up over the narrow road leading from the marshes towards her house. Seen from a distance of about 90 m (295 ft) away, it floated slowly towards her house just over the rooftops at a height of around 9 m (30ft). Agnes said later that, upon seeing it, she got 'a bit on the worrying side in case they might fire against the houses'. She described the flying object as a flat, round platform, similar to the base of a children's roundabout. It had two sets of what looked like brass handrails, one set higher than the other, the kind you might see on the deck of a ship. Even more unusually, on board the airborne platform stood a group of men who were holding on tightly to the top handrail as it flew slowly and silently past Mrs Whiteland's bedroom window and over the roofs. (The lower handrail was level with the men's knees.)

Whiteland later described the platform as being much larger than a table big enough to seat six people. It looked to her as if the men on board were in control of the peculiar flying vessel, but she was at a loss to explain how because she could see no visible engine or machinery that they were operating to power or steer the silent craft. The passengers all looked like male humans and Whiteland thought they might be something to do with the British Royal Navy because of their blue uniforms. She described their head attire as 'little round hats, not unlike sailors' hats'. Later, in an account of the case written for her son, she said that the men 'were ordinary men just like us'. This wording could imply that someone had at least suggested to her that these were alien beings. At the time, she was not able to reliably say how many men were on board the flying platform but later estimated that there were between eight and 12 uniformed passengers on board.

An unusually agile craft

To Agnes Whiteland, it seemed that the men on board were not aware she could see them, nor did they appear to be surreptitiously manoeuvring their craft, even though they would have been spotted by many more witnesses if it had been a busier time of day. Perhaps they had chosen this time to fly their machine precisely because it was a quiet time. She watched the flying platform slowly move down the road past her house and towards the Railway Inn public house and a two-storey shed building around 7 m (23 ft) tall directly opposite. The platform abruptly turned right over a junction, still at rooftop height, and just managed to fly over the shed roof. It continued past this building and flew out towards the sea. It was a clear, sunny afternoon with good visibility and the encounter lasted approximately four minutes.

The sharp 90-degree turn executed by the platform is an interesting feature of Agnes Whiteland's story because such a manoeuvre has often been reported in connection with UFOs; people who have seen

UFOs have frequently said they performed the same move but at much higher speeds. Another detail is that she did not observe the passengers rocking to one side as a result of the sharp right-hand turn. The object, or 'platform' as she kept referring to it, was only travelling at the speed of someone running or a slow-moving car. This would have given whoever, or whatever, was on board ample time to view the scene below as they flew over. As it hovered out towards the sea, Whiteland lost sight of the object. She never told anyone except her son about the sighting and did not report it officially to any authorities.

Enemy airship

After Agnes Whiteland's son, Alfred, wrote to the *Daily Mirror* newspaper in 1968 – by which time Agnes was 84 – many people came forward with potential explanations. The most frequent was that his mother had seen an observation carriage lowered from a propeller-driven Zeppelin airship. Her strange sighting occurred while the First World War was raging in Europe. During the conflict, Zeppelins were launched from Germany and their crews would throw bombs from the cockpit area beneath the balloon. The ships also had a small observation carriage about the size of a small car, which could be lowered from the main airship via a cable. In thick fog, this would allow the pilot to lower another man clear of the fog to act as an extra set of eyes and navigation aid.

There are reasons to discount the airship theory. According to the renowned aviation historian and author, Charles Gibbs-Smith of the Victorian and Albert Museum, the Zeppelin's observation platform was so tiny it could only take one man and it would not have been lowered so close to the ground because the observer could then be shot by ground-based snipers. UFO researcher, Carl Groves, who saw Alfred's letter published in the *Daily Mirror*, wrote to Mr Whiteland in 1968 to find out more information, asking a list of questions and requesting sketches of the object she had witnessed. Some of his questions were very well thought out:

Could the strange platform Mrs Whiteland saw have been a Zeppelin?

Would you please provide a drawing/drawings of one of the men?
Would you please provide a rough sketch map of the area, indicating your mother's position and the object's flight path, etc. (+ scale.)?
Did the men appear quite normal in facial appearance? And in size?
How fast was the object moving, as compared with a car or a man?
How high was the object above the ground? Were the men doing anything? What were they looking at?

Despite Grove receiving answers from Mrs Whiteland and sketches of the platform, he was never able to come up with a plausible explanation.

Another hypothesis put forward by researcher John Harney was that Mrs Whiteland saw an actual Zeppelin crash that occurred nearby at Holly Tree Farm, Theberton around 10 km (6 miles) north of Aldeburgh, on the night of 17 June 1917. Sixteen of the airship's crew burned to death and were buried in the local churchyard. It was speculated that Whiteland had seen this and somehow screened the horrific details from her mind, instead constructing a more palatable image of the German aircrew floating in a controlled way on their round platform. However, the crash location was too far away to witness the details from her bedroom window. She may have seen Zeppelins before in person or at least known what they looked like from newspaper reports, so she would probably have been able to tell a Zeppelin from a round floating platform with handrails. 'Is it possible that her apparent observation of the flying platform was what some psychologists call a screen memory?' said Harney. Screen memories, continued Harney, are 'a protection, a defence against the recollection of other memories that they hide. It's easy to see why Mrs Whiteland might have wanted to hide whatever memory she had of the fate of Zeppelin L48. In view of the facts that the object reported by Mrs Whiteland obviously had only a conceptual connection with airships and that no one else reported seeing the object, or anything resembling it, some kind of psychological explanation seems to be indicated.'

However, when asked by Grove by letter if there were lights on the platform, Agnes replied, 'What, in daylight at 12 o'clock?' In his letter to *Flying Saucer Review*, Grove pointed this out. 'I think this testifies to the fact that to Mrs Whiteland the object was real and solid, and did not have the quality of a dream or hallucination.' Zeppelins would be significantly larger than the craft Agnes said she saw, plus they would have lights. Would a screen memory created in her mind mimic those attributes, if screen memories do work in the way suggested?

Grove summed up his thoughts on Mrs Whiteland's sighting as: 'Duration, about 3-4 minutes. Speed of object, 5-10 mph. Since the road is about 45 feet wide, at its nearest point the object must have been no more than 25 feet from the witness. The turn came suddenly, and the radius of the turning circle must have been in the order of 10 ft. Witness did not see men's boots until it had passed close over the roof of the building beyond the 30 ft gap through which it had passed.'

It was clear following Grove's line of inquiry that it could not have been anything like a Zeppelin simply because the platform had too many men on board.

'Apart from purely physical reasons' he said, 'why should the Germans, or anyone for that matter, drop an observation device within 30 ft of ground level on a clear, sunny day, and place in it 12 men when 4 could have done the job?' Zeppelin excuses might have served those questioning a sighting of something strange in the First World War, but when something similar showed up many years later, a very surprising reason was giving to explain the object.

A second platform

The strange airborne platform might have remained simply a part of the Whiteland family's oral history, had a certain clergyman not taken an unforgettable train journey some 40 years later. On the afternoon of 18 October 1955, Reverend Rupert Pitt-Kethly was travelling on the Uxbridge train line in northwest London towards East Harrow. As the train waited at West Hampstead viaduct, he saw what he would later describe as a reddish-brown-and-grey flying platform, which was the size of a small bus. Aside from the 'platform' description, there were other parallels to the Aldeburgh sighting. The craft was silent and stayed in sight for three or four minutes. It was described as travelling around 37 m (120 ft) off the ground and, in this case, at about 32 km (20 miles) per hour. There were also passengers all in similar dress; Reverend Pitt-Kethly counted 20 men dressed in khaki uniforms and helmets standing on the 'platform'.

One contention was that the reverend had actually seen the reflection of a double-decker bus. However, he firmly replied that he 'did not doubt the evidence of his own optics'. London buses have always been red in colour and the platform reported by Pitt Kethly was reddish-brown and grey, with men all stood around the platform. It was a clear day with only minimal haze, and definitely no rain, according to historical weather reports. Another point is that some reports said that Pitt-Kethly was travelling on the train to East Harrow and some people have pointed out that there is no such station. However, it might be feasible that they could have been referring to Harrow on the Hill station, which is east of Uxbridge. Heading out of Uxbridge, a passenger would be heading eastwards to Harrow. It's not known whether Reverend Pitt-Kethly and Mrs Whiteland ever knew of each other's sighting, but it would have been a useful exercise to compare both witness's accounts to see if there are other similarities.

A water connection?

Another interesting feature linking these cases is that both craft were observed near water. The Aldeburgh craft was first sighted coming off nearby watery marshland before eventually turning right and heading out to sea. Reverend Pitt-Kethly's sighting occurred by the viaduct. Could the presence of water be a connecting factor? In several instances, UFOs have been spotted either near water, including coming out of lakes or diving down into them, or appearing to suck up water.

In certain cases where people claim to have been abducted by extraterrestrials, they have spoken about beings known as 'The Greys': small, grey humanoids that have indicated their base of operation is in the sea or under large lakes. While the passengers on both flying platforms looked human, their purpose was not clear. Arguably, the platform construction could suggest such a craft would not fly high in the atmosphere as it would lack a pressurized hull. At altitudes above 10,000 ft (3,048 m), aircraft need to protect passengers and crew from the effects of low air pressure. Agnes Whiteland's recollection of seeing no visible steering equipment could indicate that they were short-range craft only. Rather than diving into the water, perhaps another structure emerging from the water would act as a larger landing area for these flying platforms, which could also have a submarine-like ability to go beneath the waves.

A future military force?

Is it possible that the travellers on these curious flying platforms could actually have been humans? In both accounts, the witnesses thought they were men in similar dress resembling some kind of military attire, although the Aldeburgh passengers wore blue uniforms, whereas the Reverend identified khaki-coloured uniforms with helmets.

One fascinating suggestion presented by certain researchers is that such craft are piloted by humans – except that these are visitors from the future on a military operation that demands they travel back into the past. This is not a new idea, but one that has been debated by researchers and UFO experts for quite a while, given that the main argument against travel from other star systems would take hundreds of years, depending on how fast you are travelling and where in our galaxy you might be travelling from. Scientists currently suggest that the speed of light cannot be exceeded. But perhaps the physics of aliens could be assumed to be far in advance of our own understanding. However, a lot of debate in recent years has thrown the alternative suggestion of time travellers into the mix. One such book, *Identified Flying Objects: A Multidisciplinary Scientific Approach to the UFO Phenomenon,* published in 2019 by Michael Masters, a professor of biological anthropology at Montana Technological University in Butte, suggests that future humans could develop the knowledge and technology required to return to the past.

Describing the beings on these craft as 'extratempestrials' rather than extraterrestrials, Masters points out that typical close-encounter accounts describe UFO occupants as 'bipedal, sometimes hairless, human-like beings with large brains, large eyes, small noses and small mouths. They also have the ability to communicate with us in our own languages and possess technology advanced beyond today's technological prowess.'

A more human-like encounter with something or someone aboard a flying saucer occurred around 5.45pm on 21 October 1954. It was a clear day and it had just started to get dark when Mrs Jesse Roestenburg and her two sons, eight-year-old Anthony and six-year-old Ronald, witnessed a UFO hovering just above their cottage at Vicarage Farm, Ranton, Staffordshire. The flying saucer was initially sighted by her children, who were outside the house. Mrs Roesterburg heard a whooshing noise and, initially thinking a plane had crashed, she went out to investigate. She saw her two young sons lying flat on the ground, 'lying prostrate and terrified' – half-expecting the thing above them to crash, hence lying down on the ground as one might do in an air raid. The boys were shouting out to their mother to look up at the 'flying saucer' just above them. At first, she disbelieved them but looked up and saw a 'Mexican hat'-style silver disc tilted at an angle. It was 'about 15 to 20 feet in diameter', hovering just above the roof tops of the family home. On board the vessel, they could see two occupants, both human-like in appearance.

Roestenburg described seeing two beautiful-looking humans with long golden hair with 'page boy'-style haircuts, looking down at her through the clear top-dome section of the saucer. They were wearing ski-style, one-piece suits, blue in colour. Their foreheads were slightly larger than average humans she noted, but the rest of the face she described as 'normal'. They were also wearing something like a helmet, a transparent fish-bowl-type contraption, similar to headwear worn by astronauts.

Gripped by fear, she said she noticed they had a look on their faces of complete empathy. They did not seem intent on causing any harm, but were merely looking down at her, like the men on the Aldebrough platform did as they flew over the street. She looked down very briefly to check on her two sons and when she looked up again, the craft was, she said, 'gone', vanished in seconds. However, her two sons pointed upwards to the silver disc, which flew three times around the house and then shot away from the site 'faster than any jet plane'.

If this account is true, could these beings possibly be from our future? They, too, wore something like a uniform, blue again in colour. Their dress sense could be described as almost military or service-like, perhaps from a future army or air force… or even a space force? This could explain why the attire of the Aldebrough platform 'crew' made Agnes Whiteland think of Royal Navy uniforms. Mrs Roestenberg did at first wonder if this craft was a secret Russian craft sent during the Cold War years to spy or possibly invade Britain. But there are no

Russian flying saucers that we know of. There is also no evidence that the German or British armed forces had flying platforms back in 1916.

Alternatively, if the beings on these platforms were alien, what was their purpose? There is no shortage of UFO sightings during wartime. Human conflicts, including the First World War, could be a subject worthy of study, although in 1955 Britain was not at war on the home front. Craft have been sighted over military bases, atomic or nuclear research establishments and power stations; some have landed in school playing fields and those on board have interacted with children.

When questioned by 'abductees', those who have been taken on board these craft, the beings themselves turn out to be a little cagey about where they come from, and don't give definite answers. If they are from our own future, it may be that by telling us now about things happening in our distant future, it could actually change our destiny. We might then go and do something to try and avoid that particular pathway, which could affect the visitors or time travellers, if they are such, themselves. By saying little to us, it might do the least harm. Could the occupants of the London 'platform' have been the same crew from the Aldeburgh platform 40 years earlier? Perhaps not, as they were in different-coloured dress and there were around 20 people on board the London 'platform'. However, both 'platforms' appeared to be similar in design, suggesting they might have come from the same place.

Steering questions

Given the platforms, as described, were both at a low altitude, there was presumably some wind effect upon the passengers. The men were not tethered to the craft in either case, but merely held on to the handrails, which seems a rather strange way of staying on board a flying platform, certainly for longer journeys. Maybe the passengers were controlling the direction of the craft by leaning and using their weight, as was the case with prototype flying platforms developed here in the 1950s. The Aldeburgh platform turned suddenly at a 90-degree angle; on a 'normal' craft, as all the passengers shifted their weight to the right, it would have been seen to dip as the change in balance happened.

But Agnes Whiteland did not say anything about how they steered the craft: indeed, all the men just seemed to be calmly observing the landscape while holding the handrails.

Human-made flying platforms

Were the craft sighted by Whiteland and Reverend Pitt-Kethly some kind of secret prototype aerial machine? Was there anything in official development that could explain them? In the early 1950s, Charles H. Zimmerman, an engineer specializing in unconventional aircraft at NACA, the main precursor of the National Aeronautics & Space Administration (NASA), conceived an individual flying platform. The platform was flat with the rotor blades of a helicopter placed underneath and the pilot would steer it just by shifting or pitching his weight, which Zimmerman called 'kinesthetic control'. The aim was to develop craft that could be flown with very little training. After testing the concept, flying platform prototypes from three aeronautics companies – de Lackner, Bensen and Hiller – reached speeds up to 22 km per hour (12 knots) and altitudes of up to 3.6 m (12 ft), enough for them to be put forward as contenders for further development.

The US Office of Naval Research then contracted the Hiller design for a one-man flying platform, which made its first flight in February 1955, and was named the VZ-1 Pawnee. The Pawnee's pair of contra-rotating rotors were powered by a 30 kilowatt, two-stroke engine. The single pilot stood above the duct covering the rotors, surrounded by a circular handrail and secured to the machine by a safety harness. He controlled the speed with a twist-grip throttle similar to that on a motorcycle and by leaning to steer the platform left or right. The Pawnee performed very well in initial test flights and was later modified with longer landing-gear legs to increase the height from the ground on landing and eight vanes (similar to wings) underneath the duct to improve overall flight control.

While there are minor similarities with the strange flying platform described in Aldeburgh, the two flying machines cannot be the same. The Aldeburgh platform flew silently according to Agnes Whiteland,

The VZ-1 Pawnee, a flying platform first used in 1955.

and there were at least eight men aboard. If what she saw was real, it appeared to be far more advanced technology, with no spinning blades, air currents or dust kicked up.

In the decades since the two sightings, no one has come forward to say they served as a pilot or crew member; no blueprints have surfaced. Unfortunately, nor have any further encounters with these strange self-flying platforms been reported. To all intents and purposes, both these strange airborne craft have vanished as mysteriously as when they first appeared.

BIGFOOT

In the early-19th century, explorers' reports of a strange new kind of large bear spotted in remote Chinese mountains were dismissed by European zoologists because the creatures described were black-and-white bamboo-eaters, not brown or black carnivores. It took decades, and the production of a live cub, for western science to accept the existence of the solitary Giant Panda. Today, many 'Bigfoot' enthusiasts and hunters point to a history of similarly derisive attitudes about the existence of a huge, hairy, ape-like, possibly hybrid human that walks upright and is rumoured to live a reclusive existence in the deep forests of northwestern America and Canada. Just because we haven't seen Bigfoot in a zoo, does that mean it isn't a living creature?

The name 'Bigfoot' went mainstream in 1958, when journalist Andrew Genzoli of the *Humboldt Times*, covering the county of the same name in northern California, highlighted an amusing but, he suspected, made-up story in a letter from a reader called Jerry Crew. Crew was part of a bulldozing crew who cleared logging trails with his road-building team in Bluff Creek in the Six Rivers National Forest. One day, they found footprints that seemed almost human but were massive, measuring 16 inches (40 cm) long and 7 inches (18 cm) wide, with stubby toes. The depth of the print was about 2 inches (5 cm), whereas Crew measured his own tread to go down to about one inch only (2.5 cm). In his column of 21 September, printed alongside the letter, Genzoli joked to his readers that perhaps a cousin of the 'Abominable Snowman' of the Himalayas was lurking deep in the Californian forest.

However, the account fascinated readers so much that Genzoli and fellow journalist, Betty Allen, published further in-depth articles about the footprints. They reported the nickname the loggers had given to the creature which might, or might not, have left the large tracks – it was 'Bigfoot'. Crew said to Genzoli, 'I don't know what this thing is; nobody does. It can't be a bear as there are no claw marks.'

Crew said he had seen a lot of these footprints, but never actually seen what caused them. Two years previously in 1956, something visited Crew's logging camp one night in Klamath River Forests and threw 50-gallon oil drums about like firewood. A former employee who worked with Crew, logger John Auman suggested that maybe the origins of the tracks was no big deal. 'If your rig was parked overnight, you might as well figure it would have no tires in the morning,' said Auman, suggesting that his prankster boss Ray L. Wallace was Bigfoot and he was the one who planted the tracks around equipment to scare off worksite thieves. 'That's why this all started.'

This story of a so-called Bigfoot was far from the first suggestion that powerful humanoid beasts stalk our world. Such huge, hairy hybrids appear in the folklore of various Native American and indigenous Canadian peoples, stealing food or other belongings. It's thought that another name for Bigfoot, 'Sasquatch', may derive from *sas'quets* ('wild man'), from the Salish languages of indigenous peoples in British Columbia. Other cultures also feature their own share of legends of large, hairy, ape-like men, which is how they are typically described, including Australia's Yowie, Russia's Almasty and the Yeren from China, to name a few. But the best-known of course, is Bigfoot, or Sasquatch as it is commonly called by the Native Americans of Canada. Bigfoot is said to live in the large, deep forests of the American Pacific North-West, Alaska and Canada.

The many sightings of these strange part-ape and part-human creatures commonly describe them as very tall, with broad shoulders, long arms, no visible neck and covered in black or brown hair. In some countries, they are described with reddish hair, particularly in the Far East. Often, those who claim to have seen them have claimed the creature's eyes glow yellow or red at night. Their reported heights are often up to 3 m (10 ft), although some are smaller.

The abominable snowman

The Snowman, or Yeti in Tibet, was first brought to European attention by Lieutenant-Colonel Charles Howard-Bury, who in 1921 led the British Mount Everest Reconnaissance Expedition to find a route up the world's highest mountain. In his book about the journey, Lt. Col.

Howard-Bury wrote an account of crossing Lhagpa La ('Windy Gap'), a mountain pass at an altitude of 6,400 m (21,000 ft) about 7 km (4.3 miles) northeast of Everest. There, he discovered footprints that he believed were likely to have been made by a huge 'loping' grey wolf, which in the high snow formed twin tracks similar to those of a barefoot man.

Howard-Bury's Sherpa guides told him the tracks were actually made by *Metoh-Kangmi*, or 'The Wild Man of the Snows': *Metoh* was translated as 'man-bear' and *Kang-Mi* as 'snowman'. They also told him that these wild men of the mountains had been spotted crossing snowy peaks by mountaineers, usually in search of food in the lower valleys. When Sherpas were later interviewed by reporter, Henry Newman, for *The Statesman* newspaper in Calcutta, India, he mistranslated *Metoh* as 'filthy', and so substituted 'abominable', so the Abominable Snowman became synonymous with the legend of the large hairy wild man of the Himalayas. Could the tracks found in the high-up Himalayas be faked though?

'Big people living in the mountains'

The developing legend of a Bigfoot creature in the Pacific Northwest region of North America was augmented by new accounts. After Bigfoot became a media sensation in the late-1950s, one man, who had kept his story to himself for more than 30 years, decided to speak up, initially to friends and relatives, and then later on his story first appeared in print in a newspaper called *The Agassiz-Harrison Advance*. The man was cross-examined by the police and signed a solemn declaration that affirmed the story was true under oath and also by virtue of the Canadian Evidence Act. The story appeared in *The Province* newspaper in British Columbia in 1957. Two years later in 1959, the man related his strange encounter to Queen Elizabeth II when she visited his province. Swedish-born Albert Ostman was a contractor and logger in the 1920s when, in 1924, he decided to try his hand at gold prospecting. He gathered camping equipment and provisions and hired an old Native-American man as a guide to get him as far as the remote Toba Inlet on the coast of British Columbia, the westernmost province of Canada. Before leaving Ostman to carry on his journey alone, the old man warned him to be very wary of the 'big people living in the mountains'.

Ostman laughed it off since he had never heard of anything like a Sasquatch or Bigfoot type of creature. However, when he set up basic camp on his hike into the mountains, on three consecutive days when he emerged from his sleeping bag in the morning, he found that during the night his belongings had been rifled through and items taken. Ostman then decided as a precaution to keep his loaded rifle with him in his sleeping bag. On the fourth night, something disturbed him and he woke up. He found himself being picked up by something large and carried in his sleeping bag over its back. He tried to figure out in the darkness what the creature carrying him might be and even wondered if he was maybe slumped over a horse, but he could only just breathe through the opening in his sleeping bag, which was held in an iron grip.

After about three hours of being carried, Ostman said he was eventually dumped on the ground where he was able to crawl out of the sleeping bag. As dawn broke, he realized that he had been carried to a small valley or basin surrounded by high mountains. The most amazing thing was the creature who had carried him there. Ostman described it as a huge, hair-covered man about 2.4 m (8 ft) tall, with a massive barrel-shaped chest, a large hump on its back and extremely powerful shoulders. It also had immense biceps and its forearms were longer than those of an average human male's, but well proportioned. The creature was hairless on the palms of its hands and the soles of its feet. Interestingly, the upper part of the nose and eyelids had no hair either. Ostman said he never saw the ears since the Bigfoot's hair covered them. He quickly figured out that he must try and escape and said, 'I am going to have to get out of here even if I shoot my way out.'

The Bigfoot, claimed Ostman, was not alone: indeed, he appeared to be male and the 'Old Man', as Ostman called him, of the group. There was also the 'Old Lady', an older female who was similar in height to the male, and a younger male and female, which Ostman took to be their offspring. Ostman thought the young male was around

11 to 18 years old and about 2.10 m (7 ft) tall. He felt that the young female appeared to be very gentle in her manner and, despite her strength, would probably not hurt anybody. Ostman recalled that he considered attempting to kidnap the young female and taking her back to civilization but decided against it. He asked the strange group of creatures, 'What do you fellows want with me?' He got no reply, but they seemed to chatter together in a language of their own. If Ostman couldn't escape, then he considered shooting at them from a distance with his rifle but decided against the idea. 'I saw a moving picture (film) of three men trying to shoot a mountain gorilla once, with a high-powered rifle, and despite their shooting, it did not bring it down.' He figured the attempted shoot-out might not work and would only make the 'Old Man' very angry.

Ostman claimed that he could not escape from the Bigfoot family straight away because the large male would stand in his way every time he tried to get up to leave and he said, 'It just kept saying, "Oohka Oohka" to me,' presumably a direction to mean no or get back. Although they did him no harm and seemed fairly placid, he did not want to make the mistake of angering them. He described them as smarter than humans in many ways and thought they usually tried to avoid people.

When asked in a rare Canadian public radio station interview in 1971, what did he think they wanted with him, Ostmam laughed and said, 'Well, I believe the old man wanted me to be a sweetheart to his daughter!' However, it seemed Ostman wasn't intending to stick around and become part of the family. Eventually, after six days he claimed his potential in-laws became quite friendly towards him and were interested in his coffee and snuff tin. Ostman seized his chance when the two males opened his tin of snuff. The 'Old Man' ate the whole of it and began to get sick, his eyes rolling in his head. During the ensuing commotion, Ostman grabbed his rifle and sleeping bag along with some food and ran for the opening in the rocks.

He fired a warning shot at the 'Old Lady', who tried to pursue him, and she turned and ran back in fear. Ostman ran down the mountain as far as his strength allowed him, saying he 'must have broken the world record for running at top speed', then he walked for two days, eventually encountering some loggers at Sechelt Inlet, northwest of Vancouver. He said nothing to them about his Sasquatch 'kidnap', concerned that they would think he was crazy. Ostman was asked in the 1971 radio interview why he kept the story to himself for 30 years. 'I would try and tell it to locals and friends, but they just used to laugh and wondered what I had been drinking!' he said. He found more sympathetic listeners in the Native Americans, he said. They were more willing to take him seriously. He never believed in these creatures before his encounter, assuming anything like that would have died out thousands of years ago. 'There may not be many,' said the Native American who first guided him to the remote Toba Inlet, 'but there are still some out there.' Ostman said the guide informed him, 'They have hair all over their bodies, but they are not animals. They are people. Big people living in the mountains.'

Ostman was willing to be interviewed by police, who published an affidavit about his story. On 20 August 1957, police magistrate A. M. Naismith wrote, '… I found Mr. Ostman to be a man of sixty-four years of age; in full possession of his mental faculties. Of pleasant manner and with a good sense of humour. I questioned Mr. Ostman thoroughly in reference to the story given by Mr. Green. I cross-examined him and used every means to endeavour to find a flaw in either his personality or his story but could find neither.' Ostman signed a Solemn Declaration indicating that his account of the Sasquatch story was true. Ostman was even hooked up to lie detector machines, which found he was telling the truth. Small details that Ostman observed about the Bigfoot were later compared to footage of primates in the jungle, which were not widely understood in the 1920s. For example, Ostman noted that the younger Bigfoot would play by himself and roll over and over, holding the tips of his toes as he did so; this was similar to behaviour which has later been observed in both chimpanzees and gorillas.

Some are naturally sceptical of the Ostman encounter, despite the fact he passed a lie detector test. The primatologist, John Napier, stated in 2009 that 'Ostman's story fails to convince me primarily on the grounds of the limited food resources available.' However, do we really know what Bigfoot eat? Bears are in the same territory and consume fish, plants, fruits, nuts, insects and small animals. Presumably, they might be competing for the same resources. Ostman made the following observation during his encampment with the Bigfoot group. 'The following day I did not see the Old Lady till about 4.00pm. She came home with her arms full of grass and twigs and all kinds of spruce and hemlock as well as some kind of nuts that grow in the ground. I don't think this valley was their permanent home. I think they move from place to place as food is available in different localities. They might eat meat, but I never saw them eat meat… or do any cooking.' After his bizarre encounter, Albert decided he had had enough of prospecting. 'That was my last prospecting trip, and my only experience with what is known as Sasquatches.' Albert Ostman died in 1975, and maintained his story was true all his life.

The Patterson-Gimlin film of 1967 Bigfoot

The most iconic event in the history of Bigfoot or Sasquatch encounters occurred in October 1967. Cowboys, Roger 'Patty' Patterson and Bob Gimlin, were out trying to film Bigfoot in Bluff Creek, northern California. If you recall, it was back in Bluff Creek that Jerry Crew and his road-building, log-clearing team had come across Bigfoot tracks around ten years earlier. It was now October 1967 and both men had heard that some large footprints had been found in the area recently, and so they decided to camp out with horses and explore the area in the hope of finding Bigfoot tracks. They had been camping and riding for about a month when, on the afternoon of Saturday 20 October 1967, they were riding slowly up the creek at walking pace. As they turned, they came around a corner. Their horses reared up in fear and Patterson almost fell off to the ground. He managed to land on his feet and, spotting a large Bigfoot by the water's edge, he quickly pulled out his hired 16mm cine camera (an older, lower-resolution version of a video camera, which used film rather than video tape) and began filming what he saw.

He ran towards the creature to try and get a better shot and fell over, which was why he ended up filming by resting on his elbows as he tried to steady the shot. They saw the Bigfoot walking away from them. It was about 60 m (200 feet) distant. As the creature walked off, it swayed its long arms and looked back over its shoulder towards Gimlin and Patterson with what they later described as almost a look of disgust or annoyance at them. Patterson managed to film just under a minute of footage before the large creature disappeared into the dense forest. Later, the men were also able to identify its footprints and managed to get casts made of them. These measured approximately 35.5 cm (14 in) in length.

What is less well known, according to researcher and author, Lloyd Pye (see below), is that Patterson went back to the location the next day, calling on experts in zoology and anthropology to come out and help him track the creature down and to bring hunting dogs. Pye said in his book, *Everything You Know Is Wrong*, that if it was a human in a suit, the dogs would happily hunt the scent down. However, with Bigfoot he said, that dogs hated the smell of Bigfoot, as the stench is described as quite awful, and the dogs would refuse to follow the trail. Unfortunately for Patterson, according to Pye, none of the experts whom he called to support him in his quest agreed to help. They did not want to be drawn into something so controversial.

Real or fake footage?

Pye also pointed out that Patterson did the thing most fakers do not do, and that was to be completely open to everyone about where the film was shot. Patterson also called on scientists from the British Columbia Museum to come out and investigate the scene. Would someone who had faked critical evidence really behave in this way?

Sceptics will say yes because as a Bigfoot enthusiast Patterson may well have wanted to add to the legend and become part of it himself. However, Pye points out that someone who'd made a fake film would not disclose the location because they would know the film could be analysed for discrepancies. Close examination of the environment could be made, to then compare it against the Bigfoot onscreen. In this way, for instance, the legs could be measured, or the overall height of the creature could be matched against trees, which would definitely be known once the location was released. If you measured a tree, you would maybe find that your alleged Bigfoot was not so tall after all. The prints in the ground could also be analysed. All this was done in the Patterson-Gimlin film of 1967 and, for years, people have been examining the footage as well as visiting the location.

Bob Titmus, a taxidermist from Redding, California, was called out to the area and he took plaster casts of the prints. Ten years before, Titmus had a taxidermy shop near where Jerry Crew had found Bigfoot tracks and he helped advise him about the plaster-of-Paris needed to make his famous cast of one of the 40-cm (16-in) prints that kept showing up on the dirt road above Bluff Creek. By the depth of the prints, he estimated that the Bigfoot must have weighed 270 to 320 kg (600–700 lbs), far heavier than an average man of around 91 kg (200 lbs). Titmus was the first investigator to go the 'Patty' site at Bluff Creek and what he found left him totally convinced that the movie was genuine.

It is interesting to note that another point to consider about whether they faked the film or not, was the fact that Roger Patterson eventually made sure that poor Bob Gimlin was cut out of any money deals that were made when rights to the Bigfoot film were sold. Patterson died five years after the film was shot, and yet Gimlin has to date never come forward to say any of it was faked.

Even though the two the men fell out over the iconic film, Gimlin never went running to the media to declare that it was a piece of fiction as revenge on Patterson. In fact, he mostly shied away from publicity and only recently came forward to tell his side of the story because by now he is ageing and only has so much time left to tell the story as he sees it. Gimlin initially did a radio interview with Patterson soon after their encounter in 1967. The next time he was seen doing an interview was for *Arthur C. Clarke's Mysterious World* programme in 1980. By that time, Patterson had died of cancer and Gimlin perhaps wanted to set the record straight. Then, he went off the radar for around 12 years, returning to be interviewed in his own home in 1992 by journalist Roger Green.

Prior to his encounter with the 'Patty' Bigfoot in 1967, Gimlin said in his 1992 interview with Green that he had previously been a sceptic but was persuaded to ride out with Roger to search for Bigfoot. He was asked whether the film could have been faked and said he did in fact wonder at one stage whether Patterson might have secretly hired an actor to dress up in a suit to portray the female Bigfoot. But given that Patterson asked Gimlin to cover him with his rifle should the creature attack during the 1967 encounter, he had had to ask himself whether he was prepared to shoot a human in a suit. Would Patterson have risked that, Gimlin wondered? He decided that this was definitely not the case. Gimlin also noted how big the creature looked and how enormous its muscles were as it walked. He noticed the face was smooth with a human-looking nose, but the skin was a dark brown colour. He also said the creature in real life was a lot lighter in colour than what you see on the film, probably due to contrast adjustments when the print was made. Both Patterson and Gimlin agreed that, with the benefit of hindsight, they should probably have shot and killed the creature instead of filming it, both for financial reasons and to silence the sceptics.

Good but not that good!

The film has proved to be controversial ever since it was shot. Some suggest it is totally faked, while others back the idea that it is a real Bigfoot. Another interesting detail is that the alleged Bigfoot in the Patterson-Gimlin film appears to have breasts. If someone was going to fake a sighting of something like a Bigfoot and make or hire an ape-type costume, it's unlikely to have been female because in films of the 1960s, apes were typically depicted as male.

In the sci-fi *Planet of the Apes* films, apes were shown as clothed beings. Only the masks and ape hands had to be manufactured, not full ape costumes. Ironically then, by the time he was safely retired and in a nursing home in the 1970s, John Chambers, the award-winning, special-effects artist responsible for the ape make-up in *Planet of the*

Apes, was asked by a researcher if he, with all his skills, could have faked the creature in the Patterson-Gimlin film. He replied that he was 'good, but not that good'.

A man in a suit?

By the time the film was made public in 1968, it appeared that others wanted a piece of the money as well as the attention it generated. A man named Bob Heironimus, who was a retired Pepsi bottling factory worker from Yakima, Washington State, claimed he was the man in the Bigfoot costume in the Patterson-Gimlin film. He said he hadn't spoken up previously about his role in the alleged hoaxing because he hoped to be paid eventually by Patterson. Based on legal advice from his lawyer, he also said that since he had received no payment for his part in the apparent hoax, he could not be held accountable for any fraud on his part.

Philip Morris, the proprietor of Morris Costumes in Charlotte, South Carolina, which make and sell stage costumes and film props, claimed that he manufactured a gorilla costume that was sold to Roger Patterson in 1967. However, he provided no evidence to back up this claim in the form of receipts, photographs or having similar costumes in stock. Looking at their website today, they only produce one Bigfoot mask, which is not likely to worry crypto-zoologists any time soon!

In 1997, after watching the Patterson-Gimlin film, Stan Winston, who supervised special effects and make-up on *Jurassic Park* and the *Terminator* films, said it was a man in a poor-quality suit, which could have been made for a couple of hundred dollars. There are unverified claims that he changed his mind after viewing the film again when the film was later digitally stabilized and enhanced. The interesting side note to this issue is that Winston praised Hollywood costume-maker, Janos Prohaska, as a brilliant gorilla/ape costume-designer. Prohaska, who had regularly been cast as aliens, monsters and apes, made his own costumes. He was emphatic in his opinion that the Patterson-Gimlin film does not show a man in a costume. In the late 1960s, he said, 'If that was a costume, it was the best I have ever seen.'

Experienced make-up and costume artist, Barry Keithan, insisted that the Hollywood special effects industry was making false claims about how easy it would have been to fake a Bigfoot creature to make themselves seem like the true experts in the field. He believed there was no fakery detectable in the Patterson-Gimlin film.

More sightings... and smells

The sensory experience surrounding huge ape-like creatures, namely smell, must be mentioned. Further south from the extreme north-western region of the US, which is supposedly home to Bigfoot, there have been claimed sightings of a 'Skunk Ape', which gives off a particularly strong smell. This is an interesting detail because many people who have claimed to encounter Bigfoot have also reported being able to smell the creature even if they haven't always seen it. Michael Rugg, founder of the Bigfoot Discovery Museum near Santa Cruz in California, himself described the Bigfoot smell as being a combination of skunk odour, the smell of dead animals and waste bins.

Over the years, many Bigfoot researchers and enthusiasts have offered evidence to prove the creature's existence, including numerous anecdotal sightings, but also photographs, video and audio recordings, and even hair samples.

In 1968, Wayne Twitchell, a government wildlife guide, found six hairs on a bush near Riggins, Idaho, after a reported sighting of two Sasquatches. Suspecting that the hairs might belong to them, he sent the hair samples to a forensic laboratory in Los Angeles. There, police lab officer, Ray Pinker, used his 36 years' experience in a police crime lab to examine the hairs. He issued a report concluding that the hairs showed a combination of animal and human characteristics. Pinker said they did not match any samples he had in his collection. The resemblance to animals included the variation in colours and thickness of the hairs from the roots to the tips. Human hairs are more uniform. But the scale patterns on the outside of the hair shaft were quite similar to those of human hair and there was no core visible in the centre as would be the case with almost all animal hairs. The samples consisted of rough coarse outer hairs and finer hairs from an undercoat. The main problem that scientists have in establishing the identification of Bigfoot hair samples is they need an actual living or dead Bigfoot with which to make scientific comparisons. Science did actually get something resembling a Bigfoot, however, and we will come to that shortly.

People out in the wilds have often reported what they believe to be the strange calls of Bigfoot. Some even claim to have made recordings of these calls. In 1971 in the Sierra Nevada mountains in California, sceptical reporter, Al Berry, and his friend, Ron Moorehead, were investigating the Bigfoot phenomenon. One night in their camp near Lake Tahoe, they woke up to hear bizarre cries. Berry said, 'Something approached camp from a ridge above, rapping on wood or rocks as it came, and when it arrived – [there were] two voices that I could discern – it vocalized, and the sounds carried through the trees as I have never heard human voices carry before or since. And it whistled, a clear, beautiful whistle like a bird might make between its kind and, at one point, back and forth with us.' He continued, 'This encounter went on for nearly an hour and a half, and another followed on the second night. I was able to get reasonably good tape recordings of the sounds and interaction, and we cast several of the foot impressions, both in pine mat and snow. I looked high and low for evidence of the joke, including searching the others' belongings while they were away hunting.'

Finding no evidence of a hoax from his fellow camp members, Berry passed his recordings over to experts who gave their opinions. In 2019, Scott Nelson, a retired crypto-linguist formerly in the Navy, told the *Hastings Tribune* that, when he heard the recordings, his 'whole world changed… it took me out of my paradigm.' He is confident that they represent an intelligent language, probably being 'spoken by a family of intelligent, humanoid beings'.

Deliberate hoax or misidentification

With over 10,000 reported eyewitness accounts of Bigfoot in the continental US alone, you would think that perhaps we should have the scientific agreement by now that something is out there lurking in the great forests. The scientific community is clear that accounts of Bigfoot, and related ape-like creatures that appear to walk on two legs like humans, originate from hoaxes or, giving the benefit of the doubt to some claimants, misidentified animals – rather than from a living but as yet unclassified ape-type animal. For instance, scientific opinion on the large footprints supposedly made by Bigfoot, which are up to 60 cm (24 in) long and 20 cm (8 in) wide, has concluded they are either faked or contain claw marks suggesting they are bear prints (bears have five toes).

Brian Regal, author of *Searching for Sasquatch: Crackpots, Eggheads, and Cryptozoology* and associate professor of the history of science at Kean University in New Jersey, told website *Live Science* that people project their own ideas onto the 'Patty' film. 'You look at it and you see what you want to believe,' he said. From that perspective, it could be argued he himself could want to believe it's not real because he doesn't want to believe it exists. Anthropologist, Grover Krantz, listened to sound recordings claimed to be from Bigfoot for his book *Big Footprints: A Scientific Inquiry Into the Reality of Sasquatch* published in 1992. After listening to ten tapes, he said he found 'no compelling reason to believe that any of them are what the recorders claimed them to be.' Despite that, Krantz did believe that Bigfoot was real. However, he did seem to have a frustration with the evidence. Concerning samples of Bigfoot hair, faeces, skin scrapings and blood, he said, 'The usual fate of these items is that they either receive no scientific study, or else the documentation of that study is either lost or unobtainable.'

Considering the point of samples going missing, there was one item, an alleged prized specimen if you will, that science had in its clutches, but it somehow slipped away. Was it a Bigfoot or some kind of unknown version of a human?

Modern Neanderthal

Could Bigfoot, and similar creatures reported around the world, be the last remaining descendants of our early human relatives? Author Lloyd

Pye, in his book *Everything You Know Is Wrong*, suggested that Bigfoot is most likely a modern version of the Neanderthal species that officially died out about 40,000 years ago. *Homo sapiens*, or modern-day humans, carry some Neanderthal DNA, indicating that some bred with the Neanderthals. Pye speculated that rather than dying out, Neanderthals in fact retreated from humans and were driven into the large, dense forests where they could live in small groups in relative peace and isolation – until recent times, when logging became a larger industry. Before this, the indigenous peoples of the US and Canada were the only humans who would occasionally come into contact with them.

Pye recalled as a boy seeing a creature promoted as 'The Minnesota Iceman' in a travelling fair, which he had come to believe was a genuine Bigfoot shot by a hunter named Frank Hanson in 1967 in Minnesota. Later, Hanson wrote that he came into contact with the creature while hunting deer around 100 km (60 miles) north of Duluth. He claimed that he initially saw three Bigfoot eating a deer he had just shot. Suddenly the male jumped straight up into the air from its crouched position, its arms held high in the air and screeching loudly as it charged towards him. He didn't remember aiming his rifle or even pulling the trigger but said a bullet must have struck the creature. He did not recall ejecting his spent shell or firing a second time.

According to Pye, instead of presenting the body to a university for scientific research – and confirming the existence of Bigfoot once and for all – Hanson froze the corpse and displayed it publicly in a glass-covered case for money. (Pye speculated that Hanson might have thought he could be arrested for murder if the creature was found to be partly human.) From 1968, it was taken around shopping malls and travelling fairs for about 12 years. Hanson, apparently, also claimed he was acting as ward of the body, which actually belonged to an undisclosed owner (widely rumoured to be American actor, James Stewart). Pye recalled that it was clear to him on viewing the creature that 'this was an ex-living dead thing'. According to him, the 'Iceman' was actually a juvenile unofficially recognized hominid – a two legged, upright-walking part-human, part-ape.

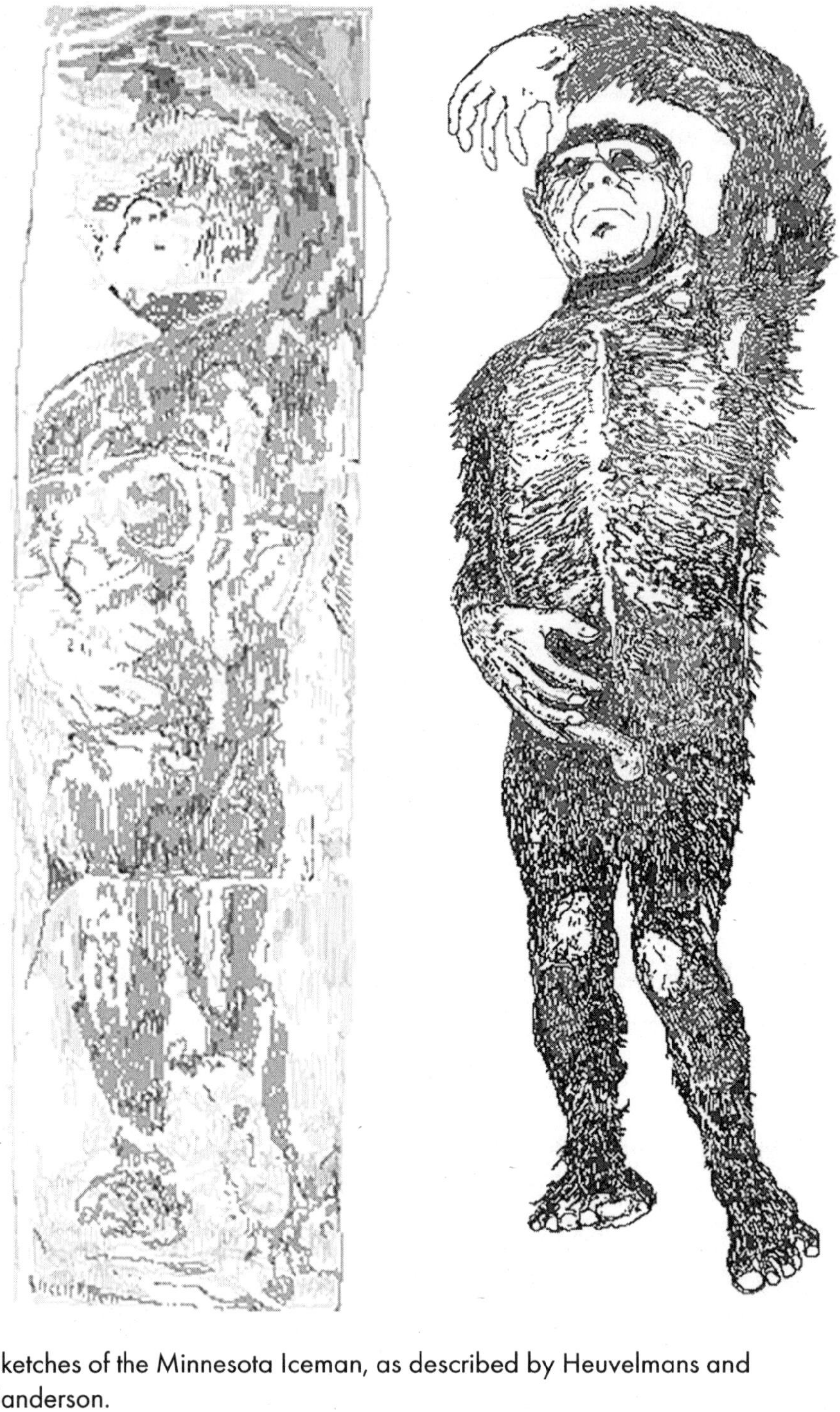

Sketches of the Minnesota Iceman, as described by Heuvelmans and Sanderson.

To give his new exhibit credibility, in December 1968 Hanson invited two scientists to examine the specimen: Ivan Sanderson, a biologist, and Bernard Heuvelmans, a zoologist. The two men made detailed illustrations and notes, which they compiled into their report. They described the frozen corpse as a strong, barrel-chested male with huge thickness to the neck and extra-large hands and feet. Sanderson and Heuvelmans also noted its giant hands with thumbs that were slender, tapered and long, adding that it had a broad, flattened face with a short, turned-up nose and high ridges on its brow.

During the investigation, the protective glass cover over the case cracked and a smell leaked out that was described as that of decomposing flesh. This was further proof to Sanderson and Heuvelmans that, whatever they were looking at, it was very real. They published their research in 1969 in a Belgian scientific journal, identifying the creature as a new species of the human genus that they named *Homo pongoides*, or 'Living Neanderthal'.

Heuvelmans declared that their discovery of a brand-new species of Neanderthal-like man was a historical breakthrough. This type of hominid, he said, was thought to be extinct for over 40,000 years, but it was now proven to be alive today. The hunt for rumoured 'missing links', he said, was now a success. Dr John Russell Napier was a leading primatologist/anthropologist, who read the report on the Iceman but never unfortunately got to examine it in person. What he noticed about the report was interesting. He noticed the hairs on the iceman, in certain parts, contained patterns like stripes on a tiger or the tail of a monkey. This patterning is called *agouti* and Napier said of the hairs, 'The *agouti* pattern of hair colouration is also extremely common amongst the primates. It is seen in the monkeys of both the New and Old Worlds; but at the higher levels of primate evolution – among the apes and man – it is completely unknown. That the Iceman should possess *agouti*-patterned hairs is a zoological improbability of the highest order. If we can take this observation of Sanderson's as valid, and there is no reason why we should not, then the likelihood that the Iceman is an artefact – a man-made object – is high.' But would someone faking fur go to the length of inserting individual stripes within its fur? It would be an unenviable task to say the least!

Over time, Hanson is said to have replaced the real 'Iceman' with a model version, supposedly in case he was ever arrested for killing the creature. Its last owner was the Museum of the Weird in Austin, Texas; unfortunately, today the original model 'Iceman' is missing. What happened to it is a complete mystery. Some accounts even allege that the FBI switched the real corpse for the model to prevent the public becoming aware that such a creature existed. The Iceman story, while very interesting, is clouded in confusion. Perhaps some people intended it to stay that way.

The Proof Is Out There

In 2021, a television show called *The Proof Is Out There* brought together Dr Jeff Meldrum, Professor of Anatomy and Anthropology at Idaho State University, computer scientist, Isaac Tian, and Bill Munns, a Hollywood costume and special effects designer, to apply their expertise to the iconic Bigfoot footage filmed by Roger Patterson and Bob Gimlin in 1967. They used artificial intelligence, computer technology and costume manufacturing knowledge to investigate the footage, and so identify minute details that had previously been overlooked.

By examining the creature's feet, they studied how Bigfoot interacted with the ground while walking. They noted a flexing in the middle of the foot, typical of apes but not humans. Meldrum mentions the casts made from the footprints at the location where the Patty Bigfoot film was shot. 'One of them shows a very distinct pressure ridge. A push off that comes about as a result of the very flexible mid foot.' This distinctive characteristic is very strong evidence for Meldrum as he's seen that pressure ridge in foot samples taken across the decades. Meldrum shows the Patty film footage to his students and asks them to point out landmarks of surface anatomy and muscle mass that you can identify on the alleged Bigfoot. He said, 'They started at the head and they can see the trapezius muscles, they can see the deltoid muscles, they can see the lateral and long heads of the triceps. They can see the *erector spinae* (the spine) down the back, they can see the shoulder blades moving under the skin. I mean just go on and on from top to bottom and you're gonna pick out all these features, none of which ever show up in a cheap off-the-shelf costume!'

They also identified an upward turning of the toes that someone wearing a manufactured costume would not have been able to replicate.

Despite the controversy surrounding the Patterson-Gimlin Bigfoot film, it has never been successfully debunked. With the amazing digital stabilizing technology that has been applied to it, all sorts of hidden things are being discovered. Could it really be a man, or a lady in a suit? Until someone brings back a live Bigfoot for all to see, the controversy will continue around the existence of a reclusive ape-like humanoid creature in the deep woods of North America – and possibly in other remote locations too.

Maybe a clue as to why Bigfoot still remains a mystery could be found in something said by one of the army of Bigfoot hunters, which has visited the wilds of northern California so often. In 2017, Jackie Tonks from Bristol in the UK claims that, during one such visit, she witnessed two adult Bigfoot males crossing the road in front of her car and running in panic into dense woods. In an interview on *The Paranormal Peep Show* podcast, she said, 'I believe the majority of Bigfoot hunters know where these creatures are to be found and could, with careful planning, bring a body back. However, they may be reluctant to do so because, once this happens and the existence of Bigfoot is officially acknowledged, it could be the end of them.'

Like so many extinct mammals that have been devastated by man in the history of the Earth, they may, too, end up as an unfortunate statistic. Maybe, as Jackie mused, 'Hunters of this much-disputed creature do not want to be a party to its inevitable destruction at the hands of humankind.' It may be better that society continues to view Bigfoot as an unsolved mystery.

The alleged photograph of Bigfoot taken by Roger Patterson in 1967.

THE GIANT OF KANDAHAR

When one thinks of bloodthirsty giants, the biblical story of Goliath springs to mind. The champion of the mighty Philistines, his huge size and strength so terrified the Israelite army that not even its finest warriors would accept his challenge to fight in single combat – except the young David, their future king, who is famously said to have killed him with a stone from a sling. Historians still debate the truth behind this inspirational tale, including the existence of the legendary giant, but in recent years a strange story of conflict with a modern-day Goliath has emerged, this time in the mountains of Afghanistan. Could this violent encounter have actually happened?

With possible giants from the distant past in mind, we come to the present day, where a truly bizarre story emerges from the invasion of Afghanistan. In October 2001, as a response to the '9/11' attacks, the hijack of four civilian aircraft by al-Qaeda terrorists, joint United States and British forces invaded Afghanistan to overthrow the Taliban, who were thought to have harboured some of the hijackers. The resulting conflict would involve troops from more than 20 countries under a NATO banner and last for two decades, costing over 1,000 American lives alone, as well as unknown numbers of the local population. This became known as the War on Terror. Behind the daily headlines recounting the mounting casualties, drone strikes, bombings, firefights and Taliban resurgence was a deeply strange story about an encounter between US forces and a giant man.

A flaming-haired giant fighter

Kandahar province, in the south of Afghanistan on the border with Pakistan, is one of the oldest regions of Afghanistan; it was first settled around 7,000 years ago. In 2001, its capital, Kandahar City, was the last major stronghold under Taliban control. After it fell, American forces were out on constant patrol, trying to round up pockets of Taliban resistance. In 2002, according to an unnamed member of the US Army Special Forces, his unit was dispatched to find one such patrol that did not return to base or even radio back for assistance. The officer, who refused to identify himself and was known only as 'Mr K', said his team was flown to a remote area in the mountains, hiking on from there to one of the missing patrol's previous checkpoints. He suspected the patrol had been ambushed by Taliban soldiers and was not able to alert their base and call for back-up.

Finding no sign of the patrol at the checkpoint, the search team continued down the mountain via rocky pathways. As they descended, they came across the mouth of a large open cave with rocks piled up in front of it, which they thought was unusual. 'Mr K' also noticed damaged parts of US military communications equipment strewn over the area, and what he thought at a distance could be 'bone matter' here and there on the pathway. He immediately jumped to the conclusion that the patrol group had been ambushed either by the enemy or possibly a large animal and instinctively his team took cover behind the rocks, ready for combat. Before they could even get into their positions, a huge figure came running out of the mouth of the cave towards them. Then the colossus was on a ledge just above them, jumping down with alarming speed.

'Mr K' described the man as having flaming red hair down to his shoulders and a long beard. The soldier estimated this giant to be between 3.7 m and 4.5 m (12 ft to 15 ft) tall and said he was carrying a large, bladed weapon similar to a pike (a long, spiked medieval spear) and a large shield. The giant took a swipe at the soldiers with the end of his spear as he swung it around, knocking some of them over. It looked like the giant was very used to using his weapon in this way. One of 'Mr K''s team, whom he just called 'Dan', ran towards the giant with his gun raised, and the rest of the patrol began to fire at the tall figure. Unfortunately, Dan was speared through his body armour and ended up being lifted on the long weapon as the giant headed towards the other Americans.

'Mr K' recalled yelling out to his fellow troops, 'Shoot him in the face!' The squad was armed with fully automatic M4 carbines, 'recon carbines' (semi-automatic) and M107 Barrett anti-materiel rifles firing .50 BMG (Browning Machine Gun: this is the technical name for a heavy-calibre round). They began to fire at the giant's head and chest, but despite taking multiple hits, the huge man was still moving – firing was constant for about 30 seconds, although it felt to Mr K like it took them an hour to get the creature down. According to one onlooker, they managed to blow the bottom part of the giant's face off and he collapsed in a heap. Both Dan, the soldier impaled on the giant's spear, and the huge man himself lay dead in a scene resembling a sci-fi or fantasy monster film. The eyes of the creature were the size of a man's hand according to the account given by 'Mr K', who ordered the medical evacuation of the unit. Then a Chinook, a heavy-duty cargo helicopter, arrived and dropped a huge net for the men to secure the giant figure.

Six digits

'Mr K' noticed yet another odd detail about this bizarre giant man: he had six fingers on each hand and six toes on each foot. Also, the nails on each were long and curled over, which suggests the giant could have had some kind of fungal infection that causes nails to grow out and curl around. 'Mr K' also noted a terrible and overwhelming stench emanating from the giant. This was an interesting observation as it's a detail that has also been reported from many encounters with the immense ape-like 'Bigfoot' creatures mentioned earlier.

With great difficulty, the huge man was eventually positioned in the net and lifted by the powerful Chinook, then flown back to base. 'Mr K' was later told to write a report on the incident, as were others in his team. However, their commanding officers refused to accept their account of the giant and ordered them to rewrite their reports. The Special Forces team did as ordered and removed all mention of the giant. When Snopes.com asked about the 'Kandahar Giant incident' in 2016, the US government denied the claim. The Department of Defense said, 'We do not have any record or information about a special forces member killed by a giant in Kandahar.' Perhaps that's true and they don't have a record. Although the unit was asked to write out reports, they were after all ordered to change them. So perhaps an official report, if the incident happened, does not exist. Even the helicopter crew carrying the giant would, therefore, presumably have been ordered to sign a 'Non-disclosure Agreement'. I would presume it would be regarded as classified, like, say, a recovered UFO story might be treated in the same way.

Despite this denial, according to L. A. Marzulli, an American author and film-maker who researches and explains current and historical events through the lens of biblical verses and prophecies, other US military personnel who served in Afghanistan also heard the story about a giant being killed by American soldiers. Some claimed to him that they spoke to the aircrew who flew the giant's body out of Afghanistan on a metal palette transported by a C-17 Globemaster cargo aircraft. From Kandahar, it was airlifted north of Kabul to a closed section of what was then the Bagram Airfield Base. The crew flying it there had to measure and weigh the giant creature under a tarpaulin. They also noticed the six digits on its hands and feet. From Bagram Air Base, it may then have been flown to Germany and on to Wright-Patterson Air Force Base near Dayton, Ohio. Wright-Patterson is often mentioned in connection with supposed recovered crashed UFOs and other strange artefacts, with the famous Roswell UFO also allegedly ending up there.

Ancient and modern giants

The US Special Forces soldier, 'Mr K', is said to have told his story to L. A. Marzulli after speaking to film-maker Richard Shaw, who happened to be answering calls during a radio station interview in 2015 when a caller rang in and spoke about his tour of duty in Afghanistan. Shaw arranged to speak more after the show and the caller explained how he had shot this giant man in the mountains. Later, the caller was identified as 'Mr K'. Both Shaw and Marzulli secured interviews with 'Mr K' on separate occasions and they both agreed that, when 'Mr K' spoke about his friend, Dan, who was killed by the giant, he became very upset and emotional. He would 'choke up, break down and weep, and hang up the phone,' said Marzulli.

This convinced them both that he appeared to be genuine in the telling of this bizarre encounter! Marzulli said, 'There is a vetting process we do, we don't just put the guy on camera. We talked with him around four times over a few weeks and then he agreed to re-tell his story on camera.' Each time 'Mr K' spoke about his dead friend, Dan, he became emotional. 'He was certainly not acting,' said Marzulli. Both Shaw and Marzulli acknowledge that the story first broke in 2008 with researcher and author, Steven Quale, who had spoken to the pilot who had flown the body of the giant out of Afghanistan. This means that at least two US forces members had spoken to researchers from their own perspective about what they experienced.

As well as Marzulli interviewing Special Forces soldier, 'Mr K', *Giants on Record* co-author, Jim Vieira, claims he also interviewed the very same soldier. Vieira is a stonemason and was the star of the History Channel TV show, *Search for the Lost Giants*. He has collated 1,500 newspaper and scholarly accounts of giant skeletons. While he can't prove the giant story, his own deep dive research into accounts of giants suggested to him at least that there was maybe something to it.

Another author who looked into this is Fritz Zimmerman in his book, *The Nephilim Chronicles: Fallen Angels in the Ohio Valley*, 2010. He, too, suggests the same giants have ventured out into the world. He mentions a giant race called the Dinaric, whose remains have been found in Jerusalem, in burial mounds at Stonehenge and also in the Ohio Valley. As American pioneers pushed out west, they would come across these giant mounds. According to writers, they dug into them to find giant bones, with six fingers on each hand and two sets of teeth. Each skeleton was about eight to 12 feet tall or more. Could they be the Nephilim?

The Nephilim are mentioned in both the Christian Old Testament and the Hebrew Bible as mighty people who were incredibly large and strong, and possibly of supernatural origin – although scholars debate whether they were giants or fallen angels. It is also argued that the meaning of 'Nephilim' varies according to the translation. Marzulli believes that small groups of these biblical giants survived in pockets around the world, travelling to Europe, Peru, America and the east, beginning about 3,500 years ago. According to Marzulli, they were escaping the forces of Joshua and Caleb, who were part of the tribe of Israel that escaped from Egypt under Moses. Joshua, we are told in the Old Testament, led the people across the Jordan River into the Promised Land. After a 40-day exploration of Canaan, Joshua reported back to Moses, 'We went into the land to which you sent us, and it does flow with milk and honey! Here is its fruit. But the people who live there are powerful, and the cities are fortified and very large. We even saw descendants of Anak there.' (Numbers 13:27–28).

This report frightened people (Numbers 13:31–33). The Anakim/Anakites were a formidable race of giant, warlike people according to ancient texts of the Old Testament (Deuteronomy 2:10, 21; 9:2). The Anak lived in the lands of southern Israel near Hebron before the Israelites lived there (Joshua 15:13). The Anakim's ancient ancestry has been traced back to Anak, the son of Arba (Joshua 15:13; 21:11), who at that time was regarded as the 'greatest man among the Anakim.' The Hebrews thought them to be descendants of the famed Nephilim, a powerful race who dominated the pre-Flood world (Genesis 6:4; Numbers 13:33). Marzulli claims to have evidence of a massive cover-up concerning what he believes to be the remains of the Nephilim or the Anak. Marzulli, therefore, suggests that this race, possibly moving outwards into the world, became the stuff of many of the legends about giants we have heard over the years. But do they really exist?

It might sound crazy, but we can say with certainty that human giants exist. *Guinness World Records* recognizes an American, Robert Wadlow, as the tallest man ever, with an amazing measured height in June 1940 of 2.72 m (8 ft 11.1 in). His immense size and his accelerated growth in adulthood were the result of an abnormally functioning pituitary gland. Sadly, the resulting medical problems led to Wadlow's early death at the age of 22. Living alone in the mountains, could the 'Kandahar Giant' have actually been someone with gigantism resulting from a medical condition? More intriguingly, maybe he was not alone. Could he have been a descendent of the ancient race of Nephilim described in the Bible?

The idea of massive, unnaturally powerful humanoids is certainly one that can be traced back in histories and cultures across the world,

Robert Wadlow, the tallest man to have ever lived.

not only in Biblical accounts such as David and Goliath. There are also records of groups of unusually tall people living in groups that appeared to be a race. In *The Nephilim Chronicles* author Fritz Zimmerman covers around 300 historical accounts of excavated giant skeletons. Many were associated with the earliest mound sites discovered in America, but stories also emerged from the hunter-fisher cultures of northeastern Europe and in the Middle East: for instance, 'Red Paint People' were described by the ancient Babylonians as having double rows of teeth.

The indigenous American Cherokee people referred to a race they called the 'Moon People' – huge creatures their ancient ancestors battled when they migrated from the west. These ugly cannibals were more than 3 m (10 ft) tall and lived in caves in what is now the state of Tennessee. (Cannibalism is an interesting detail, given 'Mr K's' reference to seeing fragments of bone and the fairytale reputation of giants as eating humans.) In 1857, the Comanche Native Americans described 'a race of white men, ten feet high, and far more rich and powerful than any white people now living. They inhabited a large range of country, extending from the rising to the setting sun.' There are written reports of huge bones found near the famous archaeological site of Stonehenge in southwest England. And in 1880, at a burial mound site near Plano, Texas, enormous human bones were found, including femoral bones nearly 13 cm (5 in) longer than that of a typical adult human.

Giants of America

In their book, *Giants on Record*, Jim Vieira and Hugh Newman documented what they believe to be an ancient race of giants in North America. Covering a period of more than 200 years, they examined thousands of newspaper reports, town and county historical records, letters, photos, personal diaries and scientific journals. They claim these records show that human skeletons ranging from 2.1 m (7 ft) up to a staggering 5.5 m (18 ft) tall have been found at prehistoric mounds, tombs, caves, burial sites and ancient battlefields.

Recovered skulls had peculiar anatomical anomalies such as double rows of teeth, elongation of the skull and even in some cases protrusions that looked like horns. The authors allege these immense remains were all taken at various times by archaeologists to the Smithsonian Institution, the national US museum and research centre in Washington DC, and quietly disposed of there. They also claim the Smithsonian's own records describe at least 17 giant human skeletons in annual reports relating to its collections. It's not clear if the bones or full skeletons were hidden or destroyed, however. Some of the authors even suggested the bones of the giants were dumped out at sea!

More giants in Afghanistan?

Returning to Afghanistan, the 'Kandahar Giant' may also not have been the only living example of his kind – whatever that kind may be. Ex-serviceman and author, Nick Orton, has collected many strange tales, including possible giant stories involving the military. One story he mentions occurred in 2008, when a newly deployed and unnamed US soldier was using a night vision scope – this enabled clear vision through a telescope in the dark and it could display temperature variations known as heat signatures – to spy on suspected Taliban fighters hiding out in the mountains. Scanning the valley, he came across a very large heat signature on the night scope. He assumed it belonged to a group of Taliban fighters huddled around a fire but was then surprised to see the heat signature rise, as if one person had suddenly stood up. The trees in the immediate area were around 3–3.7 m (10–12 ft) high but the signature was much taller.

The giant figure then appeared to stride along in a very relaxed manner, covering the ground very quickly, and eventually moved out of the night vision's field of view. The soldier recalled in his interview that he thought that what he saw was a member of an 'ancient race of giants that descended from fallen angels… Or it could be something like Sasquatch. I'm not sure.' Could a fault with the night vision scope, or a misjudgement on the part of the operator, explain the height discrepancy?

It would be easy to dismiss this story, given the lack of photographic or video evidence and the anonymous source. However, Orton has collected numerous accounts of bizarre sightings and encounters from soldiers, sailors and air crew for a book, *Tales From The Grid Square*, featuring interviews conducted on the basis of anonymity. One concerns yet more giants in Afghanistan. During the 'War on Terror', this story tells of a drone operator working remotely for the US Air Force in the northern part of the country. On one occasion, when he was flying a drone looking for the Taliban hiding out in caves, he was able to steer the craft via a joystick and view live video from its camera on his computer terminal.

The drone operator said that he saw three giant figures, each standing roughly 3.7 m (12 ft) tall. Their height was calculated by a measuring tool on his computer screen and, as this happened at night, the drone's camera was operating in infrared, so the figures showed up as black humanoid heat signatures. The operator watched them for about 10 minutes, during which time they sat by their fire and performed chores. 'The only interesting thing was the size,' the operator wrote. 'The goats looked like cats next to them.'

Clearly, this account was remarkably similar to the description of the Kandahar giant. If giants do exist and hide out in caves, then a drone would be a safe way of viewing them. Drones were used routinely to search for and track Taliban soldiers, so hearing stories about military personnel capturing other things on their screens besides the enemy would be plausible. It could be argued that the drone operator who saw these things was just tired and misjudged the scale of what he saw. However, it would also make sense to anyone who operates these drones to record and later review the footage. We know from news programmes that much drone footage was recorded during the War on Terror. They reviewed the footage for tactical reasons and possibly legal reasons, too, so any potential oddities would likely have been recorded for verification.

In another account, an Australian officer, on sentry duty at a NATO military base in Afghanistan's central Uruzgan province, allegedly spotted an extremely tall, thin humanoid in strange clothing walking near the compound, perhaps looking for scraps of food or water. Using the building as a reference, the officer estimated the giant to be nearly 2 km (1.25 miles) away from him. The officer discreetly followed the figure through field glasses for about five minutes then lost sight of him. He estimated the giant to have been around 3.7 to 4.6 m (12–15 ft) in height. Not knowing whether anyone else had seen it, the officer said that he didn't have the nerve to tell anyone else about this odd experience, but he had never forgotten it.

But do soldiers really come across giants and ghosts during war? Dr Simon H. Walker, of Walker Military and Institutional Mental Health Research Network, suggests that psychological stress under combat, grief, fear, adrenaline and hunger could all combine to create these illusions. But if you have recorded something on a drone, could it be called an illusion?

What stands out in the description of the Kandahar giant are details like its red hair and curved nails. If someone was going to make it up, would they have specified the hair colour as red? Truthful people will often mention specifics that stick out as odd in their observations of people or situations. The description of fungus-infected toes was another small but pertinent observation. Would someone make up these kinds of unusual details to 'sell' a story, or could they be true?

In the absence of hard visual evidence, the likelihood that a tribe of giants is living in remote areas today can only rest on the personal testimonies of those who claim to have seen them. But there are also local legends that seem to support the tales related here by western military personnel. Ray Rahem, a New York resident and US citizen who was born in Afghanistan, backed up the possibility of the existence of giants in 2023 in a Youtube interview with Terry Carter. Rahem said that his grandmother, a native of Kandahar, knew of the so-called giants in the region and warned him when he was younger not to venture into the caves. She would frequently take goats to the mouth of certain caves in an effort to keep the giants from coming into the village to look for food. Although he never personally encountered a giant, Rahem's father also told him that he once saw a huge human footprint in the desert in Afghanistan, which made him very nervous.

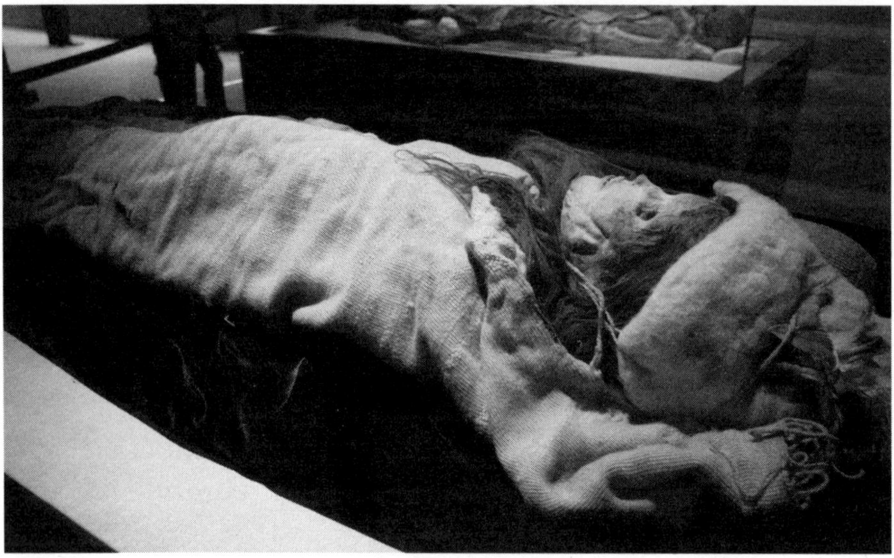

Princess of Xiaohe mummy, found in the Taklamakan desert. Buried approximately 3,800 years ago, she has European and Siberian genes and has white skin and red hair.

With nothing but oral evidence, we simply cannot tell whether the intriguing idea that giants are stalking the remote mountains of Afghanistan – and maybe other locations around the world – has the ring of truth. Even if they exist, and until scientists are able to study such beings, we can't be sure whether they are descendants of a biblical giant, early humans like the Cro-Magnons who migrated east to west many millennia ago, or something supernatural. Hopefully, in our age of smartphones and drones, someone will soon capture clearly visible footage that will at least help us begin to solve this mystery.

HAVANA SYNDROME

Many of us are lucky enough to suffer illness only occasionally and, when we do, we can access medical care that diagnoses the problem quickly and sets out a clear pathway of treatment. But if you are suddenly struck down, it must be extremely unnerving if you find that many of your colleagues are presenting with the same symptoms, and even more so when medical authorities can't isolate the cause. This is what hundreds of American diplomats and other government officials stationed abroad claim happened to them, starting in the mid-2010s. The existence of a mysterious mass illness, now known as 'Havana Syndrome', has been disputed, not to mention the controversy that arose around its possible causes. What is Havana Syndrome, or 'anomalous health incidents' as the grouping of symptoms has also been called, and was it triggered by vaccinations, psychological stress or malign attacks using 'invisible' weapons?

In May 2016, several American officials working at the US embassy in Havana, Cuba suddenly began to experience intense headaches, ringing in their ears, nausea and fatigue. For some people, it was even worse, with cases of cognitive impairment being reported. One lady working there said she felt a 'low hum and intense pressure in her skull'; while another worker felt a constant pulse of pain. Covering their ears apparently made no difference to the sound they could hear. Others reported dizziness and fatigue lasting for months. The symptoms were initially reported by a few people in the last few months of 2016, but these began to escalate in the following year and, it seemed, the problem was not just limited to workers at the embassy there.

The illness started to affect family members of embassy staff living in Havana. Rumors began to spread that some embassy workers thought sufferers were crazy and it was 'all in the mind'. Although most believed the syndrome began in Havana, there are reports that it possibly started two years earlier in Germany.

Since then, there have been more than 1,000 cases of the mysterious illness. These were reported by civilian and military employees of the US government from locations as far-flung as China and India, Europe and Hanoi, as well as inside the United States itself, including Washington DC.

'Like drilling on steroids'

While specific effects have varied, one notable common factor was the sudden onset of neurological symptoms, with people hearing loud, localized loud sounds. As well as harsh metal scraping sounds, there were screeches, bird-like chirps, clicking sounds and high, piercing

The Hotel Nacionale in Havana, Cuba, where many visiting American diplomats and government officials experienced symptoms of Havana syndrome.

grating noises. In a recent television documentary for the American channel CBS, a sufferer named only as 'Carrie', an FBI agent, described being hit with full force by the illness at her home in Florida. 'Inside my right ear, it was like a dentist drilling on steroids,' she recalled. 'That feeling when it gets too close to your ear drum… It was like that but times ten.'

Sudden afflictions like these were reportedly followed by chronic health problems, with symptoms varying between different sufferers. Carrie, for example, said she went on to have problems with her concentration and memory. According to Ali Asadi-Pooya, in 'Havana syndrome: a scoping review of the existing literature' (December 2023), 'More than half of the afflicted said they also experienced blurry vision with a sensitivity to light. Other sufferers also reported feeling highly intense pressure feelings or vibrations in their head, coupled with ear pain and headaches, and alongside such symptoms as forgetfulness and poor concentration. Around one-third reported ear pain, tinnitus (ringing in the ears) and a reduction in hearing, while others were affected by spells of dizziness or unsteadiness while walking, aka POTS (Postural Orthostatic Tachycardia Syndrome).'

'A very unusual attack'

In 2017, the US government expelled two Cuban diplomats from the United States. Government spokeswoman, Heather Nauert, said, 'The two Cuban diplomats were "asked to leave" in May 2017', but she said their departure was not a reciprocity action over the incidents. Cuban officials, however, said that it would 'never allow its soil to be used for actions against diplomats and that it is willing to cooperate with the US to clarify the incidents.' Cuban officials said expelling their diplomats was 'unjustified and baseless'.

While the US the government was unwilling to blame potential attacks on any single country or adversary in public, voices in Washington rose in complaint against certain parties. Republican Senator, Marco Rubio, said in a statement, 'The Cuban government has been harassing US personnel working in Havana for decades. This has not stopped with President Obama's appeasement. Personal harm to US officials shows the extent the Castro regime will go to and clearly violates international norms.'

Then, in September that same year, the government removed non-essential staff from its embassy in Havana and warned US citizens not to travel to Cuba in case they came under similar attack. President Donald Trump later said he believed that Cuba was responsible for the strange spate of weird symptoms, suggesting it was a 'very unusual attack'. The general speculation at that time was that the Cuban government – or a faction of it – was opposed to improving US and Cuban relations and might somehow be responsible for this. Nervous Cuban security services were allegedly worried about an influx of US personnel and wanted to keep their eyes on things.

Many government and non-government agencies over the years have conducted investigations into the 'anomalous health condition' as some officials dubbed it. Those who investigated the AHIs – as the US government calls 'Havana Syndrome'; it's short for 'Anomalous Health Incidents' – including the State Department, the Department of Defense and the Central Intelligence Agency (CIA) to name a few, did their best but none of their investigations has been able to determine the cause with absolute certainty. And few were willing to point to a specific government or particular foreign agency as the possible culprit. UK intelligence has suggested to media outlets like the BBC that perhaps Cuban intelligence was seeking to hamper or track electronic devices using microwave technology and this might be affecting staff caught in their vicinity. Another suggestion from insiders at British intelligence was that electronic high-tech equipment might have malfunctioned, causing microwave or electronic pollution, leading to bad reactions in some people.

In January 2022, the CIA denied foreign governments were involved in most of the 1,000 cases it had reviewed. However, there were around two dozen cases that could not be ruled out as having a hostile cause, whether that was due to foreign governments or criminal activities. On the other hand, some people suggested the syndrome was just a flight of fancy, with Senator J. D. Vance, a close Trump ally, writing on Twitter, 'Feels like a lot of journalists have lost their minds,' after reading about Havana Syndrome in the press.

For their part, Cuban scientists wondered if the American Embassy had succumbed to some kind of mass hysteria. Speaking to the *Washington Post*, Mitchell Valdés-Sosa, director of the Cuban Neuroscience Center, said, 'If your government comes and tells you, "You're under attack. We have to rapidly get you out of there," and some people start feeling sick, there's a possibility of psychological contagion.' But why would the US government want to do such a thing?

By March 2023, the office of the Director of National Intelligence (ODNI) issued a later redacted report, saying it was 'very unlikely' that AHIs were caused by any foreign adversary. This report understandably caused considerable upset and anger among intelligence officers and their family members. They claimed they had suffered very significantly and, in a lot of cases, suffered irreversible health consequences at the hands of an unknown enemy force. Many of the victims apparently felt let down by their government for neglecting to protect them as well as in failing to identify the cause of their predicament.

Does Havana Syndrome exist?

The US National Institute of Health (NIH) conducted a five-year study of patients between 2020 and 2024. 'Our goal was to conduct thorough, objective and reproducible evaluations to see if we could identify structural brain or biological differences in people who reported AHIs,' said Leighton Chan, MD, acting chief scientific officer at the NIH Clinical Center. However, he was still unable to offer a clear idea of what happened. Chan stated that patients with Havana Syndrome do have very real symptoms, adding that these are both disabling and difficult to treat. They believe critics of the NIH's five-year-long study may have missed clues due to the limits of existing technology. The NIH tests involved MRI brain scans and other blood tests as well as visual and auditory assessments of those who believed they were affected.

But this 'does not exclude that an adverse event (such as an energy beam) impacting the brain occurred at the time of the AHI,' said Carlo Pierpaoli, who led the study. David Relman of Stanford University, who has led previous research into Havana, was critical of the long study and said the NIH study 'was flawed as not all brain injuries were detectable with the tests used'.

The NIH study was not designed to assess the likelihood of the symptoms associated with Havana Syndrome possibly being caused by the use of a weapon. It looked at many possible causes.

Sonic or directed-energy weapon

Could a secret sound- or energy-based weapon deployed by a hostile nation like China, Russia, Cuba or North Korea against American and Canadian government workers be the cause of a seemingly related set of symptoms reported by different people around the world?

In 2019, some US officials suggested that unidentified and unknown technologies, such as ultrasound or microwave-based weapons, were the likely cause. In the early years of the syndrome, in 2016 and 2017, US intelligence services and government officials were reported in the press as suspecting that Russian military intelligence was responsible.

The US Navy has carried out research into directed-energy weapons, which it defines as electromagnetic systems capable of converting chemical or electrical energy into radiated energy. This focused energy causes the target physical damage that degrades, neutralizes or finally destroys it. Through its research into this area, the US Navy's goal is to protect sailors who might be exposed to such an attack. Could foreign powers use similar systems to cause Havana Syndrome?

Before the Havana embassy was ever reported as a target for a syndrome, a US government employee stationed at the consulate in Frankfurt in 2014 was mysteriously knocked unconscious by something like a strong energy beam. The victim was later diagnosed with a traumatic brain injury, but the employee believed its origin was a directed-energy weapon used by members of a Geneva-based unit known as '29155'. It's been suggested in *The Insider*, a Russia-focused, independent media outlet, that secret operatives working for Unit 29155 travel around the world under cover and some of them were stationed at strategic places just before, or at the time of, the reported anomalous health incidents or AHIs. According to a former high-ranking CIA officer, 'Unit 29155's scope is global for conducting lethal operations and acts of sabotage.'

A report published in 2022 by the US National Academies of Sciences, Engineering and Medicine concluded that pulsed electromagnetic energy or microwave energy was still the most likely culprit in many of the cases. Microwaves and electromagnetic energy are very similar to each other. Electromagnetic waves are a spectrum of waves that includes radio waves, microwaves and gamma rays.

The report also noted that Russia had a long history of studying and developing this kind of technology. In 1978, James Lin, a professor at the University of Illinois, was invited to visit a Soviet research station in the town of Pushchino near Moscow, where they were trying to test the effects of microwaves on humans. 'They had a very elaborate, very well-equipped laboratory,' he said sarcastically, 'The test subject would sit in a drum of salty seawater with their head sticking out. Then microwaves would be fired at their brain.'

The Russian scientists suspected that the microwaves interacted with the nervous system and wanted to question Professor Lin on his views. Earlier, Americans apparently could find no proof of Communist-bloc microwave weapons but later understood that they had tried out experiments where microwaves were pulsed at the throat of frogs until their hearts stopped.

Spycatching

It's well known that embassies are constantly under surveillance by their host country; there is a long history of the host's intelligence services monitoring the activities of foreign embassy officials on the assumption that some of them will be spies.

James Lewis, senior vice president and director of the Technology and Public Policy Program at the Center for Strategic and International Studies (CSIS) in Washington DC, suggested that the surveillance technology being used might be too highly powered for the task. Reports in the 1970s, about health problems at the US embassy in Moscow that bore similarities to those reported in Havana, could have been the result of microwave-based surveillance devices that were not working correctly. Lewis told the *Guardian* in 2017, 'It was much more likely that a sonic surveillance device, designed to remotely pick up the vibrations caused by speech, could have been wrongly configured and emitted harmful sound waves as a result.'

In his infamous 1987 book, *Spycatcher*, which was initially banned by the UK government for its revelations about the world of espionage, former MI5 agent, Peter Wright, described an ingenious surveillance device placed in the main meeting room of the Russian Embassy in London as a gift to the Russian Ambassador. It was a model of the Kremlin in Moscow crafted from thin wood, so that when Russian officials spoke to each other it would quietly vibrate and create soundwaves, rather like the body of an acoustic guitar. The model's 'tune' was played to

MI5 agents across the street, aiming at a highly sensitive receiver that converted the vibrations into audio. This allowed them to listen to the Russians covertly without an electronic bug, which was more likely to have been discovered. Years earlier, in 1945, the Russians had presented the Americans with a similar device known as 'The Thing', concealed in a carved wooden Great Seal of the United States. It wasn't discovered until 1951 when surveillance operators at the British Embassy accidentally overheard American conversations on an open Soviet Air Force radio channel as the Soviets were beaming radio waves at the US ambassador's office to pick up vibrations from 'The Thing'.

If the Russians had such capabilities in 1945, it would not be surprising that, decades later, they had developed technologies that could be aimed at sensitive buildings such as embassies. Perhaps the splitting headaches, memory loss and other symptoms complained of by Americans in embassies around the world were side-effects of a beaming device that was not designed to make people ill, but rather to listen in to conversations, but which may have been too powerful and also might have been used excessively over a long period of time.

In Moscow, during the 1970s, staff at the American Embassy were subjected to waves from a nearby transmitter. For around 25 years, beginning sometime in the early-1950s, the 10-storey US Embassy in Moscow was exposed to a beam of low-level microwaves. Dubbed 'the Moscow signal', most people working inside the building were totally unaware of what was going on. Microwave beams from an antenna on the balcony of a nearby Soviet apartment were directed to pass through the upper floors of the embassy. There, the ambassador's office and more sensitive work was carried out. The Americans became aware of its operation from the 1950s on, and plans were made to monitor the antenna from a room on the 10th floor. It was kept top secret from all but a few inside the building. 'We were trying to figure out just what might be its purpose,' said Jack Matlock, senior diplomat at the embassy in the mid-70s. However, things began to come out when the new ambassador, Walter Stoessel, arrived to take over in 1974. He wanted everyone to be told the truth and threatened to resign if they were not. 'That caused something like panic,' recalled Mr Matlock. The US State Department played down any risks, however. Sadly, Stoessel later died of leukaemia at the age of 66, with symptoms that included bleeding from the eyes.

Perhaps there was a malign intent behind the device; it could have been a covert method of assassinating specific officials, such as ambassadors or suspected spies, who would get increasingly sick over time, eventually appearing to die a natural death that in fact was triggered by regular energy or soundwaves beamed into their office and homes. It's worth remembering here that families of those affected were also sometimes affected by Havana Syndrome-type symptoms.

Vaccine side-effects?

The US Embassy in Havana reopened in 2015 after extensive renovation. This could have provided ample opportunity for devices to be installed into the building structure by agents posing as building contractors that would monitor or even harm people working there. However, that does not explain the other cases reported around the world. Another explanation might lie in the vaccinations that were given to embassy staff prior to their postings to various countries.

While vaccines offer protection from various tropical diseases, they can and often do have side-effects. Could the various issues reported as Havana Syndrome come down to a bad batch of vaccines, or their side-effects on certain vulnerable people? A major study would be required to either rule it out or count it in.

Physical or psychological factors

Certain studies in 2021 suggested that psychological factors lay behind Havana Syndrome symptoms, while others pointed towards environmental triggers. Some scientists have even suggested pre-existing medical conditions as possible causes of these distressing health problems.

One interesting scenario was presented by medical sociologist, Robert Bartholomew, co-author of *Havana Syndrome: Mass Psychogenic*

Illness and the Real Story Behind the Embassy Mystery and Hysteria. He suggested that the mysterious syndrome resulted from what he called 'classic mass psychology'. High-status embassy personnel working in a foreign country and in a stressful environment would report the initial symptoms, which alerted other officials in embassies elsewhere. This could have created a 'ripple effect', making others think they, too, might be ill, resulting in psychological (rather than physical) injury – that is, a psychosomatically induced syndrome brought about through stress, leading to a widening health scare fuelled by what Bartholomew called 'moral panic'.

If this is true, then it suggests a modern version of the hysteria witnessed during the witch trials in 17th-century Salem, New England, where there was also a fast-spreading, large-scale mysterious 'affliction', whipped up by a clear thread of moralizing and panic. Could Havana Syndrome have been an extreme reaction to the stress of living and working in a foreign environment, fully aware that one is being monitored at work and probably at home too? Or was something, or someone, more sinister actually targeting those individuals with some kind of invisible force – a mystery and a curse of a very different kind.

THE MYSTERY OF THE GOLD LEAF LADY

The mystery of the 'Gold Leaf Lady' is particularly intriguing, not least because its details were so unusual. It could be compared to accounts of stigmata, wounds, scars or blood that suddenly appear on someone's body in locations corresponding to the crucifixion wounds of Jesus Christ. This story concerns a woman who also seemed to be able to manifest something on her body, except in this case it was a kind of metallic substance rather than blood or injuries (although it's reported that she did once manifest stigmata-type of reddish patches on her skin in the shapes of a cross and of a butterfly). For many people in our age of social media, maybe the most baffling element of this mystery is that this particular woman did not seem especially keen to share and display what many believed were genuine psychic abilities.

We do not know the full name of the woman who became known as 'The Gold Leaf Lady'. She presented herself in 1987 as a candidate to study under psychologist, Berthold E. Schwarz. She preferred to be known only as 'Katie', and she is reported to have been living in Florida when the weird manifestations happened.

Katie undoubtedly had a very tough life; she was described as functionally illiterate and was barely able to write her own name, having only been educated to first-grade level (around age seven). This was because, at that young age, she had dropped out of school to care for her poorly mother, who reportedly suffered with serious psychogenic paralysis, itself an unusual condition where the sufferer loses motor function after psychological or emotional trauma.

The mother's illness was brought on by family stress and could be connected to her daughter's later manifestations. Katie's very first supernatural experience occurred when she was 18 years old in 1974, when she claimed that she saw an unknown man walk past her and literally disappear. A few days later, while looking through an old family photo album with her husband, Katie flicked over a few pages and recognized a familiar face in one photograph, the ghostly man she had seen walk past her and vanish. The odd thing was that it was her deceased father-in-law, whom she had never met. With a shudder, she realised that he was the ghostly man that she had seen walking past her.

Over the next few years, Katie's psychic experiences and her own abilities gradually increased. Under observation initially from Schwarz in 1985 and then a few years later with parapsychologist, Stephen E. Braude, emeritus professor of the philosophy department at the University of Maryland, Katie demonstrated the bending of spoons, the ability to germinate seeds in her hand, writing in French quatrains like medieval French mystic Nostradamus – remember, she was functionally illiterate – and helping the police to solve burglary cases. However, when Braude tried to converse with her in everyday French while she was in a trance, she had no idea what was being said. This does not mean she was a fraud; it just means that a certain part of her was perhaps able to do certain tasks while other conscious parts of her mind were switched off.

If this sounds confusing, perhaps consider yourself consuming a meal. Part of you does the conscious act of chewing, say, an apple, then you swallow it. But if someone was to ask you, how do you then digest it, most people, including yourself, would not fully understand the process. Yet it is still your own body going through that process, while the waking self is unconscious. It is automatic. Equally, the process Katie employed in writing is known as automatic writing, it works in some far-off reach of the brain – Katie just held the pen and her unconscious mind did the rest. For example, many mediums have spoken in foreign languages to those able to understand them, yet when they come out of the trance state that they previously entered to speak in those languages, they often have very little memory of what was said or even how to speak in another tongue.

'Sweating' metal

Katie claimed that she began to display the strange physical effects that earned her the unusual nickname around 1986. Her body, she said, would begin to glisten slightly, taking on a gold sheen or tone, then revert to normal after an hour or so. At other times, droplets of a gold colour would appear on her body and these droplets would form into a foil-like 'gold leaf' covering areas of her skin. The leaf appeared on her face – then around her eyes, on her ears and lips and on her limbs, stomach and back. It was recorded as having manifested more than 100 times. Despite Katie's claims to other psychic abilities, it was the mysterious sweating of gold leaf that most interested parapsychologists.

Psychic materialization?

For the parapsychologists, one fascinating question was whether the leaf was being produced by Katie's body or being psychically materialized or 'apported' on to her skin from elsewhere. An apport is supposedly a psychic transfer of a physical object or matter from one place to another; often these happen in a séance setting and typical apports are old coins, newspapers and flowers, rather than 'gold' leaf. The metallic leaf that was appearing on Katie's body was later analysed and found to be brass, an alloy comprising 80 per cent copper and 20 per cent zinc. A sceptical take on this is that the alloy leaf would have been cheaper to purchase than real gold leaf, if indeed the materialized leaf was not genuinely paranormal.

Sceptics suggested that Katie had taken a brass-type material, dissolved it in a liquid and applied it to her body – then, when the liquid evaporated, witnesses would see the golden-colour leaf appear on her body as if by some mysterious force. Scientists at the prestigious Johns Hopkins University in Baltimore studied the material and pointed out that, if that this is what happened, the metal would show as a crystalline structure. But in fact it displayed a granular structure more akin to foil.

As well as manifesting on Katie's body many times, in one instance the gold leaf reportedly appeared around a framed photograph of her deceased mother. This could be significant because when Katie was a young girl her mother suffered a family trauma – Katie's sister leaving and taking her own baby with her – that had the effect of leaving her physically dependent on Katie.

If her mother was effectively becoming the 'baby' to be looked after and manifesting her own psychological hurt as paralysis, could Katie also be psychically producing phenomena of some kind as an emotional response? She might have subconsciously manifested the gold leaf around her mother's photograph, perhaps to signal that her mother was the most important person in her life.

Katie's youth and lack of education meant she was not able to provide financial security for her mother, so this could be a way of showing her mother's value to her and also of displaying visually the value of her own abilities. Her emerging psychic abilities enabled her to help others, for example by aiding police investigations and by doing psychic readings for people in her community. But could the fact that the 'gold leaf' was nothing more valuable than brass be another visual reflection of her refusal to take money for helping others, so she couldn't be accused of, or feel guilty for, satisfying her own selfish desires? Katie claimed that she didn't welcome the gold leaf phenomenon; it often happened while she was out shopping, which she found embarrassing. It also caused itching and, after it faded away, a redness would appear on her skin where it had materialized: maybe this was some kind of psychic eczema.

Physical or emotional causes

Sceptics also suggested that Katie was hiding the material somewhere on her body and using sleight of hand like a magician, would place it on her face or other parts of her body. However, in practice, this kind of fine metallic foil is hard to move around because it carries static and tends to stick to the hands. No evidence was ever found of traces of foil on Katie's hands. According to researcher, Stephen E. Braude, who wrote about the case, a skilled magician was asked to reproduce what Katie had claimed to do naturally and could not do so.

Another solution is that somehow Katie was sweating this material out of her body. Stephen Braude pointed out that if this were the case, she would have to have lethal amounts of copper within her body to begin with. She would be dead before she could sweat it out. Braude also recalled that when Katie met his wife for the first time and they hugged, within the space of a few seconds at most a piece of gold leaf appeared on Katie's face. This could suggest that if it was a true phenomenon, then the leaf was likely to manifest after some kind of social interaction or emotional change, such as the joy of meeting the wife of a trusted friend, or perhaps anxiety at meeting someone new. This might explain why Katie could not manifest proper evidence of gold leaf during videotaped sessions; there was no emotional stimulation or personal connection to produce a manifestation.

Diamond-shape object

Just as the leaf appeared around her mother's picture frame, it would mysteriously appear in sealed containers around the test laboratory as well as Katie's body. It appeared to manifest without her will being involved and was more spontaneous. Friends said they could sit with her for hours and nothing would happen, and other times it would just occur. Unfortunately, researchers never managed to capture the leaf appearing on her body on video. While a sceptic will say this was because she did not want a camera to capture her sleight of hand, those who think these events were paranormal in origin might respond that being filmed is likely to make any 'civilian' nervous, and maybe this affected Katie's ability to manifest the gold leaf.

In July 1990, researchers were able to video Katie supposedly producing a diamond-shaped object that fell out of her eye. If she was faking the occurrence, it would be much more convenient to manifest something from her mouth. It was also claimed that Katie manifested a gold chain from her ear, and other objects did appear from her mouth. Of course, she could have hidden these before they were sighted by witnesses. In tests, though, Katie was always meticulously searched by her psychiatrist, who was also her doctor, who never found anything to suggest that she was hiding any material within her person.

Poltergeist phenomena

Stephen Braude suggested that Katie, being a younger woman and because of her limited intellect, may be spontaneously and unconsciously produced strange events like a poltergeist or even a stigmatist. She was a young woman with little outlet for her thoughts and feelings due to a lack of education and opportunities. Poltergeists ('noisy ghosts' in German) are thought to haunt in attention-seeking ways, by making physical objects fly across a room by themselves, or having writing suddenly appear on walls, or causing fires to break out. Some studies of such cases propose teenagers as potential causes, especially girls. The thinking goes that they are often frustrated by societal and familial rules dictating their behaviour, at a time when they are also undergoing profound physical and emotional changes as they move from childhood to adulthood. Their pent-up emotions might erupt into psychokinetic effects, which could include manifesting gold leaf.

In Braude's opinion, Katie was unconsciously an agent of physical phenomena in the same way as a poltergeist manifests as flying objects or a stigmatist manifests wounds on their body without any apparent injury. As well as the role Katie's mother and her emotional issues may have played in physical manifestations, marriage can also be a fertile ground for emotional difficulties. If an individual's inner turmoil and frustration can stir up some kind of psychic storm, Katie's unhappy marriage might have added fuel to the fire. According to Braude, Katie unconsciously 'discharged' or projected her intense, pent-up feelings in a highly psychic way.

Shortly after Katie's marriage to her husband Tom, she told Braude that a strange knocking sound started to be heard in the house and things began to appear and disappear – one day, a set of carving knives mysteriously appeared in the kitchen. A few days after that, Tom remarked to Katie that it was no use things appearing unless it was money. That was when Katie manifested the 'gold leaf' for the first time. Perhaps her subconscious desire was to give her husband what he wanted, but another part of her thought it impossible, so she manifested a kind of hybrid 'fool's gold' to reflect that turmoil. Alternatively, the whole thing could have been a form of payback to her husband. Braude thought this allowed Katie to express her rage and anger towards her husband in a safe way, by doing so psychically. Materializing the carving knives might have symbolized her suppressed desire to injure her husband because she was angry at him.

Braude's research identified another example of what he said were the 'psychokinetic' effects of an unhappy marriage. A woman in an abusive relationship in Maryland was a keen amateur photographer. Many of her images featured unusual squiggles in the sky that were not there when she took the photos. The squiggles appeared in a photo of her husband looking very angry, forming the word 'Help'. Of course, not every teenager or person trapped in an unhappy or abusive marriage will alter images, move objects or manifest physical phenomena.

Attention-seeking

Could Katie have been faking the manifestations in some way to get media exposure or to make money? The fact that she did not agree to her surname being disclosed indicates that she wished to avoid public exposure, rather than seek it. Braude pointed out that she received no money from her abilities or fame, even when she helped police through her psychic abilities. Instead, she was earning her living as a house cleaner. She did accept expenses related to travelling somewhere to be tested, but avoided further contact with those who offered payment.

In 1990, the American television programme *Unsolved Mysteries* filmed an episode about Katie's case, again without revealing her surname. While the camera crew didn't manage to capture her manifesting the gold leaf on her body, crew members did observe small amounts of the leaf appearing on her when they were not filming.

In the programme, Paul Kurtz, professor emeritus of philosophy at the University of New York at Buffalo, claimed Katie was no more than a clever fraudster. He asked two students to recreate the gold leaf 'sweating' using dutch metal, an imitation gold leaf comprising copper and zinc that can be bought in craft shops. The students used a variety of glues and sprays to make the material adhere to their bodies, which caused it to become sticky and change colour. No such colour change was detected, nor was there any sticky residue left when the gold leaf appeared on Katie.

On the same programme, a professional magician explained how Katie could have made the diamond-shaped gem 'appear' from her eye: by secreting the stone in between her fingers under her wedding ring and then appearing to pop it out of her eye.

On the other hand, Stephen Braude claimed that he actually saw gold leaf appear on Katie when her hands were not close enough to have placed it herself. He recalled being seated across a table from Katie, about 1 m (3 ft) away. While the two were talking, a small piece of the gold leaf suddenly appeared on her face. Her hands were resting on the table when this occurred. Katie's husband, Tom, was sitting next to her and he was observed to be doing nothing at the time; had he placed the leaf on her face, he would clearly have been seen. Braude believed the gold leaf appeared without any interference from him.

'The Good Lord gave me a gift'

While some people are convinced that Katie faked her so-called gold leaf manifestations, Braude points out that sceptics were not able to reproduce the same effects convincingly. He eventually lost touch with Katie and she continued her life out of the public gaze. It's not clear what became of the mysterious woman with her highly unusual psychic talent, although a YouTube commentator claiming to be her son later said her full name was Katie Kennedy and that she passed away peacefully in a Florida hospital in March 2020. He also claimed that she was able to do things other people couldn't comprehend and that she told him, 'The good Lord gave me a gift to help people', and that her mysterious abilities were not for sale.

Thus, we can't know for sure whether Katie was an exceptionally clever and imaginative fraudster, a woman who unconsciously expressed her emotions in the most unusual way or a genuine psychic. Maybe her real gift was emotional intelligence rather than psychical power: that is, her understanding of the value that such powers afford – to help other people, rather than oneself.

CHAPTER 4

MESSAGES FROM AFAR

These days, computers are the norm in most homes. But back in the late-1970s, they were the preserve of universities, research institutes and the military. They only began to enter mass usage – and even then only slowly – from the early-1980s, when they were little by little introduced into schools and businesses. Home and business computers were, to all intents and purposes, little more than glorified electric typewriters, hooked up to very basic dot-matrix printers. Most people barely understood how these machines functioned and few were able to operate them. Imagine, then, the wonder and confusion felt when a computer in 1977 received a 'message' that seemingly came from somewhere deep in outer space – and, then again, a few years later when another early PC was involved in correspondence with another user apparently writing from Tudor times as well as with an entity sending messages from the future!

THE 'WOW!' SIGNAL

For many who remember it, 1977 was an eventful year. Queen Elizabeth II celebrated her Silver Jubilee in the UK, *Star Wars* was breaking box-office records at the cinema, Elvis Presley's sudden death shocked his fans, Apple Computers released their first home computer and the *Voyager 1* space probe was launched to explore the outer reaches of the solar system. It may have been much lower profile, but for the scientists involved there was another truly exciting, and unexplained, event that year. They received what seemed to be a communication from deep space, which they called the 'Wow!' signal. What was this unusual transmission? A greeting in a kind of cosmic code? A gleam of celestial torchlight in the darkened forest of the universe?

'Big Ear' hears something new

Instead of travelling to distant stars, today scientists and astronomers can observe the 'exoplanets' of far-flung solar systems courtesy of NASA's James Webb Telescope, which was launched in 2021 to orbit the Sun and uses infrared technology. However, back in 1977, anything heard from space came via the medium of radio waves and the 'Wow!' signal arrived via one of the electronic listening ears using this technology.

On 15 August, the 'Wow!' signal was picked up by the 'Big Ear' radio telescope as it was called, which was based at Ohio State University in the US. A famous slogan of the time, 'In Space, no one can hear you scream', adorned the poster of the science fiction horror film, *Alien*. The film-makers were indeed right, for in the vacuum of space where there is no air, the sound of screams or indeed any other noises could not be heard. Was the 'Wow!' signal friendly though? Or was it something that might, as the film poster suggested, be likely to make us scream?

Officially, we don't have the technology yet to travel to distant stars! The *Voyager 1* space probe took around 49 years travelling through our solar system, just to pass outside the influence of our Sun, and it's only now entering the area beyond our local celestial neighbourhood! We just do not have the speed to reach other far distant planets in our lifetime unless, of course, there is something hidden in a secret hangar in Area 51 that we have not yet got the memo about!

So instead of trying to travel to faraway stars, scientists and astronomers are trying to observe the universe in a number of new ways. Using the James Webb telescope, we can now view Exoplanets. These are planets that are in far-distant solar systems, beyond the reach of ordinary Earth-based telescopes. Since the first one was discovered in the early-1990s, we have found around 4,000 planets that we have officially catalogued.

A strange signal

Back in 1977, working on the 'Big Ear' radio telescope, astronomer Jerry R. Ehman noticed that their fixed array had picked up a signal anomaly while performing a routine check of data recorded by his institution's powerful instrument on a strong narrowband radio frequency. The astronomers at the university had been looking for signs of intelligent life out there in the cosmos since 1961 when 'Big Ear' was built. Now, suddenly, it appeared as if they might just have something in the form of an innocuous-looking set of letters and numbers that Ehman found when he was reviewing data from signals received by the telescope. He noticed the code, '6EQUJ5', on a computer print-out.

What this code represented to experts was a radio signal far stronger than any the 'Big Ear' telescope had ever recorded before. It appeared to have originated from the direction of the constellation Sagittarius, in a hitherto quiet corner of the Milky Way. Was it just cosmic 'noise', the kind of radiation constantly emitted by our Sun and by the billions of stars that fill the universe, or was it a sign or a message sent by some unknown extraterrestrial intelligence? Whatever it was, it was not normal – hence Ehman scribbling 'Wow!' next to the '6EQUJ5' code on the print-out. This still-unexplained phenomenon is known as the 'Wow!' message to this day.

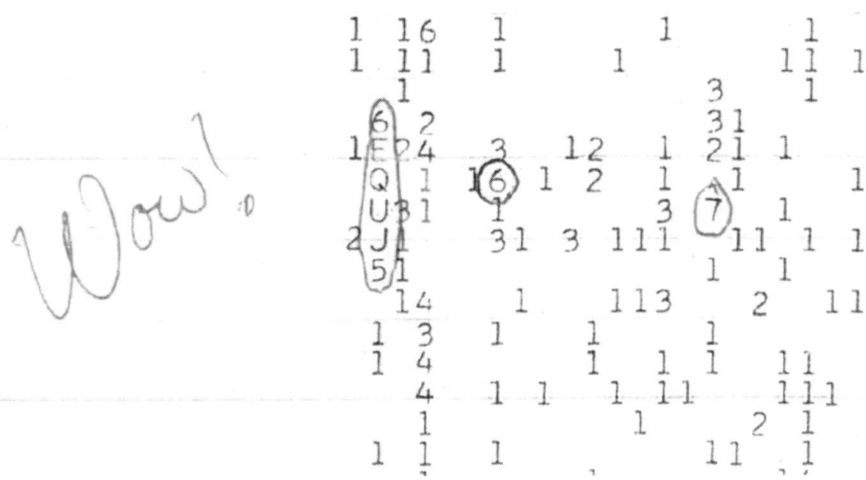

The Wow! signal, detected in 1977.

Seventy-two seconds of 'Wow!'

What made the 'Wow!' message shine out like a beacon was its intensity and its duration. For years, radio telescopes such as Big Ear had been detecting what astrophysicists today call cosmic background radiation, the faint echo of the Big Bang that permeates the universe as a constant but low-level hum, or the louder and more powerful regular pulses of electromagnetic energy that are the result of supernovae or other explosive events in space.

But neither of these things could explain a signal that lasted a full 72 seconds, came from an unexpected corner of the night sky and which happened only once. Could the length indicate it was a distant alien civilization sending out a one-off communication to any developing planets out there? Were aliens low on power maybe or could there have been some kind of hidden code within the number 72?

It seems that Ehman and his colleagues at Ohio State University were able to account for the length of the signal for a reason that was far more down to earth than alien. At twice the size of a football pitch, the 'Big Ear' radio telescope was huge. It had also been built in a fixed position in order to save money, so it could not rotate and sweep across the night sky as some other radio telescopes are able to do. It could, though, be adjusted for height to look up and down, rather than across from left to right. Due to the speed of Earth's rotation, this meant that 'Big Ear' could capture any segment of the night sky within its range of movement, but the telescope could only listen in on any given point across the night sky for a total of 72 seconds. After that, the area it was observing would move out of range as the Earth rotated and the next segment of sky took its place.

In this respect, the signal was like the beam of light from a lighthouse, which takes 72 seconds to complete one full rotation, with the ship at sea acting as the 'Big Ear' radio telescope. The ship (or telescope) would see the light (or signal) getting more intense as it moved through its cycle, to the point when, halfway through at 36 seconds of transmission, it would be at peak intensity and 'shining' directly at the ship. After that, it would gradually fade, before starting its next rotation. This is precisely how the unusual signal behaved.

The astronomers were certain they had received a communication of some kind in the form a remote, unknown kind of blip. But as for who or what sent the signal – and how – that was another story, and one that was open to all manner of interpretations.

Protected spectrum

The big question was could the 'Wow!' signal really have come from deep space, or did the transmission originate from Earth? The signal was received at a frequency of 1420 MHz, which was within the radio reception range astronomers called the 'protected spectrum'. This is part of the wavelength that Earth-bound broadcasters keep free because it is reserved exclusively for satellite communications. It's rather like a CB radio breaking channel, where users always keep their messages brief rather than chatting.

In astronomical terms, scientists have a similar frequency range reserved for research – a bit like Channel 19 in CB radio – in which Earth-based transmissions are forbidden. However, a 2010 study revealed several instances of transmissions of terrestrial-based broadcasts. These may have been either interference from nearby frequencies or someone was illegally transmitting within the forbidden zone. If someone had used this frequency to send the 'Wow!' signal, they had either done it illegally or mistakenly. Or, perhaps, the message had been sent for some secret purpose and 'Big Ear' had simply stumbled upon it.

Whatever the reason, if the 'Wow!' signal originated on Earth, it had come from a highly unusual source. That might explain why it was only received once.

It is possible the unexplained signal could have originated away from Earth. All atoms in the universe are in constant states of motion, and the range and intensity of this motion is measured as their electro-magnetic – or 'radio' – frequency. The natural radio frequency of neutral hydrogen, one of the most common elements in the universe, just happens to be 1420 MHz. Given the huge number of radio frequencies to choose from, could it be that an intelligent form of extraterrestrial life would be aware of this fact and chose to use this particular frequency to broadcast its message to Earth, safe in the knowledge it was being transmitted on the radio wavelength where it was most likely to be intercepted?

In 1977, all satellites in orbit at the time were checked to see if they were somehow broadcasting on that reserved frequency and none were found to be doing so. The 'Wow!' signal was found to be a narrow band transmission, which generally suggests it would have been artificial in nature. This was around 10Khz in range, which prevents a kind of 'spill over' into other radio bands. However, many people are reluctant to believe that aliens may have sent the 'Wow!' signal and have put forward other ideas as to its origin.

Bounced-back signal?

Could the signal have been a transmission sent on Earth that somehow bounced off a planet or celestial object, such as a moon or a comet, before coming back to us? According to experts, none of the other planets in the solar system was in that area of the night sky when the signal was sent. Nor was there any sign of known comets in the area, which could have thrown out a 'spiked' signal like that, plus comets do not emit hydrogen-type radio signals either. An alternative explanation could be a technical issue with the 'Big Ear' radio telescope. Once the signal arrived, checks were made to ensure that no technical issues existed, so that can also be ruled out.

Of course, following the 'Wow!' signal, 'Big Ear' and other radio telescopes were aimed many more times at the area of the sky from which it came. Unfortunately, they never again picked up a repeat of the message.

If it really was a one-time-only communication from an unknown alien civilization, what were they trying to say? That we will probably never know. It could even be that it was not a message as such but more a means of making contact – a cosmic handshake, as it were to let us know there is something else out there. If the 'Wow!' radio signal did come from some alien civilization, what could it possibly say? Well sadly, not much. It is more what can be implied from it. If it is alien in nature, then it says or rather shows that aliens have radio transmission capabilities and, at the very least, possess technology capable of matching ours, but of course they could very well belong to a much older civilisation and using radio could be their way of saying hello to the less-evolved creatures of the universe, perhaps meaning us!

SETI

In the meantime, has the enthusiasm around the 'Wow!' signal fizzled out? The answer is a loud 'No!' After all, this unexplained signal is just one element of the much wider mystery about whether we are alone in the universe and it's a question astronomers, physicists and analysts have been asking for decades, if not centuries. They call it the search for extraterrestrial intelligence (SETI) and it's an activity that has its own official organization, the SETI Institute, founded in 1984. This is not to mention the armies of independent researchers, ufologists and alien hunters worldwide, all trying to make contact with life beyond our planet by plugging into the vast array of online open-source data, from social media to satellite mapping.

In the years since the 'Wow!' signal was received, improvements in space technology mean that SETI investigators now have far more opportunities than ever before to explore the mysteries of the universe. Beginning with *Voyager 1*, space probes and space-based instruments, such as the Hubble Telescope (launched in 1990) and the James Webb Space Telescope (2021), have been looking ever deeper into the cosmos and sending back images and data that are constantly enriching our understanding of the universe.

Back on Earth, ever more powerful and sophisticated radio telescopes are picking up signals that date back to the immediate aftermath of the Big Bang. The Very Large Array is a group of 28 radio telescopes in New Mexico that have been listening to the skies since 1980, while the 500-m Aperture Spherical Telescope (FAST) in Guizhou, China, which went live in 2020, is the world's largest radio telescope and is collecting vast amounts of data. Until we develop the capacity to build spacecraft with the speed to reach distant stars and planets, we will continue to rely on these probes, space telescopes and radio telescopes to 'visit' them for us and send back information that alien hunters back here on Earth can pore over.

Another 'Wow!' signal?

According to one alien hunter, we have already been contacted by a non-human intelligence, although, he claims, SETI researchers have been reluctant to release the proof for years. Simon Holland is a former BBC video editor and director based in France, from where he broadcasts a regular Youtube show on space exploration. In October 2024, the self-styled 'Professor Simon' told media outlets, including the *Daily Mail* newspaper, that on 29 April 2019 an Oxford University-backed project called Breakthrough Listen, which connects up all the huge and varied radio telescopes around the world, received a five-hour-long burst of radio waves from an unknown source in a region of space channel. In other words, he believes we have actually found evidence for ET picking up that phone and making that call!

And shockingly, the SETI researchers have been sitting on that recorded message for years, withholding it from the world! Was this a cover-up? Since the first distant planet was discovered in the early 1990s, using an earlier space telescope, we have found around 4,000 new planets that we have officially catalogued! This includes Proxima Centauri, about 4.2 light years from Earth. The signal from there was detected by the Murriyang radio telescope at the Parkes Observatory in New South Wales, Australia and was, according to one of the research teams that analyzed it, 'on a par' with the 'Wow!' signal.

So why has this 'message' not been more widely publicized? 'We have found a non-human extraterrestrial intelligence in our galaxy,' Simon Holland told the *Daily Mail*, 'and people don't know about it.' While he acknowledged that scientists at the Breakthrough Listen project were right to be careful in their analysis of the signal and not jump to conclusions, he also felt that, by October 2024 when he spoke to the

British newspaper, enough time had passed for them to have worked out what they thought of it. Indeed, he even told the *Daily Mail* he believed that the Breakthrough Listen project was on the verge of announcing that what they called the BLC-1 (Breakthrough Listen Candidate-1) message could have been received from an extraterrestrial source. At the time of writing, however, no such announcement has been made.

This is frustrating, because, as 'Professor Simon' revealed, scientists operating the 'Heaven's Eye' FAST radio telescope in China also supposedly received a mysterious radio signal from the stars – and

The Murriyang radio telescope detected a remarkable signal from Proxima Centauri in 2019.

possibly from the same area of space as BLC-1. They had registered this communication in 2021 and, like the researchers at Breakthrough Listen, had been verifying the data ever since and were close to releasing a statement on the matter. In the competitive world of astronomy, both the Chinese and the Breakthrough Listen organizations would no doubt prefer to publish their findings first, especially if they contain results that prove intelligent life is out there. Only time will tell.

By the time this story is being read, it may be that there has been an official declaration from at least one respected astrophysics organization that Earth has received messages from extraterrestrial life. And if there hasn't been any such announcement, ask yourself why not. Either way, any new signal could have been heard by the huge Australian Parkes 'Murriyang' radio telescope. The signal that could be 'heard' emanating from the Proxima Centauri star region contained a narrow band signal with characteristics of a techno or artificial signature near the 982 MHz waveband. As of December 2020, research was still going on to try and rule out terrestrial or Earth-based interference.

By continually monitoring the area and filtering out other unwanted signals, such as aircraft and pulsars (rotating stars that cause radio interference), and Earth-based satellites, they located the signal that was around 12 degrees offset from the nearest star, i.e. it was likely to be from an orbiting planet around the Proxima Centauri star. The signal was consistent also with a drifting signal meaning that the planet was moving, as all planets do, around their central sun.

The researchers approached the United Nations a number of years back but only after announcing they had possibly found intelligent alien signals. They were quietly advised to go back to their arrays and dig deeper into the signals before making such announcements to the world.

So this may be, if not a cover-up, more of a check and double-check procedure as requested by the UN. Presently SETI, with the help of volunteers around the world, are looking much closer at all aspects of the received signals and checking for modulation, or if you prefer, spoken words or some kind of confirmation within the signal that it has been created artificially, maybe alien music? By focusing in on the noise, they hope to be able to prove to the world that there really is something to go 'Wow!' over.

THE DODLESTON MESSAGES

Personal computers were rare in the early-1980s. Few people owned one; fewer still understood what they were for and what they could do. 'Computers' at that time meant the large mainframe machines operated by multinational companies or powerful state-run organizations such as NASA. Things began to change in the UK when the British Broadcasting Corporation teamed up with Acorn Computers Ltd to produce the BBC Micro, a small, personal computer (PC). Released in December 1981, it was designed to be used in schools and homes for education, work and leisure. The computer revolution was under way.

Home computers like the BBC Micro were initially used as word processors. The internet – or a very early version of it – existed, but it was a primitive, file-sharing system used by the US military and by a global network, or 'web', of universities. Ordinary PC users had no access to it and their computing activity was limited to writing documents. If they wanted to share documents, the only way to do so was to save the file to a floppy disc and insert it into the hard drive of another computer. Email was not an option. Imagine the surprise, then, of one user, who in 1984 borrowed a BBC Micro from the school at which he worked and began to receive messages on it. This was unusual enough, but even more strange was who those messages came from – and *when.*

A letter through time

The computer was under the care of Ken Webster, a newly qualified teacher at Hawarden High School in Flintshire, North Wales. He had recently moved into Meadow Cottage, a 16th-century building he was planning to renovate in the village of Dodleston in Cheshire, just across the border in England. He was living there with his 19-year-old girlfriend, Debbie Oaks, and their friend, Nicola Bagguley. Ken

A BBC Acorn computer from the 1980s – much like the one Ken used to communicate with 'Lukas Wainman'.

had borrowed the computer for Nicola, who wanted to try her hand at writing comedy scripts. Having taken some basic lessons from Ken on creating and saving files, she began using the computer for scriptwriting, mostly in the daytime. As time went on, she sometimes chose not to shut down the machine in the evening after she'd finished her work, rather than boot it up each time she wanted to use it. Thus, it wasn't unusual when Ken, Debbie and Nicola returned from a Christmas night out in December 1984 and came back to find the computer switched on. What was odd was the strange message on the screen addressed to all three housemates. Written in what appeared to be an early modern form of English, it spoke about flowers seeking the light, bodies no longer in pain, and cats seeking their fortune in London. The writer identified himself as 'L.W.'

Seeing the light

The three friends believed the message to be some kind of prank, perhaps left by a musician friend of Ken's who would often pop by the house to record guitar tracks on Ken's multi-track tape recorder. But when another message appeared, and then another, Ken began to have his doubts. The messages kept appearing, even when the house was locked up and everyone was away. If Ken thought the messages would stop once he returned the computer to the school, he had to think again. When he borrowed *another* BBC Micro in the New Year of 1985, the messages resumed. As they became a bit clearer and more coherent, one informed Ken it was being sent in the year 1546 and asked him 'if he doth have a horse?'

Seeking expert opinion, Ken printed the messages and showed them to his colleague, Peter Trinder, an English teacher at his school. After examining the language, Peter estimated the text could be from the 16th or 17th century. Ken, Peter and a solicitor friend were so intrigued by the messages that they decided to compose a reply to 'L.W.', sharing some details of the year they were writing from, 1985 – including the fact that the reigning monarch was Elizabeth II. Having done this, they went to the pub. When the trio returned after a few drinks, there was another reply: 'L.W.' revealed that his name was Lukas Wainman and he was writing from March 1546. His king, he added, was Henry VIII. Lukas also told Ken that he and Debbie were living in *his* house and that he had observed Ken 'using strange lights, that were of the Devil'. If the message was real, Lukas was most likely referring to the electric lights that illuminated the old cottage.

PC pen pals

When he began to inspect the text more closely, Peter noticed some anomalies. The author, he saw, had used question marks, a form of punctuation not used in the time of Henry VIII. Did this prove the messages were a hoax? The language used was unusual, being a form of early modern English mixed with some Latin. Did this mean that Lukas was an educated man? The fact that he could write at all indicated that he must have been – if he existed, that is.

Henry VIII.

Whoever – and whenever – Lukas was, he seemed to know some details about the house that Ken and Debbie did not. As he continued corresponding with Ken, he informed him that the cottage was made with red stone. Then, the messages between the PC pen pals took a curious turn. It happened after Ken mentioned in one that the year he was writing from was 1985. A clearly startled Lukas wrote back, asking what Ken meant when he said it was 1985. Surely, Lukas said, Ken was writing from 2109 – just like 'his friend'?

This opened up all manner of questions for Ken. He remembered telling Lukas that he was living in1985, so why did he now think something different? And who was 'his friend' living in 2109? When Ken asked, Lukas told him the friend in 2019 was the person who had given him 'the strange box of lights' that he was using to communicate with. Ken was puzzled. What 'strange box of lights' did Lukas have if it was allowing him to write to two different years in his future?

Back to the future

Ken decided to find out who Lukas's mysterious benefactor was and typed a message on his computer containing just two words: 'Calling 2109'. It was not long before he received a reply, although it left him with more questions than answers. '2109', said the message, was not a single 'he' or 'she', but a 'they' – a group taking part, the message intimated, in some sort of experiment. '2109' also said that it could not say too much about the time in which it lived as this information would affect Ken and Debbie's futures, and perhaps even Lukas's.

After making contact with the mysterious '2109', Ken and Debbie began to notice bizarre things happening around the cottage. They would, for example, find small tins of food stacked up in the corner of the room rather than in the larder where they were normally stored. One afternoon, Debbie came home to find all the living room furniture piled high in the corner of the room. She and Ken heard footsteps walking across the floor above them, even though they knew there was no one upstairs. Sometimes, Debbie felt someone touching her hair or sensed an unseen presence nearby. Events took a startling twist when she began having dreams in which Lukas would appear and they would have conversations.

Believing their cottage was perhaps being haunted by a poltergeist, Ken and Debbie called in the Society for Psychical Research (SPR).

Psychic investigation

Founded in 1882, the SPR is one of the world's oldest bodies making investigations into paranormal activity and is, in its own words, the 'first society to conduct organized scholarly research into human experiences that challenge contemporary scientific models'. It dispatched investigators John Bucknell and Dave Welch to research the case in 1985. They suspected either Ken or Debbie was responsible for the communications and decided to type their own messages to both Lukas and '2109' into the computer, while Ken or Debbie were both out of the house. Bucknell and Welch also thought Peter might be involved in the hoax, so they effectively sealed off the cottage from all three friends, meaning none of them could get inside without being seen. (Nic had gone back to Bristol by this time, so was no longer involved.)

As to how Ken, Debbie or Peter might be faking the messages from Lukas and '2109', the SPR researchers had to think creatively – and wrestle with their own lack of computing expertise, given this was happening in the early days of home computing. One theory they discussed was that Ken or Debbie were somehow sending the supposed messages from the past and the future through the computer's plug. How exactly they would do this in practice, Bucknell and Welch couldn't say. Nor could they explain where Ken or Debbie acquired the scientific knowledge to do such a thing, especially as Ken was still learning to use the computer himself. With hindsight, the investigators might have been better off focusing on whether Ken and Debbie had been using some primitive form of emails. But as email and the internet were at least a decade away from public use in 1985, this was equally implausible.

Ultimately, the investigators were left stumped by what was happening with the computer. In the end, they did not even submit a report of their findings to the SPR, which was its normal policy. The first few sessions with the SPR field researchers yielded no evidence of messages from Lukas to them, despite Ken and Debbie specifically requesting that Lukas write from his time frame to Bucknell and Welch. By 21 July, the SPR team had decided that maybe John Bucknell could stay in the cottage with Debbie, while Ken and Welch went off to the local pub. After three hours, nothing had shown up, according to Bucknell, so they decided to walk to the pub themselves and bumped into Ken and Welch walking back towards the cottage. Disappointed that nothing had happened, they all went back inside. Ken decided to look at the screen in front of the others and, after scrolling through 35 pages, he found an entry from Lukas. Both Debbie and Bucknell had previously checked the PC before they left the cottage only minutes earlier and said there was nothing there.

Bucknell read the message from Lukas that was addressed to him but was not impressed. He suggested the message could have been written there in the minute that it took them to walk out of the house to meet Ken on the way back from the pub. Bucknell was therefore suggesting an accomplice or imposter had got into the cottage, scrolled 35 pages to the bottom and then typed a long message addressed specifically to him. Ken protested that no accomplice or intruder could have scrolled through 35 pages and then written a page-long message, all in under a minute. Bucknell, therefore, suggested that a pre-save disc had been prepared and placed into the computer. Yet no one observed anyone place a disc into the drive. Even that procedure alone would have caused a lot of bleeps and noises from the PC drive as it tried to access the file. Eventually, both SPR men gave up the ghost as it were and never returned. They did not even file a report to headquarters. Later, Ken learned that one of them was not even a member of the SPR! It was a message on the computer itself, however, that suggested another person to perhaps get involved in the investigation.

UFO researcher's perspective

The next person to look into the case was a UFO researcher named Gary Rowe. Bizarrely, it was '2109' that recommended Ken contact Rowe. After investigating, Rowe could not provide an explanation; he thought the computer messages probably were coming through time, although he could not say how. He was sure, though, that Ken, Peter or Debbie were not faking them.

As the various investigators were attempting to solve the mystery of where and who the messages were coming from, Ken began to find out more about his Tudor correspondent. Finally, 'Lukas' admitted in a message to Ken that he had been using a pseudonym to protect himself and that his real name was Tomas Harden/Hawarden. Tomas, as he now referred to himself, also told Ken how he had acquired the ability to communicate through time. Supposedly, one night '2109' had appeared to him in bright green light by emerging from his chimney and handed over something he called the 'leems boyste'. This, he explained, was the box he was using to communicate with Ken.

Tomas said that he simply talked into the 'leems boyste' (loosely translated as 'box of lights') and the words were produced. Where do the words 'leems boyste' originate from? 'Leems', more commonly spelt 'leam' was derived from the Middle English *leme*, from Old English lēoma: akin to Old Saxon *liomo* (gleam, radiance), Old Norse *ljōmi* (radiance), Old English *lēoht* (light). While *boist* was derived from the Old French word *boiste* (box, container). A *boist* or *boiste* would in the 16th century mean 'a jar or box (as for cosmetics, salves); also, a case or box (as for letters or bread)'. He did not need to type and could probably not have understood this method of sending a message. He said he discovered this process when his maid was singing one day and the machine began to reproduce her words as she sang. Ken would later suggest that what Tomas described was nothing less than a late-medieval version of Amazon's Alexa.

The Vertical Plane

The burning question in this strange story is why would beings from 2109 come back through time to give Tomas a computer? They had specifically told Ken they did not want to interfere and tell him everything at the risk of changing his future. Surely, though, bringing a futuristic communication device back in time and handing it to a late-medieval citizen would have some impact on his destiny? To add an extra layer of complexity, in 1989 Ken Webster published *The Vertical Plane*, a book detailing his experiences with what came to be known as the Dodleston Messages – and by its very existence, a book that would disrupt the future because of the revelations it contained. Tomas then explained that he, too, had written a book about his experiences, but had hidden it because he did not wish it to fall into the wrong hands. The beings in 2109 told Tomas the book would be found one day but could not tell him when. As yet, it has not surfaced.

As Tomas and Ken's correspondence developed over time, they began to suspect that '2109' was altering the content of their messages for some reason. Ken came to believe, for example, that the question marks that the early 'Lukas' messages from Tomas could have been added by '2109', although he could offer no reason why. Tomas himself also suggested that '2109' had somehow interfered with his earlier messages to them. To get around this, Tomas stopped using his 'box of lights' and instead began to send his letters on ordinary paper. Somehow, he was able to write a letter in his own time, which would then appear in crayon on modern paper in Ken's cottage in 1985. Tomas had no idea how this worked himself, although he did say a few clues that '2109' left him included a supply of paper which he used to write on. Somehow the computer or 'box of lights', as he called it, had to be near the paper for it to work, which suggests some potential scanner was present. He also managed to draw images for Ken and Debbie of his house and a nearby windmill from his time period. Later, messages also began to appear on the cottage's walls.

In November 1985, things took a dramatic turn when Tomas indicated that he was being arrested on suspicion of witchcraft. He had earlier told Ken that his serving maid had been tried and convicted of the same charge and that the authorities, led by the local sheriff named Sir Thomas Fowleshurst, were now coming for him.

Sir Thomas Fowleshurst 'writes'

A friend of Tomas's then began communicating with Ken. He explained that Thomas had been arrested and was being held by the local sheriff,

Sir Thomas Fowleshurst, due to his communications with the 'light box' or 'leems boyste'. It seemed now that many medieval characters were attempting their hand at the strange box of lights. Sir Thomas Fowleshurst – or person unknown – visited the cottage, which had been Tomas's home, found the strange 'box of lights' and apparently used it to communicate with Ken. Initially, Sir Thomas said he believed Ken to be the devil, but after a week or so of messaging saw that this was not case. Finally, Tomas was released, presumably uncharged, and once more resumed writing to his 'dear friends, Ken, Debbie and Peter'.

Eventually, in March 1986, Tomas wrote to Ken and told him that he was leaving the cottage in his own timeline and would no longer be able to write to Ken or Debbie. The messages stopped and Ken and Debbie never heard from Tomas again.

Keen to find out what had happened to his friend from the past, Ken did genealogical research into the name 'Tomas Hawarden' and discovered that there had been someone by that title who lived around the time in question and who had become a priest. Beyond that, however, he could find no more information. This could be because there was no more information to find – or because, as a man who in his past had been held on suspicion of witchcraft, Tomas Hawarden was keen to keep as low a profile as possible. Perhaps Tomas became a priest, as a potential cover, to hide any suspicion of his time-travelling communications.

Ken was later told by '2109' that Tomas eventually died but not before writing the book of his encounters with Ken and Debbie. There was no explanation about what happened to the 'leems boyste', the strange box of lights, or computer, that was supposedly given to Tomas by '2109'. By the end of March 1986, Ken and Debbie thought that their communications were all over. Ken had promised himself that he would never again set up a BBC Micro computer in his house. In July 1986, a new unnamed friend of a friend expressed interest in communicating with '2109'. Ken relented and showed her the computer. He was not expecting any messages, but to his surprise there was a message specifically related to her. It was so shocking apparently, that as soon as she read it, she fainted on the spot. She refused to tell Ken what the message was. Ken explained that he simply did not want to let it begin again, and he packed up the computer and gave it back.

Opening a portal

How, then, did any of this happen – if it actually happened? According to '2109', the messages could travel back and forth through time due to something called 'convexual magnetism'. They explained there are holes in the Earth's magnetic field, crossover points, which time can leak through and the ripples these cause can be picked up by sensitive individuals in the way that a psychic medium does. Thus, in his medieval time period, Tomas could also experience poltergeist activity as did Ken and Debbie in their time, since both appeared to be connecting through a possible portal or bridge through time.

But what are 'crossover' points and 'convexual magnetism'? Strange terms for us, but perhaps a being from 2109 might have them in their everyday vocabulary. Just as Tomas would not understand the words of our time, such as 'electricity' or 'microwaves', the word 'convexual' does not appear in our dictionaries. But it might suggest a joining-over point, so maybe '2109' was attempting to explain our own Earth's magnetic field, with its ebbs and flows at, say, the north pole, or magnetic north perhaps. Where streams of energy cross, you might get some kind of interference patterns, like two magnets producing variations and distortions of their fields as they come together. According to some scientific minds, time exists all at once, so that the past, present and future all exist in the present moment. Everything is happening now! Perhaps these fields, or crossover points as '2109' describes them, are where you can pick up on holes through time, as it were, and those sensitive enough may be able to use those energies, unknowingly or not, to communicate. Perhaps the location of the cottage, where these events occurred, might have been a significant factor, to do with crossover points intersecting, or perhaps lay lines interchanging. Other factors might also be present. Debbie or Ken might be the sensitive medium who enabled the flow of messages. In Tomas's time, it would have been just him probably. It's also worth noting that he found his furniture had also been moved around, just like Debbie and Ken's in their time.

Certain parties on forums discussing the book, *The Vertical Plane*, have suggested that Debbie may have been slightly mediumistic and this is what enabled the manifestations to occur. Debbie was 19 years old at the time, and it's often the case that poltergeist activity occurs around teenagers as they transition into young adulthood – in other words, that some teenagers with an excess of psychic energy experience a kind of 'psychic puberty', so to speak. Although in the Dodleston messages, it appears there was no 'spirit' as such making the furniture move or causing the messages to appear.

But with poltergeist activity, the perception has always been that there is a spirit to blame, just as Tomas was blaming the devil for causing his furnishings to move about. It suggests that perhaps researchers need a fresh approach to what a poltergeist might actually be. Tomas appeared to be a fully fledged living entity just from another time frame. From our perspective now, he is dead, but hit that BBC Micro switch and, if the conditions are right, you could in effect tap right back through time to what he was back then. The movement of objects both in Ken's time and Tomas's time suggest that it might have been a byproduct of what the actual central idea was: namely, a computer sending messages through time, which might have been initiated somewhere in the far future.

As mentioned, Tomas had a young serving maid – possibly a teenager – and it was her singing around the cottage that 'activated' the 'box of lights'. Could it be that she, like Debbie, was mediumistic and that her psychic sensitivity opened the door to the future in the same way that Debbie's could have possibly opened the door to the past? This could perhaps explain why the messages continued even after Tomas's maid had been taken away: having opened the door, she was not in control of what then came through it. She, or Debbie, may even have created a portal through which messages pass, along with poltergeist-type effects, and this may account for the furniture being stacked up in Ken's living room. Maybe this incident wasn't even connected to what was happening between Tomas and Ken and Debbie; rather it might have been a spirit or poltergeist tapping into the psychic energy at the cottage to cause disturbances.

An £87,000 phone bill

Of course, sceptics will point out that Ken and Debbie could have somehow dialled in to a basic internet and were communicating with someone else pretending to be Tomas in 1984. This is possible, but highly unlikely. As already mentioned, email and the internet were highly specialized and exclusive technologies in 1984, limited to certain parts of the academic world and to the higher echelons of the military establishment. It's not clear how a schoolteacher in rural Cheshire would have been able to access such sophisticated telecommunications.

As Ken pointed out in his book, even if they had somehow been able to get hold of a modem, given the number of messages going back and forth over 18 months, the dial-up costs would have racked up around £87,000 in today prices. If the whole thing had been a prank, it would have been an extremely expensive one for Ken and Debbie. In addition, they and whoever they were collaborating with would have had to become pretty fluent in early modern English – specifically its local Cheshire variant, while also learning some Latin for extra authenticity.

Out of This World

If it was attention that Ken and Debbie were after, they certainly got that – albeit around 10 years after the event. In 1996, the Dodleston Messages case was dramatized in the supernatural UK television series *Out of This World*. By then, Ken and Debbie had moved on with their lives. Although they both contributed to the content of the programme, they asked not to be filmed directly and actors played them in the reconstruction of the case.

Psychologist Richard Wiseman interviewed Ken and Debbie, both with their backs to the camera, and questioned Ken's friend, Peter. Asked if the incident could have been a hoax, Peter replied that it would have been a monumental task to set it up. Besides, he added, 'For what reason would you hoax such a thing?' There was certainly no money to be made from it. Wiseman had spoken to the 'two' SPR investigators and he said they had chosen not to appear in the programme, but told him they thought it was a hoax, adding they 'had no idea how it was done.' Wiseman had to concede that it 'was highly unlikely the messages were planted on to the computer before Ken brought it home from the school'.

To explore the literary and linguistic elements of the messages written by Tomas, the programme engaged the services of Dr Laura Wright, a lecturer in English at Lucy Cavendish College, Cambridge. Her opinion was that no one in 16th-century England would have written in the way that Tomas did. Furthermore, her analysis of some of Ken's writings showed what she considered to be around a 26 per cent similarity to those of Tomas. According to Ken in his book, that Dr Wright said 'nothing could be concluded from those percentages'. While this is not a high percentage, Dr Wright implied to camera that Ken had faked or unintentionally manufactured Tomas's messages, or if it wasn't Ken, then someone else had done it. However, she also said that nothing could be concluded from this analysis, although this comment was not included in the final broadcast.

It should be noted that Dr Wright only examined around 300 words of Ken's and Tomas's text. Was this enough for her to create a fair or extensive assessment? Possibly not. It was also the case that she only looked at Tomas's messages and some of Ken's. She did not assess anything by '2109', nor did she read any of the messages that Sir Thomas sent from the 'box of lights' while Tomas was supposedly in prison. When he published an updated and expanded edition of *The Vertical Plane* in 2022, Ken Webster addressed some of Dr Wright's comments on Tomas's writing style. One compelling observation was that Tomas had not been writing his messages but *speaking* them into the 'box of lights'. Few of us write in exactly the same way that we speak. In 'dictating' his messages, Tomas would no doubt have used local dialect, slang and idioms that rarely or never appear in formal written accounts of the time. That, Ken argued, could account for at least some of the stylistic or linguistic anomalies identified by Dr Wright.

Dictionary corner

Another person who conducted an analysis of the Dodleston Messages was Ken's colleague (and sometime fellow suspect), Peter Trinder. As an English teacher, he was intrigued by the language Tomas used. His initial reaction when Ken first started receiving the messages was that they were genuine and this did not change, the more he studied them. Indeed, he was intrigued enough to dive deeper into them and came back completely baffled.

Using the *Oxford English Dictionary* as his main reference, Peter examined the origin and etymology of many of the strange words used by Tomas like 'happs' meaning 'perhaps' and 'aboone' meaning 'to make good'. This convinced him that the messages did indeed date from 16th-century England. Where, though, was another matter. Most of the primary sources available from that period come from London and East Anglia. Their language did not match closely enough that of the Dodleston Messages. But according to Peter, some of the dialects used in southwest England did, and it was his opinion that Tomas may have originally hailed from, or spent time in, the area around Bristol – or 'Bristowe', as Ken wrote it when, at Peter's prompting, he asked Tomas if that had been the case. Later, Tomas did indicate he had spent time in Bristol and even described a place he had stayed, which Ken later visited.

Maybe it was this mix of southwestern and northwestern idiom-laden spoken English that made it so difficult for Dr Wright to come to any firm conclusions about the messages – that and the fact that she was being asked to authenticate whether they had been sent across the centuries by a time-travelling correspondent. She had her reputation as a respected historical sociolinguist to think of (she is today a professor of English at Cambridge University). It is interesting to speculate about what Dr Wright would have concluded had she been given more material to go on and asked to analyse it without being told of its origins or context. It is not unreasonable to assume that her knowing the message had supposedly been sent through some supernatural time portal may have influenced her conclusions, unconsciously or otherwise.

The book that Tomas wrote

Another language factor worth considering is how Ken, Peter and Tomas may have adapted the way they communicated with each other to make themselves better understood. Early modern English and modern English are in some respects two distinct languages. In their replies to Tomas's messages, Ken and Peter probably tried to incorporate early modern English words and phrases that their Tudor correspondent would recognize. In turn, Tomas, did the same thing in modern English, sometimes using the new words that had been explained to him, such as 'computer' or 'electricity'. Though the spelling may have varied from time to time.

In both cases, these attempts to speak each other's version of English would have been far from perfect and may well have resembled a mutual private language more than a recognizable dialect. Had Dr Wright had more time with the messages, and discussed them with Ken and Peter, the programme would have been able to offer a fairer assessment.

Besides, the programme made no mention of any attempt to track down the actual computers used by Ken back in 1984. While this would have been extremely difficult, since early BBC computers would probably have been replaced by Windows PCs, it is a material factor in the investigation.

It's also telling that Richard Wiseman appears not to have personally investigated the cottage where these events happened; nor did he examine the handwritten notes from Tomas allegedly found around the cottage by Ken and Debbie. These might have provided evidence to either substantiate the case or refute it further. The programme did not appear to contact Gary Rowe, the UFO investigator, who checked out the cottage and computer messages, or ask the phone line provider for possible explanations. Nor did it ask the computer manufacturer (Acorn) whether there had been a known software fault that caused spurious messages to appear on users' computers at the time. In fact, this could be compared to investigating a murder without examining the crime scene or the weapon.

More positively, some progress was made by Ken in tracking down a Tomas Hawarden in the 1546 timeline, including the record of a death in 1560. (This indicated the demise of a priest known as Tomas Hawarden from Gloucestershire.)

Some have suggested that both Ken and Debbie could have come down in the night and switched the computer on and typed out all the messages. While that is not impossible, the question remains as to why they would think up such an idea and for what reason, as Peter Trinder, their English teacher friend, put it.

A researcher posted an interesting story online in 2011 about another case from 1988, which was originally posted on a BBC website. It concerned a cleaning woman called Alice who worked in an architect's office. Finding a computer switched on one evening, she pointed it out to one of those working late there, a man called Rob, who went on to examine it. Rob decided to stay in the office the next evening and watch the computer. He was startled to find that, at precisely 9.18pm on 11 May 1988, the screen flickered on of its own volition and displayed this message: 'Thou!'. This made Rob sit up and pay attention to the computer. 'Thou!' it repeated. Suddenly, it changed its 'tune' and said, 'Thou hathe comited a grate cryme.'

Confused, Rob struggled to understand the meaning. The message wasn't over and the words kept coming. 'Thou art a godly man who hathe fanciful woman.' Rob smiled as he thought he was having his leg pulled. 'Who Dwelth in myne home,' it continued, ''twas a grate cryme to hathe stolen myne home.'

Could someone be having a joke or was it another mystery message coming down through time? And if these two sources of messages from other temporal realms exist, how many more might there be? Only time will tell, and up until now time has been guarding its secrets closely.

Ken Webster closed his comments during the programme by saying he hopes the book that Tomas said he wrote about his experiences will show up one day in the future. Until that day comes, the Dodleston Messages will remain an unsolved but extremely interesting enigma.

PICTURE CREDITS

Alamy: 83, 178

FBI: 93

Getty Images: 68, 198, 205, 240

Shutterstock: 13, 28, 52, 166

Wikimedia Commons: 31, 33, 37, 43, 53, 66, 72, 80, 96, 108, 127, 131, 142, 154, 170, 194, 210, 212, 231, 237, 242